CITY BETWEEN WORLDS

Leo Ou-fan Lee

City
BETWEEN
Worlds

My

Hong

Kong

THE BELKNAP PRESS OF HARVARD UNIVERSITY PRESS
Cambridge, Massachusetts, and London England

2008

PRINTED AND BOUND IN ITALY, BY GRAPHICOM

Library of Congress Cataloging-in-Publication Data

Lee, Leo Ou-fan.

City Between Worlds : My Hong Kong / Leo Ou-fan Lee. — 1st ed.

p. cm.

Includes index.

ISBN-13: 978-0-674-02701-5

1. Hong Kong (China) — Description and travel. 2. Hong Kong (China) — Social life and customs. I. Title.

DS796.H74L44 2008

951.25 — dc22   2007017270

To my wife, Esther, who to me embodies the best of Hong Kong

CONTENTS

PROLOGUE

City Between Worlds is not a guidebook to Hong Kong but a book guided by the roaming reflections of a long-term Chinese resident—one who, though not born in the city, has chosen to stay here, following a thirty-year sojourn in the United States. Thus, my perspective is neither strictly native nor old-colonial. Nor, for that matter, is it the viewpoint of longtime expats, whose loving sentiments for Hong Kong often run deeper than those of the former colony's Chinese population. Sometimes I intentionally combine all three perspectives, but invariably I find my sympathies entrenched on the "inside." It is largely from this angle that I choose my sights/sites and narrate my story of Hong Kong, voicing opinions, wherever possible, on behalf of a Chinese community whose members have not chosen to write about their city in English.

In 1997, after a century and a half of British colonial rule, Hong Kong formally became a Special Administrative Region (SAR) of the People's Republic of China. We might begin our exploration of Hong Kong by asking: What makes this city so "special"? A rational answer is hard to come by, for Hong Kong thrives on confusion and contradiction. Its dynamism is expressed in a variety of ways and manifested above all by a collective energy and self-imagery that does not fit preconceived categories, including the stereotype of a "capitalist emporium." This refusal to conform to outsiders' images forms the basis of what Ackbar Abbas, a Hong Kong native and scholar, calls "the politics of disappearance" in his perceptive book by that title. In Abbas's view, "disappearance" does not imply nonappearance or absence, nor even nonrecognition. It is "more a question of misrecognition, of recognizing a thing as something else." This "something else" may have to do with the Western media's image of Hong Kong at the time of the handover. The city's "imminent disappearance" as a British colony was what precipitated such an intense and unprecedented interest in Hong Kong's culture.[1]

But contrary to Western predictions of collapse, Hong Kong did not disappear. Its economy and lifestyle did not buckle under the new political regime but attained higher levels of prosperity than before. Even in 1997, when Abbas's book was published, the atmosphere no longer signified a sense of "doom and gloom" so much as "doom and boom," as he put it: "The more frustrated or blocked the aspirations to democracy are, the more the market booms." In Abbas's view, one effect of colonial administration has been the absence of outlets for political idealism or action. And as a result, "most of the energy is directed toward the economic sphere"—speculation on stock markets and real estate or obsession with fashion and consumerism.

Abbas's observations were extremely perceptive at the time, especially about the West's images of Hong Kong. But more than ten years after the handover, perhaps they need to be revisited and updated. Does his "disappearance" act still capture the energy and vitality of the Hong Kong people and culture today, now that the dread of doom is gone? Is the pursuit of money and obsession with consumerism still merely a form of "decadence"—a displaced political urge? Does Hong Kong culture continue to suffer from what Abbas calls "reverse hallucination" or "not seeing what is there"? And if so, what *is* there that we continue to fail to see?

I believe that Abbas's important and scholarly book demands a sequel and a response, but I am incapable of writing about such theoretical matters with great sophistication. The premise of my present work is much more pedestrian: to find out what indeed is (or was) there, in Hong Kong's past, that may still shed light on its culture today, and on a new wave of "disappearance" that now threatens the city both physically and spatially. In the accelerated pace of urban renewal, Hong Kong's old monuments and streets are being demolished at an alarming rate, and more reclamations of land from Victoria Harbor are being planned. Under this relentless pressure to tear down and build, Hong Kong's self-image, its collective memory, and its unique lifestyle are at risk.

This worry brings me to another work that hovers over my thinking—the concept of the "generic city" as formulated by the renowned architect and theorist Rem Koolhaas. Over the years since I first read a shortened version of his essay, which he expanded into a long and richly dense explication in his book *S,M,L,XL,* I have had mixed and often ambivalent reactions to it. Is Hong Kong becoming a "generic city" in which history is meaningless and "any regret about history's absence is a tiresome reflex," a city in which the past has become "too small to be inhabited and shared by those alive"?[2]

Unlike Abbas, for whom Hong Kong is "a post-city on the site of the ex-city," its culture a "post-culture," Koolhaas is not describing a kind of phantom mental creation but a real urban phenomenon, especially in Asia. "A large proportion of Generic Cities," he writes, are situated "in a warmer than usual climate . . . on its way to the south—toward the equator—away from the mess the north made of the second millennium." Hong Kong, being not so far from the tropical zone, is certainly one of a cluster of burgeoning South Asian cities that includes Bombay, Kuala Lumpur, Singapore, Bangkok, and Dubai. And Koolhaas's further observation about the inevitable trend toward "verticality" in these generic cities—"the skyscraper looks as if it will be the final, definitive, typology"—is another accurate description of Hong Kong's cityscape. But most important, I was astounded to realize that the three main characteristics of Koolhaas's generic city—airport, hotels, and shopping malls—were formulated using Hong Kong as his model. The city's new airport in particular—ranked number one in the world—is itself a characterless generic city in the making, and a perfect space for "transit."

Certainly the new breed of global cosmopolitans who feel equally at home in every city (which by Koolhaas's definition are interchangeable anyway) qualify as transients. But what about the people who have nowhere else to go, not even into exile? Is Hong Kong, for them, interchangeable with all the other urban spaces in South Asia, a generic place that can be "British" at one moment and "Chinese" the next with no discernible crisis of identity? On the eve of the 1997 handover, most of the seven million residents of Hong Kong had no choice but to stay in their home city, and this real existential situation—of being grounded in one place, for better or worse, like most of the world's population—seems to have eluded the global theorizers.

For Koolhaas, himself a multinational luminary, the issue of identity is passé. Identity is merely a "mousetrap in which more and more mice have to share the original bait, and which, on closer inspection, may have been empty for centuries." In his view, a person (or a whole city) should never be trapped in one identity, since all of us now have "multiple identities." As one of Koolhaas's former colleagues at Harvard University, I too aspire to be a cosmopolitan with multiple identities, and indeed I have taught an undergraduate course about contemporary Chinese culture in just that way. But does this postmodern formulation, put in pithy and sardonic if not cynical language, really solve the problems faced by Hong Kong's seven million people? The lived culture of these permanent residents of Hong Kong is part of what inspired me to write this book.

Working in the shadow of these two brilliant theoreticians, I find myself plowing away just to pick up some piece of empirical debris or the occasional relic—a few small cultural substances from Hong Kong's streets and from the material world of its everyday people. "Re-searching" this quotidian culture is not a useless gesture, in my view. I share the sentiments of another local researcher, Jason Wordie: "Wandering about Hong Kong Island's backstreets . . . one can sometimes feel like an archaeologist of the modern day working without a shovel, piecing together isolated fragments from what was here until almost yesterday to build up a picture of a very different sort." As a longtime Hong Kong citizen himself, Wordie laments the forgetfulness of Hong Kong's residents about their own past.[3]

In Koolhaas's view, the urban archaeologist will come up empty-handed, for the generic city "perpetuates its own amnesia" and "its archaeology will therefore be the evidence of its progressive forgetting, the document of its evaporation." Still, the posture of an "archaeologue" (one who pursues archaeology but with a freer interpretation) is precisely what I have adopted in this book, together with that of a local *flâneur*. The process of digging up sources and imagining what it was like for people to live in such a city has given me countless hours of both pleasure and pain. *City Between Worlds* offers my tentative report on Hong Kong's "postcondition."

EACH CHAPTER PRESENTS a slice of the city's history and culture, called up by the streets, sites, and artifacts themselves, and by associations with literature and film. I begin by foot on the streets of old Hong Kong, which in early colonial days was called Victoria City. Hong Kong island became a British possession in the 1840s, following China's defeat in the Opium War. The protection offered by Victoria Harbor, along with the prospect for gain, quickly drew British merchants, Chinese laborers, and Indian guards and policemen to this bustling port. The old police station, magistracy, and prison are still standing near Hollywood Road, along with the Man Mo Temple, the center of Chinese civic life in the nineteenth century. Today, the sights and smells of the open-air bazaars and food markets along Queen's Road Central and in present-day Sheung Wan recall a Cantonese population whose labor built this imperial outpost—under the watchful eyes of colonial masters and Chinese elites, and under often appalling conditions of life and death.

In Chapter 2 the perspective shifts to the modern part of the island, the Central Business District or CBD, where the "Central values" of present-day Hong Kong—capital accumulation, profit motive, free-market competitiveness, land development, global trade, consumerism, and pervasive efficiency—are flourishing in both business and politics. Chapter 3 moves eastward through the hustle and bustle of the island's most congested streets, in Wan Chai and Causeway Bay. A rider on the slow-moving double-decker tram can exit at any point and plunge into the crowds, searching for relics of local history and culture, and for evidence of the policies that threaten to destroy them.

Chapter 4 invites the reader to board the Peak tram for a ride up to Victoria Peak, where the wealthiest of the British colonials once lived. The writings surveyed in this chapter, penned by residents and travelers alike, offer a sense of the mentality and lifestyle of these late Victorians, who found themselves "stranded" in this exotic outpost, not yet a cosmopolitan metropolis. The old colonials seldom set foot on Kowloon peninsula or the countryside beyond, and contemporary visitors, as they enjoy the view from the Peak, can ponder the implications of such a sheltered existence.

In Chapter 5 I board the Star Ferry and cross over to Kowloon—a crowded jungle of high-rise buildings arranged in a labyrinth of streets congested with traffic. It is inhabited predominantly by Chinese, alongside a small minority of Indians. Westerners seldom venture beyond the upscale Tsim Sha Tsui shopping area near the Star Ferry terminal, and as a result they miss seeing this most indigenous part of Hong Kong. Kowloon became a British possession in 1860, following China's defeat in the so-called Second Opium War. Our path takes us through the congested streets of Mong Kok and eventually to the site of the old walled city of Kowloon, established as a Chinese administrative outpost in 1847 and demolished in 1987. During the 1980s, over 31,000 residents squeezed themselves onto less than three acres of land in this teeming city-within-a-city.

The New Territories, a large land area leased by the British in 1898 for ninety-nine years, was home to Hong Kong's first Chinese settlers—all rural villagers. A trip by train or car leads to the few remaining walled villages near the border, where an outsider can gain a "feel" (a prevalent word in popular Cantonese parlance) for local history going back many centuries. Scores of offshore islands that also provided homes and harbors for migrant clans can be reached by ferry or bridge. In Chapter 6 I provide a brief account of these early farmers and fishers, along with their religious rituals and festivals.

The book's last two chapters—on Hong Kong lifestyle and the complex relations between Hong Kong and mainland China—are based on my personal experience as a witness to the great changes that occurred during the decade after the handover. The views expressed in these chapters are at considerable variance with those found in official statements or in most Western media accounts, and the reader is forewarned of their possible bias. Yet it seems to me that most Western media, in their overemphasis on Hong Kong's role in the global economy, have not explored the dynamics of local culture and its interaction with the official political regime. This lopsided view is partly due to the language barrier and partly to stereotypes that have been glamorized in popular fiction and film. In my attempt to "set the record straight," I may have inclined toward the other extreme of localism, a position which in this age of globalization many people consider no longer viable.

While writing this book, I found myself constantly trying to draw mental maps not only from the many walks and wanderings I have taken all over these areas but from the diverse anecdotes, vignettes, memoirs, and fiction I have read, and films I have seen (which are often described in these pages). In piecing together these fragments, I do not arrive at an overall picture of this "city between worlds." What I offer is rather a smorgasbord of thoughts and impressions—a food metaphor that may not be inappropriate for Hong Kong, a city well known for its culinary delights. Readers of this book can pick and choose from its contents and read at random. I hope they find some of the dishes served here to their taste.

"It clamors with a distinctive and personal life of its own. Fundamentally and basically, its roots connect with life as a whole and yet, at the same time, it retains a number of the secrets of a world now past."

NAGUIB MAHFOUZ, *Midaq Alley*

Inside the Man Mo Temple on Hollywood Road.

1

Victoria City

Central District, as the name suggests, is the heart of modern Hong Kong, where high finance meets high fashion, and the richest bankers and real estate tycoons conduct their business in super-modern skyscrapers facing Victoria Harbor. These high-rise towers, some designed by world-famous architects such as Norman Foster and I. M. Pei, form Hong Kong's urban skyline. Especially when seen at night, outlined with flashing neon lights, these buildings make a truly dazzling spectacle. For many, this is what present-day Hong Kong stands for. But there is another side of Central that is equally close to Hong Kong natives and longtime residents. This is old Hong Kong, located mainly in the western part of Central and in the neighboring district of Sheung Wan.

The eastern and western parts of Central, together, constituted what was once called Victoria City, the first name given to the island when the British landed in 1841 before they changed its name to Hong Kong. The name Victoria refers of course to Queen Victoria, crowned four years earlier, in 1837. Not surprisingly, Victoria City's first major thoroughfare was called Queen's Road, and it in turn was divided into three sections, Central, West, and East. There is no better place to begin our exploration of Hong Kong than Queen's Road Central. In this chapter, we will cover mainly the western section of Central, together with Sheung Wan, and leave the eastern part, now commonly known as the Central Business District, for Chapter 2.

MY STARTING POINT is the corner of Pedder Street and Queen's Road, one of the city's most historic junctions. A century ago this was Pedder

Wharf, where visitors to Hong Kong first came ashore. Pedder Street and Pedder Wharf were named after the first British harbor master, William Pedder, who assumed his post in 1841. By the late nineteenth century, a well-to-do business-man or traveler who visited this Crown colony would disembark at Pedder Wharf and be taken to the six-story Hong Kong Hotel across the street. It opened in 1866, and at that time the hotel's dining room overlooked the harbor. In 1926, when a fire broke out in the east wing and raged for two days and nights, after-noon tea was served as usual in the west wing.

At the corner of Pedder Street and Queen's Road, an eighty-foot clock tower served for over half a century as the most prominent landmark in Central. It was demolished in 1913 to make way for traffic. The General Post Office, built in 1911, was also located on Queen's Road, until the construction of the Central MTR station forced its removal to Connaught Place in 1976. Today, a new up-scale shopping center called Landmark occupies the site where the Hong Kong Hotel once stood, and most of the other old buildings in this part of Hong Kong are now gone. Even the waterfront is no longer where it once was. Over the past century, some 145 acres of land have been reclaimed from Victoria Harbor along the north side of the island. Land expansion into the narrowing harbor continues today, despite much criticism from both preservationists and envi-ronmentalists.

A short walk in the westward direction along Queen's Road leads to Central Market—a Bauhaus-style building constructed in 1939. Once the most mod-ern market building in Hong Kong, it is now in disrepair and serves merely as an indoor passageway. But stairs at its unobtrusive entrance lead to the world's longest outdoor pedestrian escalator with a covered roof. Constructed in 1993, this twenty-segment 2,525-foot moving sidewalk was intended to trans-port commuters between the tightly packed high-rise apartment buildings on the hillside—called the Mid-Levels—and offices in the downtown Central Business District. Before 10:00 A.M., this outdoor escalator moves in the downward direction to accommodate office workers, and afterward it heads back up the hill. It transports some 34,000 local residents, office workers, and tourists every day.

The pedestrian escalator has transformed the urban landscape in this part of town, and offers riders a fine view of some of the oldest streets in Hong Kong. Going upward from Central Market, the first segment crosses Stanley Street, named after the earl of Stanley, who was Britain's foreign secretary in 1841, when the British took possession of Hong Kong. It then passes over Wellington Street, which honors the

English general who in 1815 defeated Napoleon at the Battle of Waterloo. At Lyndhurst Terrace, also called Flower Street, florists and prostitutes of European descent once congregated to sell their wares. One block to the

The pedestrian escalator in Central, providing access to the Mid-Levels, and not far away, one of the many "ladder streets" in old Hong Kong.

east is tiny Pottinger Street, a steep stone-paved passageway named after Sir Henry Pottinger, Hong Kong's first governor. The local Chinese have long ignored this colonial reference and called it Stone Slab Street for its physical shape. It is hard to imagine that a century ago this small alley served as a major street, where countless Chinese and Westerners made their way among roadside vendors, and hawkers vied for customers' attention.

Further up the hill, the escalator pauses at Hollywood Road—the second oldest street in Hong Kong. Its name has nothing to do with the American movie town, though in the twentieth century Hong Kong would become a film capital in its own right. The name refers to the evergreen trees called hollywood that were originally planted along the roadside. The trees are gone, and today the area appears rather dilapidated and deserted, except for tourists who patronize its many antique shops and boutiques. Still, Hollywood Road has a quaint and exotic appeal—rather like a Hollywood movie set.

Beyond Hollywood Road, the escalator ascends above Staunton Street, named after a member of the first British embassy to China in 1784 under Lord Macartney, and Elgin Street, named after Lord Elgin, who led the British expeditionary forces in the Second Opium War of 1858–1860. Elgin signed both the Treaty of Tientsin in 1858, which opened eleven Chinese ports to foreign trade, and the Peking Convention in 1860, which ceded Kowloon peninsula (south of Boundary Street) to Great Britain "in perpetuity." The escalator moves above Shelley Street, named not after the famous British poet but the auditor-general appointed in 1844 by Sir John Davis, Hong Kong's second governor. This Shelley became involved in some shady business dealings and eventually was accused of fraud. The street name in Cantonese translation becomes Sei-li Gai or Small Profit Street—an unintended but fitting pun. Still further up, as the escalator approaches Mid-Levels, we reach Caine Road, which commemorates Hong Kong's first police chief, William Caine, and Robinson Road, named after Sir Hercules Robinson, Hong Kong's fifth governor.

Thus, the escalator ride alone, like a time tunnel, provides a historical journey back through the colonial era. Yet these colonial street names carry little weight today. In busy modern Hong Kong, nostalgia is mostly a sentiment to be exploited for its tourist attraction. "History" has become a material form of commercial window-dressing that lures antique hunters and curiosity seekers. They peek into the shops lining Hollywood Road or rummage through the scattered artifacts—old photos and faded calendars (sometimes fakes), swords and coins, and other small relics of dubious value—on display in booths at the corner of Ladder Street and Upper Lascar Row (named for the first Sikh soldiers who arrived with the English colonials and settled down in this area; it is also known as Cat Street).

An antique bazaar on Upper Lascar Row.

Upscale boutiques, bars, and restaurants flourish along the entire route of the pedestrian escalator. The historical aura in this part of the city now charms both tourists and residents into leisurely consumption. The SoHo district (named for its location south of Hollywood Road, just as SoHo in New York City is named for its location south of Houston Street) has become a favored place for the international set to eat, drink, and hang out at night. Few of these pleasure-seekers would notice that not far away, on the east side of the pedestrian escalator, stands the old Central Police Station and Victoria Prison, now vacant and desolate. Does the noisy merry-making at night ever reach the ghosts locked inside that compound?

Despite rampant commercialization, the old streets in western Central and in northwestern Sheung Wan still preserve a strong sense of continuity and communal tradition. If we get off the escalator at the corner of Lyndhurst Terrace and walk west, we encounter other narrow streets running in the north-south direction down to Queen's Road—Cochrane, Graham, Peel, and Aberdeen. First constructed in the 1850s, these colonial streets house all kinds of traditional Chinese grocery stores selling rice flour, dried foods, oyster and shrimp sauce, and other products. On Peel Street (named after Lord Peel, the colonial secretary) a lively bazaar still attracts a daily crowd. Some of the vendors have spent their whole lives here, and their family shops have passed down through two or three generations.

On a recent field trip one late afternoon, I met an old woman selling traditional cakes. She told us merrily that she was born right there and married her neighbor, a butcher. But their children have moved away. Another old store selling dried food has photos of ancestors on its walls, together with a certificate of historical merit signed by Chris Patten, the last governor of Hong Kong. One bakery called Toi Cheung, originally on Lyndhurst Terrace, became especially famous because it was patronized by Patten, whom the locals nicknamed Fei Poon or "Fat Patten" because of his bulky waistline—the result of his having developed a strong appetite for egg custard, the specialty of the store. Customers lined up out front every afternoon to buy this delicacy and other fresh sweets. But in May 2005, because of a rent increase, the fifty-year-old store was forced to relocate.

Aberdeen Street was once the demarcation line for the old Chinese quarter, which lay to the west. In another nest of narrow streets, Gough Street (which in Chinese translation becomes Song Lyrics) is the place where Sun Yat-sen, the father of the Republican Revolution, went to school as a teenager, and later—as a revolutionary—held secret meetings. This quiet street still boasts one of the oldest and best noodle shops (at No. 21) and an open-air food stall. From Gough Street, a sharp stony stairway leads to Queen's Road Central, and from there it is a short walk across Hillier, Jervois, and Mercer streets to the old lower market area of Bonham Strand in Sheung Wan district. The street names in this part of town are mostly British colonial, but the memories they evoke are definitely native. Yet in the middle of all these old streets stands a brand-new seventy-three-story glass skyscraper called simply The Center. The conjunction of the old and the new is expressed in sharp relief.

In Chinese translation, and Cantonese pronunciation, British street names have, for the most part, been rendered into vernacular sounds that convey no meaning. But a bilingual observer can

Traditional Chinese foods for sale in Central's lively market just off Queen's Road, where local patrons visit their neighborhood butcher.

燒鵝 每隻168 半隻90

find a few unintended puns. In addition to Small Profit Street, Peel Street becomes Bei Lei or Modest Profit; Hillier becomes Jubilee Profit; and Cleverly turns into Quickly Blessed Profit. The profit (*lei*) motive in Hong Kong is ubiquitous. A few streets carry Chinese names, such as Wing Lok (Forever Happy), Wing Lee (Everlasting Profit), Wing Kut (Forever Lucky), or Wing Wo (Everlasting Harmony). The Chinese character Wing, which forms part of some forty-five street names all over Hong Kong, certainly connotes wishful thinking—that good fortune may last forever—and became an ironic commentary on colonial Hong Kong as anything but everlasting: a "borrowed place" on "borrowed time." This uprooted metaphor was the title of a famous book on Hong Kong published in 1976 by Richard Hughes. Like its successor, Jan Morris's *Hong Kong* (1997), Hughes's book prophecies an uncertain future for Hong Kong after the handover to China. Writing from a proud colonial perspective, Morris ends with unstinting praise for the British record: "History, I prophesy, will look back at their 150 years on this distant rock with astonishment and admiration. What a story! What an adventure! What messages!"[1]

What messages indeed! But whose story? Whose adventure? Shortly before 1997, the Hong Kong Chinese themselves, seized with uncertainties about their own identity and future, began to claim *their* histories as distinct from the colonial record. Since their future political fate as part of China was sealed, they turned to local culture for a definition of their own past—a past seen from the native perspective. A spate of books in Chinese—photo albums, personal memoirs, descriptions of old streets, as well as scholarly treatises on Hong Kong's history—appeared suddenly. What they discovered, or managed to uncover, can only be called fragments of a dismembered past, not a coherent "master narrative" like the one colonial historians constructed from their massive official archives. As if to compensate for their obvious disadvantage, creative writers rose to the occasion by inventing their own imaginative histories of the city.

Dung Kai-cheung, one of the most gifted and learned, published a semi-fictional work in 1997 whose English title (provided by Dung himself), *The Atlas: The Archaeology of an Imaginary City*, was inspired by Dung's reading of old maps of Hong Kong. Dung's fictional "archaeology" traces and remaps an entirely different Hong Kong from the one represented on colonial maps—a city he first defines in terms of abstract concepts, such as counterplace, commonplace, misplace, displace, antiplace, and nonplace. Embedded in all of these place names are the sensibilities of an intellectual writer on the fringe, with a deeply counter-colonial attitude. For the question behind these abstractions, begging to be asked, is: Who has made this place into a nonplace or displace, a subtopia or transtopia—an invisible city that can be made visible only by Dung's creative act? The answer is both the British colonials and China's imperial government.[2]

If Dung's approach to old Hong Kong is imaginary and inventive, the fiction of Hong Kong's foremost woman writer, Xi Xi, is even more so. One of her most famous short stories, "Tales of a Floating City," refers to a mirage-like city hanging in midair that can be either grounded or blown away. Her long novel is simply called *My City*. Its simple childlike characters, like Dung's ancestors, live in the plebian areas of Kowloon and work as carpenters, construction workers, and telephone-line installers. Their everyday life is described in the manner of a fairy tale that glorifies the ethos of innocence and the goodness of the human heart—qualities seldom mentioned in colonial accounts of Hong Kong, which almost invariably portrayed the local Chinese population as devious and untrustworthy.

The shared motif in all these native responses is collective memory, as opposed to official history. Because local memory, unlike historical documents, comes from both written and oral traditions that are not fully articulated, it must be brought to the fore either by an imaginary act of fiction or by a concerted effort to piece together scattered fragments into a comprehensive written record. Yet despite a recent profusion of books and articles about Hong Kong, a comprehensive history of the city's Chinese people, especially the *mentalité* of nonelites, remains to be written.

The search for native roots has continued after the takeover in 1997, and, like everything else in Hong Kong, this search has itself taken on a commercial character. Just as tourists and curiosity seekers from abroad come to this area of old Hong Kong for the pleasure of cultural consumption, a new generation of

A vendor in the Central Market area counting her profits.

local artists and artisans have come to reclaim this part of the city as the site of their own cultural production. Old buildings are being "repossessed" by local artists and artisans and turned into galleries, boutiques, and small exhibition halls for experimental art. One such venue is Para/Site Art Space on Po Yan Street off Hollywood Road. "Culture" here does not refer to the elite pursuits in the eastern part of the CBD but to a plebian heritage that flourishes in the nooks and crannies of western Central and Sheung Wan—a place where time moves at a much slower pace, and grandmothers mind their streetside shops just as they did a half century ago.

Alas, the government of Hong Kong has also seen the area's cultural/commercial potential, and in February 2007 it unveiled a major plan of urban renewal. Three blocks running north-south between Peel and Graham streets—some 57,000 square feet— have been earmarked for a HK$380 million renovation project. All the old buildings except for three will be torn down so that a brand new "Old Street" in the style of the 1920s and 1930s can be constructed. Traditional stores, such as those dealing with herb medicine, silk fabrics, and flour products, which have moved elsewhere will be brought back to give the area an authentic "feel." New buildings will be modeled after prewar traditional tenements of no more than three stories high. Tourists will be able to walk on the tree-lined Old Street and presumably relive the thrill of a make-believe old Hong Kong.[3]

Meanwhile, the Hong Kong Antiques and Monuments Office has already designated an official Heritage Trail in the area: a string of historic sites marked by small bilingual signposts whose truncated histories are dutifully repeated in tourist guidebooks. One series of signs on Hollywood Road leads to the Man Mo Temple, the old Tung Wah Hospital, and Tai Ping Shan Street, where the bubonic plague broke out at the end of the nineteenth century. But can we really obtain a sense of Hong Kong's past through this walking tour? Some of these "official sites" are dilapidated buildings; others have long since been demolished, their haunted presence marked by gaudy placards and signposts. It would require a leap of faith to imagine what these "memory sites" must have been like in the past. They offer at best a trail of disconnected histories.

The Man Mo Temple on Hollywood Road.

What follows in this chapter is my attempt to make a coherent story out of Chinese and Western interactions in Victoria City, but a story told with an awareness of the native as well as the colonial point of view. Unfortunately, sources for the former are not particularly reliable, because they stem from local legends, folklore, even hearsay. Most of the Chinese population in early Hong Kong were immigrants from the lower classes and thus illiterate. Their reactions to their foreign masters were largely mediated through a small local business elite who remained generally docile toward the colonial government. Moreover, the Chinese world in nineteenth-century Hong Kong was totally segregated from the European world. We will have to draw on both Chinese and English sources in order to gain a sense of how these two peoples interacted in this small colony, and some of our recreations will indeed require a leap of faith.

THE EXACT ORIGIN of the name Hong Kong (Fragrant Harbor) has been lost in the mists of time. Legends abound and interpretations vary. One version is that Hong Kong was the port where fresh (fragrant) water was available for ships. According to another more plausible hypothesis, sailors stopping for water on the south side of the island asked the local boat people (Tankas) what the name of their harbor was. They answered heung, meaning incense, since the port exported a fragrant incense made from local trees called kuan heung. But in Tanka dialect it was pronounced hong. So Hong Kong (Heung Harbor or Incense Harbor), in this account, referred to a small village on the south side of the island where ships anchored to load incense. The entire island itself did not have a name, though Red Incense Burner Mountain appears in Chinese characters on some old maps.

One of the earliest Chinese maps in which the characters "Hong" and "Kong" appear is the famous Coastal Map of Kuang Tung by Kwok Fei, from the late sixteenth century. Other names such as Tuen Mun, Kowloon Hill, and Tsim Sha Tsui are scattered about on this map in a maze of primitive-looking hills and ships. The lower part on the right side shows a gulf but not any island. At this time, Hong Kong was but one among a cluster of coastal islands in the Xin'an district of Guangdong province.

Like Hong Kong's colonial street names, old maps tell interesting stories, especially when Chinese mapping practices came into direct conflict with those of the West. The Qing (Manchu) dynasty rulers focused not so much on topography as on geopolitics. What its maps roughly reflected was the relationship between peripheral regions and the administrative center in Peking. The Hong Kong village that appeared on several eighteenth-century Chinese maps was a nameless dot on the southern periphery of China. Viewed from the capital city, Hong Kong held little significance in the Qing empire. This may help explain why the Chinese so cavalierly handed the island over to the British at the end of the Opium War. Early English maps, by contrast, demonstrated a clear

A view of Victoria Harbor from Kowloon peninsula in the 1840s, and a bamboo aqueduct delivering water on Hong Kong island (Thomas Allom).

perspective of space—and of its possibilities for geographical expansion. Size, shape, location, as well as distance, created an image which, in the case of the British, served as a blueprint for imperialism.

The British took possession of Hong Kong in 1841, but they had been eyeing the island for a long time before. Their trading ships had used the port for anchorage and fresh water supply, and from the many maps they drew of the coastline, the British had come to understand the strategic importance of this hilly island near the entrance to the Pearl River. Lord Macartney's famous mission to China in 1784 further enriched Britain's geographical knowledge, though it failed in its diplomatic quest. Even more accurate maps of the southern coast were drawn up in the early nineteenth century, under the aegis of the British East India Company. British imperialism in Asia was buttressed not only by its gunboats and opium trade but also by its expertise in navigational mapping.

Thus, on January 26, 1841, when a small platoon of British naval forces from HMS *Sulphur* under Captain Edward Belcher landed on the northwestern tip of the island and hoisted the British flag at 8:15 A.M., the task of producing a nautical chart of Hong Kong harbor was the first order of business. Belcher was commissioned to undertake a hydrographic survey of Hong Kong and its surrounding waters, and the masterful chart he produced was remarkably accurate, containing details that are repeated on maps to this day.

A popular legend tells the story of how some British sailors from Belcher's expedition got lost in the southern part of the island. They bumped into a local peasant named Kwan, who led them over the steep hill to the north side, where they reconnected with their mates. The Chinese phrase "Ah Kwan Tai Loo," meaning "Ah Kwan led the way," became slightly abbreviated to Kwan Tailoo, translated "Kwan's Way." This sounded to British ears like Queen's Way. Thus, according to this legend, the first major road built and named by the British— Queen's Road—actually referred, inadvertently, to a Hong Kong native.

A nice story, but most likely untrue. According to research conducted by the Chinese writer and scholar Ye Lingfeng, the term kwan tailoo in Cantonese pronunciation probably refers to kwan-tai, a sash in women's clothing, which is what the winding road may have looked like when viewed from

Kowloon peninsula. Still, this latter-day legend about the peasant Kwan proved useful diplomatically, and for more than a century the colonial government exploited it as a metaphor for Sino-British amity. The scene was engraved on official seals and, until 1962, on police badges. In the foreground were two Chinese men with queues, dressed in Qing dynasty clothing; one of them was shaking the hand of an English gentleman wearing a tall hat and tails. In the background were two ships—a Chinese junk and a British clipper. The mythical meeting is remarkably similar to equally fictive images of first encounters between Europeans and the natives of North America. All we know for sure is that Captain Belcher took possession of Hong Kong without meeting any resistance from the several thousand Chinese already living on what Lord Palmerston (Britain's prime minister at the time) described inaccurately as a "barren rock."

Belcher's expedition to Hong Kong was a direct outgrowth of the Opium War. This conflict erupted in 1839 after the Qing dynasty attempted to enforce a ban on the importation of Indian opium into China. The British resisted the ban, in part because opium sales were essential to redressing its growing trade imbalance. Silks, porcelains, and tea had been in great demand in England for over a century, but British products had proven less attractive to the Chinese. The market for opium from India, on the other hand, seemed limitless—and highly profitable. By the 1820s the British East India Company was smuggling 900 tons of opium per year into China, and in 1838—just before the war began—the number had risen to 1,400 tons.

In March 1839 the Qing emperor's new commissioner, Lin Zexu, demanded that the British halt all opium shipments going through Canton (Guangzhou), the only Chinese port open to the West at that time. When the British refused, Lin imposed a total trade embargo. At that point Charles Elliot, the British superintendent of trade, ordered all British subjects to turn over their opium stores to the Qing commissioner. When Lin disposed of several million pounds of opium by flushing it into the sea, the British government declared the action a destruction of private property and responded with warships and soldiers. The military superiority of the British was evident from the start. With British gunboats firing on coastal villages at will, the Qing army proved no match for modern cannon and muskets.

Possession Street marks, more or less, the area where Captain Belcher and his small platoon came ashore to take possession of Hong Kong. Because of land reclamation, it is no longer on the waterfront. Though the British promptly named this spot Possession Point, "possession" did not mean legal ownership. The island was not legally ceded to Britain until the signing of the Treaty of Nanking in 1842, and the treaty was not ratified until 1843. In addition to giving Hong Kong and a few surrounding islands to the British, this treaty opened five Chinese ports to foreign trade.

The British chose Hong Kong over several other possible cessions, including Taiwan (Formosa) and the Chusan islands, for a number of strategic reasons. The availability of fresh water was a factor, but the major one was military defense of Britain's commercial interests in nearby Canton. There, influential merchants (taipans) in the opium trade—men like Lancelot Dent, William Jardine, and James Matheson—immediately saw great potential in this small island just off the coast. Over the initial objections of Lord Palmerston and his foreign secretary, the earl of Stanley, Jardine and Matheson persuaded London to take Hong Kong by force. Six months after Captain Belcher hoisted the British flag, Henry Pottinger declared that Hong Kong's harbor would henceforth be a free port for international trade.

Once Hong Kong was open to foreign commerce, it began to attract ships from Canton and also from the Portuguese colony of Macau, on the other side of the bay. British taipans built warehouses, called godowns, along the harbor for storing opium, and they gradually moved their factories from Canton to Hong Kong. Within a decade, almost the entire waterfront—from Possession Point to East Point in Causeway Bay—was flanked with two- or three-story godowns belonging to the big trading companies. Wherever British military imperialism led, British mercantile capitalism soon followed.

A map drawn in 1842 and credited to Pottinger provides a detailed sketch of the northern section of the island shortly after possession. Clear demarcation lines parceled the land into lots numbered 1 to 68. In addition to Dent's Pier, the map shows the future building sites for various government offices and houses of high officials. The curving line of Queen's Road is clearly marked. A square-shaped area called "Magistracy including Jail" occupies a strategic position on the hillside overlooking the old Chinese quarter. Together with three subsequent maps—Gordon's Map, attributed to A. Gordon, the first land officer, in 1843; the City of Victoria–Hong Kong map taken from Lieutenant Collinson's Ordinance Survey in 1845; and the Plan of Victoria from 1856—this map clearly indicates a vision of urban development held by the early colonists.

In the 1856 Plan of Victoria we can see some of the familiar buildings that embodied British colonial power, and a few are still standing in their original location today: Government House (home of the governor), St. John's Cathedral,

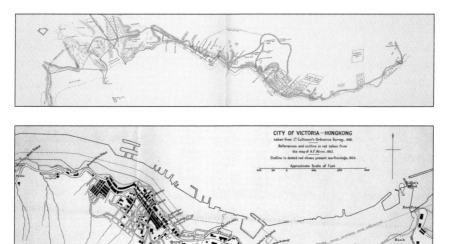

Top: Pottinger's map of the city of Victoria, 1842. Bottom: City of Victoria–Hong Kong, taken from Lieutenant Collinson's Ordnance Survey, 1845. Changes in the waterfront are shown for 1862, 1923, and 1991. Reclamation continues today.

the Central Police Station, and the Court House. By this time, banks—the bastion of British mercantilism—had also made their appearance: the Oriental Bank (first established in 1845), Agra Bank, Mercantile Bank, and the Bank of India, Australia and China. Perhaps the most important of all and the flagship of Britain's overseas capitalism—the Hong Kong and Shanghai Bank—would be established in 1865. Its first building occupied the appropriate address of No. 1 Queen's Road.

If we compare the 1856 plan of Hong Kong with plans of other British colonial cities in Asia (Singapore, Penang, and Kuala Lumpur, for instance), we notice that the basic design of all these Victoria Cities or George Towns is essentially the same. It is a plan drawn from necessity—transportation and self-defense, embodied in a major thoroughfare and in military forts and barracks situated on strategic points, often at the top of a hill. But these towns were also designed for the display of British imperial power. Most of the public structures were edifices in stone and marble built in the imposing neoclassical style of nineteenth-century England and strategically placed in an equally imposing location. Each colonial possession was a small replica of London and an expression of the majestic power of the metropole.

TO PUT THESE BRITISH AMBITIONS in perspective, it helps to look at some population statistics. In 1841 the Chinese population of the island numbered about 7,450 (as compared with a few hundred Westerners in these early years), of whom about 2,000 were boat people earning a meager living by fishing. Others were stone-cutters, coolies (unskilled laborers), small vendors, and peasant farmers. The village of Chek Chue (Stanley) on the southern tip of the island had about 800 Chinese residents and 180 shops. It was a small port for merchants trading in dried fish and other products from Canton. A village for stone-cutters at Shau Kei Wan on the northeast corner of the island had 1,200 residents. In 1842, after Hong Kong formally became a British colony, the island's population increased sharply to 12,361 souls, half of whom lived on the north side in what was first known as Queen's Town and soon renamed Victoria City. Most of these Chinese immigrants had flocked to Hong Kong from the mainland to seek work in this newly declared "free port." By 1844 the island's inhabitants had increased to 19,000, of whom 13,000 lived in Victoria City and nearby. A year later, of the 23,817 inhabitants on the island, 22,800 were Chinese. Among them were 7,460 stone-cutters and construction workers, about 10,000 laborers, 3,600 boat people, and 1,500 servants. In 1851, the population reached 32,983. The ratio of Chinese to Westerners was well over 20 to 1.[4]

The Chinese population on Hong Kong island was generally poorer and less settled than their compatriots across the harbor on the Kowloon peninsula. There, since the seventeenth century, and with the encouragement of the Qing government, waves of settlers had emigrated with their families to work in the salt fields and in farming. By contrast, Victoria City was considered unsuitable for family living, and most of the Chinese employed in colonial Hong Kong were single men. Public security was weak, and theft and robbery were rampant. On April 26, 1843, some burglars even ventured into the governor's mansion. Two days later, in one evening, three of the leading British firms—Dent's, Jardine's, and Gillespie's—were robbed. In reaction, the colonial government imposed a rigid curfew: no Chinese were allowed to go out after 10 P.M., and no ship movement was permitted after 9 P.M. Every Chinese was required to carry a lantern and a pass when walking on the streets at night. This racist policy was in force until 1897.

In the early 1840s, most Chinese resided in the Lower Bazaar area of Jervois Street and Bonham Strand on the north side of Queen's Road in Sheung Wan, which soon became the focus of Chinese community life. As city construction got under way, the growing Chinese population was relocated to what became known as the Upper Bazaar area at Tai Ping Shan—an area of less than half an acre. According to one story, the name Tai Ping (Peace Hill) commemorated the peace of 1810, following the final battle between the legendary pirate Cheung Po Tsai (fighting alongside his "Dragon Lady of the Seas," the wife of the deceased pirate leader Cheng Yat) and the combined forces of the Qing imperial navy and the Portuguese fleet. Cheung Po Tsai was a Robin Hood figure whose large fleet and heroic feats were recounted from generation to generation through a rich oral tradition. Many "retired pirates" settled on Tai Ping Shan Street, which was bedecked with gaudy brothels.

In the second half of the nineteenth century, as more immigrants arrived, the Chinese community expanded into a veritable city of its own. From its center on Tai Ping Shan Street, it stretched all the way downhill to the shoreline, its narrow streets filled to the brim. Today, Tai Ping Shan Street is lined with half a dozen temples dedicated to local gods, and on a small side street, Water Lane, is a shrine for an Earth God that was once stolen and then retrieved from Shau Kei Wan on the eastern end of the island. The god apparently revealed his whereabouts to true believers in a dream—an episode that reflects a long history of clan warfare in old Hong Kong.

In addition to being a magnet for coolie labor, the island attracted wealthy Chinese merchants from the mainland, who sometimes had two shops: a primary shop in Canton and a branch in Hong Kong. A rich merchant might also keep two residences: a home in Canton where his family under his principal wife lived, and another house in Hong Kong where he kept a concubine or *yi-nai* (second wife). Hence, the Cantonese expression *bao yi-nai* or "keeping a second wife." According to popular legend, one clever concubine concocted a special soup to keep her master in her house, and the phrase *yi nai lien tang* or *ah yi lien tang* (appetizing soup from the second wife) stuck in the popular imagination and later became the name of a restaurant chain. One can be found near the pedestrian escalators at Lyndhurst Terrace. According to legend, Yi-nai Lane (its official name is On Wo Lane), off Gough Street, got its nickname because a rich merchant was enamored of a beautiful and intelligent courtesan who became his *yi-nai* and bore him a son. In gratitude, he bought her all the houses on the street.

Less privileged Chinese workers who could not afford a second wife resorted to brothels (as did British soldiers). What the early maps, with their leased lots, army barracks, and government buildings, did not show was a red-light district on Possession Street, near where Colonel Belcher's platoon first landed. The Chinese name of the street was Shui Hang Hao Gai (Water Puddle Mouth Street), at the border between Central and Sheung Wan. By the end of the nineteenth century, this area was thriving. Among the scores of brothels were four famous courtesan houses named Brocade Hall, Joy House, Strange Flower, and New Flowers. Alongside were gambling houses, opium dens, and more than a dozen restaurants where Chinese merchants wined and dined and talked business, especially those engaged in the export-import trade with China.

Like its counterparts in Shanghai, this was a world of taste and decorum as much as a playground of the flesh. It became the custom for rich merchants to request the company of courtesans at banquets—cultured women who were appreciated for their beauty and talent in singing as well as other favors. Courtesans aspired to a high public standard of behavior governed by rigid rules, even though their social status was low and their family background poor. By the early 1920s, the brothels and courtesan houses were relocated from Shui Hang Hao Gai to Shek Tong Tsui on the northwestern part of newly reclaimed land in Sheung Wan. During its heyday, this new red-light district had over a thousand workers in no fewer than eighteen restaurants. Some fifty brothels of various sizes employed more than two thousand prostitutes and two thousand servants. But the splendor did not last long. In the late 1930s, the government banned prostitution, and Shek Tong Tsui receded from history into legend and film.

The behavior of wealthy Chinese merchants offers a partial answer to a question raised by some Chinese historians: Why, given such disproportionate numbers in the population, did no large-scale insurrections occur among native workers before the early twentieth century? The answer is that before the Opium War, Canton's trade system had made some Chinese merchants exceedingly rich, and their ranks swelled with additional fortune-seekers when Hong Kong became a free trading port in 1842. British colonials rewarded their Chinese collaborators with money and recognition, and even outcasts could achieve high social status—a luxury seldom attainable in traditional China— by working faithfully for their Western overlords.

Two of these men—Loo Aqui and Tam Achoy—were engaged by British forces to supply water and food during the Opium War. After the British took possession of Hong Kong, Loo and Tam were rewarded for their service with land grants, exclusive trading rights, and opium monopolies that brought them instant wealth. Later on, the status of the Chinese elite was legitimized with

British honorific titles such as justice of peace and even knighthood. Thus, in addition to law and punishment, collaboration became a winning way to keep Chinese leaders submissive, and through the British system of indirect rule these men in turn kept the local population under control.

With this system, a few representatives of the Chinese elite served as middlemen between the colonial government and the Chinese population. The rest of the natives were left alone, to be managed by these Chinese gentry through their own social organizations and neighborhood security system. The natives were free to observe local customs and rituals with little interference from the colonial government, as long as law and order were not disturbed. This form of local self-government was far from democratic, however. For their influence, the Chinese elite relied on a paternalistic system derived from Confucianism. Lower-class Chinese willingly obeyed, their socialization reinforced through close observation of custom and ritual. The essential conservatism in these popular traditions was precisely what the colonial government counted on for maintaining civil and political stability.

The new social status of the Chinese elite also brought with it a sense of obligation to the local community. In 1847, with contributions from Loo and Tam, the Man Mo Temple was constructed on the western end of Hollywood Road. It was intended for worshipping the gods of civil and martial arts, but eventually it became the site where local disputes were settled—a Chinese alternative to the British courts. Certain religious rituals had to be performed in the temple before the proceedings began. These included swearing a vow by burning incense, and cutting the head of a rooster right in front of the temple gods—a ceremonious act performed by both the accuser and the accused. This was a long-standing custom of the boat people carried over into the Man Mo Temple and reportedly also adopted by the judicial courts. The task of arbitration and final settlement was entrusted to a few respected elders, whose judgment was almost invariably obeyed.

The Man Mo Temple quickly became the center of Chinese social and civil life. Some local historians consider it to be the first Chinese institution of civil government in Hong Kong, but this use of temples was not unusual: they had long been a part of informal government in China. Temples created an invisible web of social cohesion and coercion that was deeply conservative precisely because the community needed these cultural traditions to protect itself and its interests while under foreign rule. Even a radical revolutionary like Sun Yat-sen, who was Western-educated, still had to work within these social bounds in order to solicit support for his cause.

CONTRARY TO MOST Western interpretations, the record of colonial rule in nineteenth-century Hong Kong was not glorious. Still, the trials and errors of the British—and their subsequent efforts to correct their mistakes and missteps—left a legacy that endures in Hong Kong today.

The first order of business in the new colony was to establish law and order. Charles Elliot, who negotiated the ceding of Hong Kong, proclaimed on February 1, 1841, that different laws and punishments would apply to Chinese and Westerners. Because he was busy handling trade affairs with China from his base in Macau, Elliot appointed Colonel William Caine to serve as chief magistrate and police officer of Hong Kong (a post which in Chinese eyes was similar to the familiar country magistrate in China) and First Lieutenant William Pedder of the battleship Nemesis to serve as harbor master. This division of labor worked fine as far as colonial administration was concerned, but in legal matters it was far from satisfactory. There was as yet no judiciary system, no court house, and no lawyers. All of these needs were left to Hong Kong's first governor, Henry Pottinger (who served only one year, 1843–1844).

Pottinger had negotiated the Treaty of Nanking in 1842, and the final ratifications were duly exchanged in Hong Kong on June 26, 1843. He welcomed the Chinese envoy Qiying in a lavish banquet, during which both men sang their native songs. Pottinger was enthusiastic about the new British possession and predicted that "within six months of Hong Kong being declared to have become a permanent Colony, it will be a vast Emporium of commerce and wealth." This statement is where the legend of Hong Kong as the emporium of the East got its start.

But like Elliot, Pottinger was too preoccupied with important affairs in his dealings with China to be concerned with the day-to-day administration of one tiny island. Run-of-the-mill matters were left to his deputy, Alexander Johnston. The legal basis for Hong Kong's colonial government was laid down in the Hong Kong Charter of April 5, 1843. Under its terms, the governor (who until 1859 also held the more important position of superintendent of trade for China) ruled the island with the advice and assistance of two bodies, the Legislative Council and the Executive Council. Membership in the two councils was deliberately kept small, each consisting of only three appointees named by the governor. Empowered to initiate and pass laws without the consent of the two bodies "should the necessity for such a proceeding arise," the governor held extraordinary influence. As a consequence, from a British point of view, the history of colonial Hong Kong was principally the story of the twenty-eight men who were appointed governor and the seven men who served as acting governors. Down to the Second World War, the colonial government was basically run by a very small group of thirty-three administrative officers filling twenty-three offices.[5]

Pottinger also established Hong Kong's first High Court, with himself as chief justice and General George Charles D'Aguilar as his deputy. The first court house was situated at Queen's Road Central near D'Aguilar Street and later moved to Statue Square. D'Aguilar tried Hong Kong's first case, which involved a Filipino sailor. He was found guilty of manslaughter and received the death penalty, though later pardoned. The first public execution—the hanging of three English sailors—was performed in 1859 on Hollywood Road in front of two thousand native spectators. It was clearly meant as a warning to other troublemakers.

But from the beginning the court had considerable difficulty in taking Chinese offenders to trial and sentencing them. To what extent should native practices be taken into account in meting out punishments? For example, a traditional sentence for minor crimes was $15 or twenty strokes with the rattan and cutting of the hair tail (queue), which was considered a great humiliation. By 1870 the penalties became more stringent. The use of the so-called "Nine-tailed Whip," which could inflict severe injuries on prisoners, was not only condoned but encouraged.

In 1841 William Caine had organized an informal police force consisting of three English officers and 160 policemen (78 Europeans, 48 Chinese, and 34

Indians). In 1844 Governor Davis formally signed it into law and recruited Charles May to organize a larger police force. Its ranks were soon filled with Sikh soldiers, who were deemed more trustworthy than Chinese. By 1868 the police force had 633 men, of whom 113 were Europeans, 328 were Indians and Sikhs, and 192 were Chinese. They arrested so many locals that in the 1860s two new wings had to be added to Victoria Prison, which could now hold 600 prisoners. But Chinese and Western prisoners were not treated equally—Chinese inmates were crammed into dirty, congested cells, significantly smaller than those occupied by Western inmates.

Two buildings to serve as police headquarters were added in the early twentieth century. The entire compound, consisting of some seventeen buildings, occupied a large block flanked by Hollywood Road on the north and Chancery Lane on the south. Situated on Tai Ping Hill overlooking the Chinese quarters not far away, it had a commanding presence. The police-prison-magistracy complex was modeled after London's Old Bailey, and to reinforce that fact, the steep slope on the west side was named Old Bailey Street. But the locals quickly nicknamed it Fate on a Slant Street, since the fate of prisoners in the jails facing Old Bailey Street hung on sentences handed down from the magistracy nearby. Blatant bribe-collecting characterized the police force for over a century, until the ICAC (Independent Commission Against Corruption) was established in the 1970s specifically to investigate corruption.

Today, the old police station, long unused, is at the center of a heated debate over the preservation of historic sites. Several locally prominent families offered to buy up the entire compound and turn the buildings into a memorial museum. Through its century-long history, especially during the Japanese occupation (1941–1943), some of China's most illustrious political leaders, intellectuals, and writers were detained there, together with common criminals of all kinds. The museum proposal was turned down by the government, which hopes to develop the area for tourism. As of late 2007, the case was still unsolved, and meanwhile the gates of the compound have remained closed. Uncertainty over its future has elicited much critical opinion about the government's neglect of the city's historic sites. Every day, throughout the city, more and more old buildings and streets are threatened by the same fate: demolition in the name of urban renewal and commerce.

In the early years, law enforcement and the judicial system were impeded by a lack of reliable translators. All court deliberations involving Chinese natives had to be done by English interpreters who knew both Chinese and Cantonese. For many years after the 1840s only one man was qualified for the job—Daniel Caldwell, registrar general, who married a Christian Chinese woman and was reputed to be an excellent "colloquial linguist." But Caldwell had surreptitious connections with gambling joints and even with Chinese pirates. He was fired but then reinstated, despite his questionable character, because his skills were so desperately needed.

When the famous sinologist James Legge, who had translated the Chinese classics, happened to be at a trial and corrected a mistake by the court inter-preter (probably Caldwell himself), Governor Hercules Robinson formally made a motion at the Legislative Council that London should send students to Hong Kong to study Chinese and become interpreters. The plan was put into motion but with little long-term success, because the first three students were appointed to other posts as soon as they arrived. An independent juridical system was gradually developed in the early twentieth century, in part because more Chinese interpreters and qualified barristers and solicitors were available. Some of them eventually were appointed judges. They also became prominent leaders of the local Chinese elite.

THE MID-NINETEENTH CENTURY was an unsettled time for main-land China, and rumblings were felt on the nearby island of Hong Kong. One unexpected outcome of a joint British and French invasion of the mainland in 1858–1860 (the so-called Second Opium War) was the ceding of Kowloon peninsula to Great Britain (finally ratified by the Convention of Peking). This invasion, along with internal turbulence created by the Taiping Rebellion in southern China (1850–1864), sent yet another wave of immigrants to Hong Kong, including a number of wealthy Chinese merchants. In 1861, when Kowloon was added to the census, Hong Kong recorded a population of 119,321.

With sixty-nine Chinese merchant houses (hongs) in the city, Hong Kong replaced Canton as the major port for foreign as well as domestic trade. The largest of these trade houses was Nam Pak Hong (North and South Store), with shops located on today's West Bonham Street in Sheung Wan. The Chinese traders organized themselves into various hong-wai, or self-governed trade associations. As with the first generation of Chinese elites, the elevated social status of these new immigrants brought with it a sense of obligation to the larger community.

A group of prominent Chinese merchants formed a committee in 1869 to meet a dire need—the colonial government's failure to provide suitable medical facilities for the Chinese population, who distrusted Western medicine. On Po Yan Street, a few blocks from the Man Mo Temple, the Tung Wah Hospital opened in 1872. The Chinese merchants built it at their own expense. At the inaugural ceremony, officiated by Governor Richard MacDonnell, all thirteen members of the hospital's board of trustees were attired in the formal gowns worn by the lower ranks of Chinese officials. Following common practice, they had purchased their titles from the Qing government.

The lavishness of the ceremony indicated that the role of the Tung Wah Hospital was not limited to medicine. It was in fact a civic center involved in such philanthropic activities as caring for the destitute, sending remains of the dead back to China for burial, repatriating kidnapped laborers and women, and running an insane asylum. And like the earlier Man Mo Temple, the Tung Wah Hospital became the place where civil and commercial disputes were settled, allowing the Chinese to avoid the unfamiliar and often corrupt clerks of the British courts. In short, the Tung Wah Hospital was the first association that represented the interests of Hong Kong's entire Chinese community. It still exists today as a large-scale philanthropic organization consisting of hospitals, rehabilitation centers, and nursing homes for the aged.

Because Hong Kong was a free port, custom duties could not be levied, and so Hong Kong's governors had to raise revenue by leasing land. Legally, land in Hong Kong belonged to the government, as it still does today. Though Hong Kong's third governor, Sir George Bonham (1848–1854), deeply distrusted the local Chinese, he made land available for housing construction by both Westerners and natives for a lease period of 999 years, instead of the 75 years decreed by his predecessors. The Chinese gentry welcomed this move because they could now build houses for occupation by their sons and grandsons practically in perpetuity. But Bonham's law also set a precedent for the government to enrich itself by land sales, in collusion with real estate developers. Today, Hong Kong's housing market is among the world's most expensive, thanks in part to this historic pact.

Bonham also removed the hated poll tax and tried to endear himself to the leading British merchants by appointing two of their representatives to the Legislative Council. This move ensured that one representative from Jardine & Matheson would sit on "Legco" until the end of the First World War.

DESPITE MUCH STRATEGIC COLLABORATION between rulers and ruled, the situation in early colonial Hong Kong was fraught with mutual distrust. No matter how successful Chinese merchants may have been in their business dealings, they were not permitted to occupy residences on Victoria Peak, which was reserved for Westerners. When this practice was proclaimed law at the end of the nineteenth century, it institutionalized racial segregation even between wealthy Westerners and wealthy Chinese. The notion that Hong Kong prospered as a result of the enlightened policies of British liberalism and laissez-faire economics was in large degree a myth of colonialism.

The segregation of the Chinese and European communities in early Hong Kong reflected British colonial practices around the globe. But in Hong Kong's case, it had fatal consequences. In 1894 an epidemic of bubonic plague broke out in the Tai Ping Shan community, and by the time it was extinguished, twenty thousand lives had been lost in Hong Kong, most of them Chinese. Despite warnings from homeland experts in London, the deplorable living conditions of the Chinese population on the island were not addressed by the government, and in such an environment a natural catastrophe was inevitable.

In Chinese households in Hong Kong, hygienic conditions had been poor from the very start. The shabby tenements (called tong lou) were always overcrowded. An eye-witness account by the journalist-intellectual Wang Tao, who at that time lived in Hong Kong, included this vivid description: "The Chinese tenements are as small as snail's shells and as thick as beehives. With about 10 dollars for monthly rent, often 7 or 8 families lived in one room—or two or three families at the very least. They lived together but cooked separately. A family of husband, wife, children and grandparents squeezed into an area of less than 10 square feet, sleeping, eating, washing, and bathing together, like silkworms caught in a cocoon or ants in a hole. This is definitely not for human habitation."[6] These oblong tenements, usually two or three stories high and between 10 and 60 feet deep, were built back to back, so that only one side had windows and fresh air.

What Wang Tao failed to mention is that toilet facilities were nonexistent. Women and female children used night containers hidden under their beds; men and boys went out to public toilets administered by the government. The night soil from these toilets was transported back to Canton, in a lucrative trade arrangement. The tenements also housed large numbers of domestic animals, which slept under beds and in the shared kitchens. Goats and cows were kept to supply milk to European households; and when meat was needed, livestock was butchered on the spot. No fresh water was available in the tenements, and the only sewers for waste water were open ditches running down the middle of the road. Water supply was a perennial problem in Hong Kong, and the government's new reservoirs on Pok Fu Lam Road and in other parts of town were insufficient for the island's constantly growing population.

Needless to say, rats thrived under these conditions, and the plague they brought to Hong Kong was part of a large-scale epidemic that eventually swept across South Asia and other parts of the world. In Canton, by some estimates, more than a hundred thousand people died. When the epidemic reached nearby Hong Kong in the spring of 1894, more than a hundred residents succumbed on one day, and more than five hundred perished in the first month. The plague did not come to an end in Hong Kong until 1924, and by then total deaths from this disease exceeded twenty thousand.[7]

While the colonial government did nothing to prevent the outbreak, it acted

quickly to dispatch teams of unarmed volunteer soldiers to sanitize the Tai Ping
Shan area. "You should try to imagine the armed volunteer soldiers . . . carrying
brushes, whitewash, carbolic, and spades to disinfect the houses and remove
the rubbish," Patricia Lam writes. "They were instructed to locate victims of
the plague—those still living—to get them into isolation hospitals and the dead
for burial . . . The hated soldiers would be storming the front door while the
plague sufferers were hurriedly transferred by the back door to neighboring
houses. When the soldiers found a victim, they would empty the house of all
its contents, furniture and clothing in a bonfire on the street, and then whitewash the interior with lime while the unfortunate ousted residents stood watching in horror. Rumors circulated that eyes from the plague-ridden bodies, taken
by the soldiers for burial in lime-filled pits, were being used to extract medicine
for the royal family in England."[8] When Governor William Robinson finally
made the decision to purchase and raze 350 houses and redevelop the rat-in-
fested area, at the considerable cost of HK$821,000, almost half of Hong Kong's

Chinese population, temporarily homeless, left the city, bringing commerce at the port to a stand-still.

The plague became the backdrop in the first chapters of a fictional trilogy on Hong Kong history written by the contemporary novelist Shih Shu-ching in 1993.[9] In the first installment, the Chinese heroine, a prostitute named Wong Tak Wan (Cloud-Getting), encounters a British official, Adam Smith, on the slope of plague-ridden Tai Ping Shan. Smith, assigned to clean up the mess, has his first glance of the beautiful Cloud. Smith's family intervenes in the romance, of course; he acquires an English wife; and he keeps Cloud as his mistress in another house downhill for the occasional tryst. Eventually (and predictably) he abandons her, and the later chapters of the novel shift to her own struggles to sustain her life through other men. In the second novel of the trilogy, she gives birth to a son from her union with Smith, and eventually the family rises in Hong Kong society. At the end of the trilogy her offspring all become members of Hong Kong's new elite, one a Supreme Court judge.

Was this trilogy—of a lower-class prostitute, ravaged by British colonialism, who struggles to climb up the social ladder through her own efforts—intended as a parable of Hong Kong itself? If this work carries any message beyond its well-wrought narrative and its vivid descriptions of the difficulties faced by Hong Kong's Chinese population, it is certainly that we should not belittle the "low" origins of Hong Kong's culture, which contain the seeds of its real strength.

Reflection of the backside of the HSBC bank building in Central.

2

Central Values

The heart of modern Hong Kong is the Central Business District, or CBD. Here, in an area of less than a square mile, the edifices that have given Hong Kong its image as "Asia's international city" are clustered together in all their dazzling splendor. Yet situated at the very center of this bustling district is a tiny, somewhat antiquated plot of ground known as Statue Square. Until recently, the most spectacular way to arrive at Statue Square was to take the Star Ferry from Kowloon, which docked at the nearby Edinburgh Place pier. Alas, this legendary pier, known to tourists and locals alike for half a century, was closed in November 2006, to pave the way for a new highway designed to service yet more land reclaimed from Victoria Harbor. The nearby Queen's Pier suffered the same fate, over mounting protest, in July 2007.

The removal of the old Star Ferry pier signaled a radical change in the urban landscape of the CBD. The Star Ferry now docks at Piers 4–7 to the west, near the International Finance Centre (IFC) and Exchange Square, and pedestrian traffic has shifted in that direction. Meanwhile, construction is under way on a huge government compound on the waterfront in the Admiralty area directly to the east. Located between these two beehives of commercial and administrative expansion, Statue Square has begun to lose much of its significance for modern Hong Kong. Already it has a somewhat abandoned look, and in a few more years it will probably be displaced altogether. Yet, paradoxically, as Statue Square retreats from the present and recedes into history, the role it once played at the center of the city's economic and political life becomes more fascinating to an urban "archaeologue."

FROM THE CORNER OF Queen's Road and Pedder Street, where our tour of old Hong Kong began, the short walk to Statue Square can be overwhelming to a first-time visitor. Traffic is hectic, as fast-moving taxis and automobiles, along with double-decker buses and trams, compete for narrow street space. Crowds of shoppers and office workers at ground level jostle their way through the maze, sometimes ignoring stop lights. The Central Business District is not conducive to a leisurely walk. One has to pace oneself according to the tempo and rhythm of the crowd's movement—certainly not at the normal walking speed of *andante* but faster, more like a perpetual *allegro*, or, just before 9, even *presto*, as office workers rush to their posts. These mostly-young men and women in their smart black suits (the CBD uniform), talking nonstop into cell phones, seem to be always in a hurry to make appointments and meet deadlines.

An hour later, when the district's upscale boutiques open their polished doors, another single-minded crowd—intrepid shoppers this time—descends on the CBD. And at noontime, the narrow pedestrian streets that lead uphill from Queen's Road to the restaurants of Lan Kwai Fong—streets such as D'Aguilar and Wyndham—present a different kind of congestion, especially when human traffic in both directions must yield to wheeled carts pushed by laborers yelling "Make way! Make way!" in Cantonese. Aside from a few marked areas controlled by traffic lights, most major thoroughfares in Central are sealed off with steel railings that prevent people from crossing streets at ground level. Pedestrians get around by using elevated footbridges and enclosed passageways, reachable by stairs or escalators from entrances that are not always well marked. For instance, at Pedder Street and Connaught Road, an unmarked stairway leads to a web of footbridges that head off in various directions—northward to the IFC and the new Star Ferry pier, eastward to Statue Square and City Hall.

Alternatively, a guest staying at the world-famous Mandarin Oriental Hotel close to Statue Square can go up from its lobby to the second floor and find an indoor passageway that takes him to Prince's Building. There, a right turn over to Alexander House and a walk through a glass-enclosed bridge leads to Gloucester Tower in The Landmark shopping center. And from that location, another set of indoor corridors through Chater House brings him to an exit at several elevated footbridges leading to Exchange Square, the IFC, and the piers. This weblike system of indoor passageways represents a complete inversion of the conventional concept of "path." It is mostly indoors, it runs *through* buildings instead of skirting around them, and it is elevated rather than at ground level. An ingenious model of design and modern engineering, Hong Kong's enclosed, air-conditioned passageways and open-air covered footbridges make maximum use of the CBD's limited urban space.

A footbridge near the IFC in Central.

The name Statue Square has become a misnomer, for Queen Victoria's statue, after which the square was named, is nowhere to be found. It was removed during the Japanese occupation and later reinstalled at Victoria Park in

Causeway Bay, where it stands, forlornly, in a corner across the street from the public library and next to a busy soccer field. The only statue left in Statue Square is that of Sir Thomas Jackson, the energetic founder and first chief manager of the Hong Kong and Shanghai Banking Corporation (HSBC), whose headquarters stands right behind him along the southern edge of the square.

In a way, Sir Thomas's statue is a more fitting memorial to the former Crown colony's financial prowess than the dowdy queen resting on her throne. Almost no one in this city, and certainly not in the CBD, has ever doubted that "capital" is the engine behind the "Hong Kong miracle." Although Statue Square is the private property of the HSBC, by specific agreement with the government in 1901 the bank allowed it to be reserved for permanent public use. Of course, the true purpose of that agreement was commercial and even ideological, since this open space made the bank's prominence in this most central area of the Central Business District all the more visible. Today, the dramatic skyline along the island's northern rim is formed almost entirely by bank towers like the HSBC and corporate headquarters of international businesses.

The architectural inventiveness of the forty-seven-story HSBC building, designed by Sir Norman Foster, is striking. Its construction took four years—a long time by Hong Kong standards—and cost HK$5.2 billion (US$668 million). When it opened in 1985, it was billed as "the most expensive singular construction in the world" and one of the ten most significant works of contemporary architecture. The bank's three previous buildings at the same address (1 Queen's Road Central) were also impressive in their day. The second one (1886–1933), built in Victorian style with a colonnade and a large octagonal dome, exemplified the pretensions of British imperialism. It was demolished to make way for a third building designed in the Chicago School style of Edward Sullivan. This was the first building in Hong Kong to be fully air-conditioned and was said to be the "tallest building between San Francisco and Cairo"—a fitting epithet that bespeaks the bank's growing financial prowess in the "Orient."

As the bank's name indicates, the HSBC's two centers of operation were in Hong Kong and the British concession in Shanghai. The fates of these two cities were linked in an intricate matrix of economic and cultural activities throughout the nineteenth and early twentieth centuries, until the Communist takeover of China in 1949. And even then, the HSBC remained a symbolic link between them. In front of the bank's headquarters in both Hong Kong and Shanghai were a pair of bronze lions, which were said to bring good luck to the bank and its customers. The lions in Shanghai had been brushed to an everlasting shine by the hands of numberless passers-by before they were removed to a museum after 1949. In Hong Kong, the lion on the left, with its mouth open, was named Stephen after the Hong Kong bank's general manager, A. G. Stephen, and the lion on the right was named Stitt after the general manager of the Shanghai branch at that time. Whether these statues have brought good fortune is anybody's guess, but it is widely believed that the bank's location in Central has better *feng shui* (literally "wind and water") than its giant neighbor to the east, the Bank of China.

Sir Norman Foster's Hong Kong and Shanghai Banking Corporation headquarters.

   The old twelve-story Bank of China building, standing right next door to the HSBC, was dwarfed by Foster's mammoth tribute to Western capitalism. Not to be outdone, the Bank of China engaged I. M. Pei—a native of China whose father was himself a prominent banker—to design a new seventy-floor tower on Garden Road behind the old building. It was completed in 1989 and opened for business in 1990. At 1209 feet (including its two masts), it was the tallest building in Hong Kong and in all of Asia until the Central Plaza building in Causeway Bay was completed in 1992.

   Some say that the faceted glass façade of Pei's building resembles two sharp blades like Chinese cleavers that cut into the aura of the HSBC. Its reflective glass on the back side is also said to hold the image of Government House (the official abode of the governor) in captivity. In the 1990s, as the handover of Hong Kong loomed, the political symbolism of this Chinese bank towering over these two bastions of British colonial power was hard to miss. But *feng shui* practitioners argued that the sharp edges and the numerous X-shaped crosses in Pei's original design had negative connotations. He modified the façade to some degree, but the effect is still the same.

No *feng shui* master seems to have objected to the strategic placement of the bank's neighbor: the Cheung Kong (Yangtze River) Center, home of the number-one billionaire in Hong Kong, Li Ka-shing, whose empire of real estate, supermarket chains, power companies, and other investments has reached into every sphere of Hong Kong life. His two sons, Victor and Richard Li, are also major tycoons, the latter owning the largest telecom company in the region. Li Ka-shing's company had a hand in building the seventy-three-story skyscraper in west Central called The Center. One can ponder the significance of such unimaginable wealth and power while resting in the beautiful, secluded Cheung Kong Garden, where trees and plants and a small gurgling stream, designed with classical Chinese grace, offers a temporary haven from the fiercely competitive free-market jungle all around.

If we look up at the Bank of China building from this resting place, we will find that its architecture reveals Pei's own Chinese roots. By imitating bamboo shoots in the framing, he probably intended to convey a sense of upright majesty. By contrast, the lower part of the building (especially when viewed from inside the lobby) resembles the shape of a Chinese emperor's tomb. Presumably Pei's motif reassures the bank's customers that their deposits are in safe hands, but it lacks the dynamism that twenty-first-century financial transactions seem to demand.

Its contrast with the HSBC is striking. If the Bank of China appears stolid and enclosed, anyone can pass through the open base of the HSBC. Foster's postmodern design, unlike Pei's high modernism, allows this corporate space to merge with the public space in Statue Square, in a seeming transparency of interaction. While tourists frequently stop to admire the bank's façade, few of

The secluded Cheung Kong Garden in Central.

them ever venture to enter the building. From ground level, an escalator takes visitors up to the bank's business counters and offices, as if entering the belly of a gigantic whale. Inside, the atmosphere seems surprisingly cold and a little frightening—like a set from the science fantasy movie *Brazil*, which happens to be an allegory of a future totalitarian society. Surveillance is ubiquitous, and photography is not allowed in most areas. This alienating effect is surely not what the architect intended.

As we look around—furtively, by necessity—we see bank clerks working feverishly but quietly, with astounding efficiency. The same working style can be found in every bank in Hong Kong—even at small bank branches. Local customers take this level of efficiency for granted, but first-time customers from overseas are often surprised to find that opening an account, with the help of mostly bilingual clerks, is effortless. By comparison, banking in American cities can be a disagreeable chore.

WITHOUT A DOUBT, smooth, efficient functioning in all spheres of life, especially the economic sphere, is the hallmark of modernity, Hong Kong-style. However, the cool rationality behind all kinds of "service" in this city—in banks, hotels, restaurants, other service industries, and certainly the government bureaucracy, whose various branches are also called "services"—gives one pause and may even inspire one to ask: Efficiency at what price? No one working in Central seems to have pondered this question until it was raised by a concerned outsider, Lung Ying-tai, the former chief of the Cultural Bureau of the city of Taipei.

In a public speech delivered to a capacity audience in Hong Kong on November 9, 2004, Lung used the term "Central values" for the first time as an epithet for modern Hong Kong.[1] In her view, this value system is dominated entirely by the operational logic of capitalism. The key words are money and power, profit-making and commercial competitiveness, efficiency, development, and globalization. The functioning of the entire system is sustained not only by the capitalist free market system, of which the banks and multinational companies in CBD are emblems, but also by a huge government bureaucracy. It consists of three top officials, a large Executive Council, and eleven civil service bureaus—but nothing resembling a Bureau of Culture. In Lung's view, this absence signals the utter neglect, if not disdain, of cultural preservation on the part of Hong Kong's elite. For wealthy business leaders and officials in the CBD, cultural preservation means, paradoxically, the effort to preserve a few old streets and buildings that are themselves colonial sites. Other local relics from the city's Chinese history and collective memory—temples, markets, street bazaars—have their civic champions, but these activists have had to struggle against a relentless governmental policy of phased demolition in the name of urban renewal.

Ironically, the decisions to preserve or destroy landmarks are reached in an elaborate bureaucratic process—instrumental rationality carried to the extreme, one might say. Certain old buildings of value, historical or otherwise, can be earmarked for preservation, but the process from petition to deliberation to final approval is so daunting that it is more difficult to preserve than to destroy. In Taipei, Lung Ying-tai took the opposite approach: she initiated new laws that made it more difficult to destroy anything old, including old trees, than to preserve them.

In Lung's view, these artifacts of the past are not just part of the "aura" of a city; they are its very lifeblood. Cultural inheritance is crucial to the character of any city, to its identity. Even colonial relics must be preserved in order to re-examine and remember them critically from a native, postcolonial perspective, she maintained. The obvious case for comparison is Macau, where the government has successfully preserved a cluster of old churches and other historical buildings, and UNESCO has recognized them as treasures of the world's cultural heritage. Hong Kong does not have a single entry on UNESCO's list of 851 World Heritage Sites.

Lung's plea for cultural preservation was welcomed with enthusiasm by many in her audience, but to powerbrokers in the CBD, cultural heritage has the negative connotation of traditionalism. Many found her views disagreeable. Why excoriate Hong Kong for upholding the values of capitalism, they asked, since those very values have made the city what it is today? What is wrong with thinking that making money is the main purpose in life? Typically, the government made no formal response, pro or con, to her remarks, although several high officials attended her talk. Lung's status as an unsolicited outsider did not work to her advantage. She was not one of the invited foreign "experts" or consultants whom the government regularly engages, sometimes at enormous cost, as part of its bureaucratic process of "consultation." Their advice, good or bad, is often followed, and things can change only *within* the structure of this "due process." Pressure from the outside—when it exists at all—has little effect.

This system was established by Hong Kong's British masters and inherited by the city's postcolonial Chinese elite. And the simple truth known to all is that since 1841 the leaders of Hong Kong have pursued two vital interests: trade and land. The land is owned largely by the government, which sells or leases it to the highest bidder, sometimes far above market rate. In so doing, the government secures for itself a tidy income, in addition to taxes. To justify this high cost, the developer who wins the bid tries to reap the maximum profit within the shortest length of time. Especially since 1997, most people in Hong Kong believe that real estate tycoons and government leaders have colluded to exploit this system.

Only in the last few years has the notion of sustainable growth begun to catch on in some circles—"sustainable" as opposed to unchecked growth. Yet the big developers still cast all caution to the winds in their singular pursuit of profit. To be fair, in Hong Kong, with its burgeoning population and limited, hilly terrain, verticality (building upward) has become both an architectural style and a necessity of life. But in Lung's view, the price paid for this expensive system of land sale and lease and rapid development is an increasing disparity between rich and poor.

Lung offered an alternative vision of a humane and truly democratic urban culture that is deeply concerned with the social well-being of its people and with the preservation of their culture—a vision now being realized in Taipei. But then and now, it is abundantly clear that Hong Kong's government follows a totally different set of rules, according to which problems must be approached and solved on the basis of economic considerations alone. Thus, to solve the problem of increasing disparity between rich and poor, according to a recent "Manifesto for Progress" issued by chief executive Donald Tsang, the government must push for more economic development so as to create more jobs, reduce unemployment, and increase wages—in short, to make the rich richer and the poor not quite so poor. No long-range program was laid out to build up what one local commentator calls the "social capital" of civic engagement, collective responsibility, and mutual trust.

A calculated balance between investment and profit underlies all real estate development in Hong Kong, not just tall buildings. The most recent example of this "logic" at work is the functional approach to traffic and roads. As the city expands into the harbor through land reclamation, new roads are needed. And the solution to building new roads is more land reclamation. The rationale is simple: reclamation has been going on since the mid-nineteenth century, and because a rapidly growing population requires more land, why not "finish the job" by narrowing the harbor even further? The problems of increasing pollution and diminishing scenic beauty are duly noted but are considered of secondary importance.

What these rational bureaucrats have failed to gauge, however, is a subtle change in popular sentiment, a gradual and barely perceptible shift from acceptance of unchecked development to awareness of historical preservation. At least a small part of Hong Kong's "Central values" is being put to the test, and a potential battle between the government and civil society is now looming. One recent incident serves as an indication: the relocation of the Star Ferry from its old pier at Edinburgh Place.

The Star Ferry was founded by Dorabjee Nowrojee, a wealthy Parsee merchant who made a fortune in the bakery business and owned several hotels in Hong Kong. In the 1880s he bought a small ferry service from a certain M. Buxco. Inspired by a line from Tennyson's poem, "Crossing the Bar": "Sunset and evening star, and one clear call for me!" he named the service Star Ferry. This may be an urban legend, but in any case Nowrojee turned his two ferries—called *Morning Star* and *Evening Star*—into a regular service for natives who lived on Kowloon peninsula and worked on Hong Kong island. The legend may have persisted because it so perfectly fit the natural beauty of Victoria Harbor, especially around sunset.

In 1898, when Nowrojee retired to India, he sold the service to Kowloon Wharf, which went public under the name of the Star Ferry Company, Ltd. Currently, a fleet of all-star ships (*Morning Star, Day Star, Night Star, Celestial Star, Twinkling Star, Meridian Star,* and so on) crosses the harbor continuously between Kowloon and Hong Kong island. Over time, the ships changed from steam power to diesel and electric power, and from single-deckers to double-deckers with two separate classes. The fare has always been low, and even a modest increase in 1966 triggered a hunger strike followed by riots—an event that some local historians hailed as a milestone in Hong Kong's social movement.

The *Celestial Star* ferry, on its way from Central to Kowloon.

The Star Ferry pier on Hong Kong island was relocated several times as the shoreline encroached on the harbor. A pier built in 1911, at the foot of Ice House Street, was moved in 1957 to Edinburgh Place at the northern end of Statue Square, which was itself reclaimed land. The most remarkable feature of that pier was its clock tower, a gift to the city from John Keswick, a tycoon of Jardine, Matheson & Co. The clock's iconic status in the everyday lives of Hong Kong residents was apparently overlooked by the rational planners of the government's Urban Renewal Authority when they cavalierly decided to demolish the Edinburgh Place pier and replace it with an Edwardian replica at Piers 4–7 further west. Ironically, a survey commissioned by another branch of the government, the lower-echelon Antiquities and Monuments Office, had already sent

The Edinburgh Place clock tower, demolished in late 2006, with the Jardine building in the background.

a warning: "No other ferry pier along the harbor could possibly perform such a symbolic function as this clock-tower pier. The removal of the Star Ferry Pier to Piers 4–7 leading to its destruction would likely raise public objection and dismay."[2] The prediction came true, but the scale of public outrage was unexpected.

Some 150,000 protesters and onlookers gathered on November 11, 2006, to witness the Star Ferry's last trip between Edinburgh Place and Tsim Sha Tsui in Kowloon, and to condemn the government's decision to relocate the ferry service and destroy the old clock tower and pier. Emotions ran high as citizens marched through the area, carrying posters and shouting slogans. Speakers and musicians voiced the sentiments of the crowd about the value of preserving the city's collective memories and the negative environmental impact of reclaiming more land from Victoria Harbor. This unexpected eruption of opposition and nostalgia sent a clear signal to the government: Hong Kong might be on the verge of a cultural awakening.

Interestingly, no visible protest was made when the government announced the plan to destroy the old pier or when construction on the new pier was under way. It was just at the last moment, when the public woke up to the realization that the government was going to destroy rather than remove the old clock, that a spontaneous demonstration suddenly broke out. The bureaucracy had miscalculated public sentiment. Even members of Hong Kong's architectural community came out publicly to condemn the move. Clearly the government's philosophy of rational instrumentality was being challenged.

The message of the protesters was obvious: no more senseless demolitions that threaten to destroy the harbor landscape. The next site slated for destruction was Queen's Pier, in front of City Hall, and local activists immediately formed groups to protect it. The government, after some protracted deliberations and considerable loss of money (payment for delays due in its contractual agreement with a reclamation and construction company), finally decided to act by its own final deadline of July 31. But the protesters, now calling themselves a "movement for native power," were well prepared. Three months earlier, throngs of them had already begun to "take possession" of the pier. They also collected more than four hundred signatures from prominent local scholars, writers, and cultural workers (including myself). The film star Chow Yun-Fat and some other famous personalities appeared in person to lend their support.

On the evening of July 27, three of its young protest leaders began a hunger strike, which was followed by an all-night vigil. The government

Signs were posted throughout the Star Ferry terminal on November 11, 2006, protesting its relocation and the destruction of the Edinburgh Place pier and clock tower. "Our clock tower, and we can't keep it at last?!"—a bilingual sign speaks for itself.

this time adopted a more conciliatory attitude by sending a civil servant to attend a public forum to engage in a "dialogue" with the young protest leaders—but neither side gave in, of course. On the final night of July 31, the protesters staged an all-night carnival, with speeches and singing that drew considerable media attention.

The politicians from the Legislative Council were absent and silent, since they had all, regardless of party affiliation, voted to support the government's plan to destroy Queen's Pier, presumably to build more highways and ease the traffic jam in Central. Their action was entirely in accordance with "due process" and law, but their utter lack of preservation consciousness was once again blatantly clear. Finally, in the late morning of August 1, the last of the protesters were dragged away by police, and the drama ended.

Despite its failure, which even the activists expected, this movement of civic protest certainly marked a turning point in Hong Kong. At the very least, it brought the entire issue of preservation vs. development to the forefront of people's thinking. There are visible signs that the government is seeking to make some compromises in other urban renewal projects, including the imminent demolition of a six-hundred-year-old village compound in the Wong Tai Sin area, the last of the old villages in urban Kowloon—ironically, over objections from the contracted development company that already bought the land. Obviously, the government is caught between the competing demands of land developers and local protesters. How to balance these two conflicting forces—development vs. preservation, money power vs. "the people's power"— remains to be seen. This will surely be a most exciting "spectacle" to watch, even for visitors.

THE OPENING OF A NEW "retro" Star Ferry pier to the west of Statue Square came just three years after the completion of Hong Kong's tallest skyscraper in the same vicinity. This tower, Two IFC, is the crowning glory of the International Finance Centre, billed as "an integrated commercial development on the waterfront of Hong Kong's Central District." Designed by the Italian architect Cesar Pelli and opened in 2003, Two IFC is eighty-eight stories tall (considered a very lucky number)—the seventh tallest building in the world and the third tallest in the Greater China region.

Two IFC invites comparison with its architectural counterpart, Taipei 101, which assumed the position of tallest building in the world at the time of its completion in 2004. In the eyes of detractors, both buildings are shaped like phalluses—an apt image, perhaps, for the capitalistic ambitions of their developers. Even those who reject this imagery concede that the IFC is much less glamorous than Hong Kong's second-tallest skyscraper, Central Plaza in Causeway Bay, which displays a playful art deco flair, especially at night when it is bathed in multicolored neon light. Viewed from Kowloon peninsula, the two buildings shine like gigantic beacons in this city of mammon, inviting investors from around the world to enter the harbor and make a fortune. No wonder that the American economist Milton Friedman held up Hong Kong as his favorite model for a free market economy.

But as Lung Ying-tai pointed out in her 2004 speech, capitalism cannot thrive in Hong Kong without the complicity of the city's large governmental bureaucracy. On the east side of Statue Square stands the Legislative Council building, a two-story granite edifice in the neoclassical style designed by Sir Aston Webb, who was also responsible for the eastern façade of Buckingham Palace. It is no accident of history that this low-rise building shares with the HSBC some of the most expensive real estate in Hong Kong. British colonialism would not have been successful without the underpinnings of law as well as capital. In the absence of a modern legal system to make and enforce contracts, trade and land development on a vast scale would have been impossible. And conversely, it is not surprising that Central values—capital accumulation, profit motive, free market competitiveness, land development, global trade, consumerism, and pervasive efficiency—have permeated the city's political life.

The Legco building opened in 1912 on reclaimed land where the colony's Supreme Court once stood. Above its main entrance stands a statue of the blind-folded Themis, goddess of Justice—a replica of the figure erected at the Old Bailey in London. There is nothing unusual in this colonial application of

The Legco building, before the statue of Queen Victoria was moved to Victoria Park in Wan Chai.

an architectural style inspired by the democratic ideals of ancient Greece: neoclassical buildings in Hong Kong (including the first HSBC building and old City Hall), Shanghai, and elsewhere were blatant expressions of British imperialism and power in the Victorian era. Most of them have long since disappeared in Hong Kong, leaving only a few marked for historical preservation, the Legco building being one. Today, as sixty legislators sit in its chambers to deliberate delicate matters of democratic government, the troubled ghosts of colonial law and justice still hover over the site.

The kind of government practiced inside the Legco building is an elitist form of parliamentary democracy, Hong Kong-style. The Basic Law for Hong Kong, formally approved by the National People's Congress in Beijing in 1990, made sure that Legco's composition would reflect a broad spectrum of Hong Kong's population in terms of both district and professional representation, thereby defeating any possibility of a fully popular representation by direct election. Although Article 68 of the Basic Law stipulates that the "ultimate aim" is the election of all Legco members by universal suffrage, it does not specify the date at which this goal will be realized. The popular demand for direct election is circumscribed by this ingeniously devised "system" and, of course, by Beijing's cautious policy.

Only half of Legco's sixty members are directly elected from five designated "geographical constituencies" (Hong Kong Island, Kowloon East, Kowloon West, New Territories East, and New Territories West). The other half are representatives from twenty-eight "functional constituencies" representing various sectors that supposedly played a crucial role in Hong Kong's development. They are: village council, agriculture and fisheries, insurance, financial services, transport, accountancy, finance, education, legal, information technology, medical, health services, architecture, surveying and planning, real estate and construction, social welfare, tourism, commercial (two groups), industrial (two groups), import and export, wholesale and retail, textiles and garment, sport, performing arts, culture and publication (all in one group), catering, district council, and labor.

This list claims to be comprehensive and representative, but real estate, commercial, and industrial interests predominate, and their "elected" representatives (drawn mostly from the Liberal Party) are pro-government and largely pro-China. The majority party, the Democratic Alliance for the Betterment of Hong Kong, openly supports Beijing. Members of the "opposition" minority largely represent the legal and academic professions, and they belong to the new Civic Party or to the Democratic Party, whose once-commanding position has shrunk.

This practical arrangement is a form of "controlled democracy," whose checks and balances are viewed by the commercial sector as a safeguard against political extremism at the grassroots. But to members of the Democratic and Civic parties, Hong Kong's government is certainly no democracy, and they clamor for popular election of all representatives, including the chief executive. So far, their goal remains unrealized. The vague prospect is that popular election will happen in 2012, but no one is sure. The final decision rests with Beijing.

The defenders of the Basic Law are quick to point out that membership in the Legislative Council has been undemocratic from the earliest days of British colonialism. The first charter of the Crown colony (1843) was a sparse document hastily drawn up in London that took no notice of the local population. There was no Chinese representative until 1880, when Governor John Pope Hennessy appointed Ng Choy (Wu Ting-fang) as a temporary nonofficial member for three years. In 1896 Chinese membership was increased to two, out of a total of seven official and six nonofficial council members. The former were appointed by the governor and the latter were chosen from the British business community, including a permanent representative from Jardine & Matheson. The size was increased again in 1925 to nine official and eight nonofficial members, of which three were Chinese. The Legislative Council approved the annual budget and wrote "ordinances," but its powers could be curtailed by its chairman, the governor himself, who cast the decisive vote in a tie and could even overrule the entire council, so long as he had the backing of Whitehall in London. Legco members were dismissible by the governor at any time.

The current membership is predominantly Chinese, and this fact alone represents a major improvement in representation over the colonial past. But as the Oxford scholar David Faure, himself Hong Kong born and raised, remarked in 1998: "The politics of appointment created men who were adept as appointees. What you don't find in this community is the voice of the under-privileged being represented," except in the municipal body of the Urban Council, which has no major policy-making powers.[3] With Hong Kong's increasing disparity between rich and poor, and with political power almost entirely in the hands of the rich, clearly a price has been paid in this game of capitalism-driven politics.

ON THE EAST SIDE of Statue Square, across Connaught Road from the Legco building, stands City Hall. The old city hall, built in 1869 and demolished in 1947, was a Renaissance-style edifice with a fountain in front donated by Dent & Company. The new City Hall, opened in 1962, was the first truly modern public architecture on Victoria Harbor. Designed by Gordon Brown, the founder of the University of Hong Kong's Architecture Department, the two-building complex is laid out on a clean and unadorned plan characteristic of the International style. It stresses "functional" form as opposed to decorative motifs, and as such it matches perfectly the public mission of the buildings themselves. At night, like other structures along the waterfront, City Hall comes alive with continuously changing patterns of colored light.

The two components relate to each other asymmetrically, one standing tall and the other lying flat on the ground. In between is a quiet square garden commemorating those who died during the Second World War. The tall building with twelve stories houses a number of government facilities, including a library, exhibition gallery, and a marriage registry. The low building contains a 1,434-seat concert hall on the ground floor, modeled after London's Festival Hall; on the second floor is an exhibition space and a 463-seat theater. The concert hall is used heavily as a performance space by the Hong Kong Sinfonietta and other groups, and it boasts better acoustics than the much larger concert hall of the Cultural Center in Kowloon, which was built in the 1980s.

As a longtime Hong Kong resident, Matthew Turner, has observed: "Against the monumental, colonnaded architecture of Central District's clubs, courts and banks, it was a startlingly light and open building, from its extensive public areas to its exposed glass stairwell. The association of the cultural with the political and the civic was also unusual." In Turner's opinion, the new City Hall symbolized the colonial government's determination in the 1960s "to draw together the people of Hong Kong into an integrated community . . . characterized by a fusion of European and Chinese traditions."[4] During the two decades after its opening, the building was the only public venue for public and cultural functions in Hong Kong. It became a favorite gathering place for all kinds of civic activities: meetings, performances, and marriage ceremonies. The Urban Council had its offices there until it was abolished after the handover.

In the late 1960s and early 1970s, the concert hall and theater doubled as a cinema known as Studio One, which showed European—particularly French New Wave—art films. These screenings nurtured a generation of Hong Kong directors, including John Woo, Tsui Hark, Ann Hui, and Alan Fong. Every Sunday, the public grounds around the building—indeed all the public spaces in nearby Queen's Pier and in the entire CBD area—fill up with thousands of Filipino maids on their day off. Sitting in small, densely packed groups, chatting, eating, and singing, these women express a new kind of urban solidarity appropriate to this hopeful civic space. In late July 2007, some of them joined the Queen's Pier preservationists in their protest carnival, in a show of shared community values.

Up the hill from Statue Square, between Upper Albert and Lower Albert roads, is the protected compound known as Government House, where the current chief executive, Sir Donald Tsang, resides. Hong Kong's first Chinese chief executive, Tung Chee-hwa, who assumed office in 1997, refused to live there, probably because of its associations with colonial governors. Since Tsang, unlike Tung, is a product of Hong Kong's civil service bureaucracy, it seems somehow fitting that he should choose to live and work in the house of his former masters. Tsang is the driving force behind the construction of a new government complex on reclaimed land facing the harbor in Admiralty. This new administrative site will centralize the government's many bureaucracies and will house the Legislative Council—once again changing the geographical and political landscape in Central.

Hong Kong's civil service bureaucracy, consisting of some 162,000 members, is the largest in Asia, closely followed by that in Singapore. Its offices are scattered all over the territory (hence presumably the need to put them under one roof). In its early years the Crown colony was governed by about two dozen British officers with such titles as colonial secretary, colonial treasurer, attorney general, colonial surgeon, postmaster general, and superintendent of Victoria Goal.[5] In 1861 Governor Hercules Robinson established a competitive examination system to recruit and train British administrators. This innovation produced Hong Kong's first crop of professional civil servants, some of whom were conversant if not fluent in Chinese, and they quickly formed the backbone of the colonial government.

The civil service allowed colonial governors in the last quarter of the nineteenth century to be only moderately capable and still govern effectively. An exception to this rule of mediocrity was John Pope Hennessy (1877–1882), one of the few nineteenth-century governors to call for a partnership with the local Chinese. Known for his sympathies with the "underdog," he openly claimed that he had "often taken counsel with my Chinese friends as to what would be the best course to adopt for this colony."[6] He appointed Ng Choy to be an unofficial member of the Legislative Council, over strong objections from the European community. This did nothing for his popularity with the "Peakies," but he was an Irishman, and perhaps his own "minority" status helps to explain his sympathy for the plight of the Chinese. As a result, he was the least liked by the Westerners, who did not show up to say farewell at his scheduled departure.

The civil service went through a series of reforms and restructurings, especially under governors Mark Young (1941–1947) and Alexander Grantham (1947–1957). The year 1946 marked the beginning of "nativization" or "decolonization" of the civil service bureaucracy and the involvement of more local Chinese in running the government. Before 1946, most of the high offices were reserved for "overseas" personnel. In 1951, 10.75 percent of the senior-level offices were staffed with Chinese. By 1971, 52 percent of the 2,872 senior officials were native Chinese. Yet despite this trend, the salary scales and other bonuses were structured to discriminate against the "locals": "overseas" personnel were given higher salaries and more privileges, presumably to compensate for their "hardship" while working in a foreign outpost. The same unequal treatment extended to the judicial system. When Patrick Yu became the first Chinese to be appointed Crown Council in 1951, he found to his dismay that not only was his salary lower, without housing allowances (because of his so-called "non-expatriate" status) but he was barred from attending a trial of a Western criminal, on the pretext that he might be racially prejudiced![7]

After the handover in 1997, the civil service bureaucracy remained intact, but more new offices were added. Still, the efficient and elaborate bureaucratic procedure remained the same: opinion papers were written, memorandums were signed, detailed agendas were drawn up, and frequent meetings were called. All of the documents were still written in English, with wooden Chinese translations. As "due process" was added to the list of Central values, the ironic result was a reduction in the effectiveness of decision-making. Bureaucratic efficiency returned under Donald Tsang, but other problems persisted. A century and a half of colonial rule had nurtured what Faure called a "dependent" mentality—an ability to master an elaborate system of rules and procedures but a reduced capacity for initiative and creative thinking.[8]

LOOKING BACK on Hong Kong's history in the twentieth century against this bureaucratic background, we can detect a widening gap between political activism on the mainland and conservative inaction among the colony's leaders. The early decades were troubling times for Hong Kong. As rising nationalism threatened and finally toppled the Qing dynasty in 1911,

British colonialists and Chinese businessmen tried to maintain the stability and harmony of Hong Kong, just as their present-day counterparts do. But the winds of change swept over the colony nevertheless.

When news of the Revolution's success reached Hong Kong, several thousand citizens cut their queues in celebration. Barbershops even offered free queue-cutting services. The jubilation was shared by all classes, from rich merchants and compradors to clerks and coolies—the same people who had joined in honoring the coronation of King Edward VII in 1901. When the provincial government of the Republic of China was established in Canton on November 10, 1912, two Chinese members of the Legislative Council petitioned Governor Frederick Lugard (1907–1912) to have a day off so that some Chinese could go over to attend the ceremony. Lugard reluctantly agreed, after the petitioners assured him that the celebration had nothing to do with politics.

Lugard's successor, Francis May (1912–1919), had served as a colonial administrator in Hong Kong for twenty-eight years before his appointment as governor, and during that time he became universally disliked by the Chinese community. On the way to his inauguration ceremony on July 4, 1912, he barely missed being hit by an assassin's bullet. While the attempt was the act of a frustrated man with no revolutionary connections, May found himself in a political vortex. Not all Chinese residents in Hong Kong were in favor of the new republic, particularly because the Canton government was itself corrupt. And as regional organizations, such as clan associations and chambers of commerce, mushroomed, the business community in Hong Kong was torn with internecine conflict. Not wanting their nascent nationalism to interfere with their long-term interests as colonial subjects, they adopted both patriotism for China and collaborationism with British colonials. Among the lower classes, anti-British and antiforeign sentiments were more strongly felt, and the growing rage of the dispossessed triggered a series of strikes and boycotts after 1911.

The tram boycott of 1912–13 originated with a foreign-owned tram company that refused to accept the newly minted coins from the Canton government. Some of the regular passengers, mostly lower-class employees, received their salaries in Canton copper coins, which were lighter and cheaper to make than

Hong Kong currency. A thousand protesters surrounded the tram station at Shau Kei Wan on November 24, 1912, and another thousand openly clashed with the police at Des Voeux Road in Central. Governor May summoned 150 Chinese businessmen to a meeting and urged them to ride on trams themselves to set an example. It turned out that some of them owned shares in the tram company.

The tram episode was a prelude to more riots and strikes, all connected with Hong Kong's burgeoning labor movement. A typical example was the seamen's strike in early 1922. The large number of Chinese seamen in Hong Kong were employed by foreign ship companies, working more than ten hours a day at miserably low wages as deck cleaners and cooks. Foreign seamen, who were given less arduous jobs, were paid five times more. The demands for higher wages by the Chinese seamen's unions were rebuffed repeatedly, and the Chinese Chamber of Commerce refused to mediate on the seamen's behalf. A general strike was finally called in January 1922, and thousands of seamen walked off their jobs and returned to Canton, to a hero's welcome. Dock and transportation workers soon joined the strikers, swelling their ranks to some thirty thousand. Yet both the government and the ship owners refused to budge.

The policy adopted by Governor Reginald Stubbs (1919–1925) was severe repression, which resulted in the exodus of thousands more Chinese back to Canton. When the companies tried to recruit new seamen from Shanghai, Singapore, and other places, the strikers staged an embargo that practically closed down the harbor and brought shipping to a standstill, thus causing the price of rice and other commodities to rise.

By late February, 120,000 additional workers and laborers had joined the strike, including Chinese cooks and servants employed in foreign households. Yet Hong Kong's Chinese businessmen urged the government not to compromise. Some merchants charged that the unrest was instigated by Communist agents from Canton, but the newly founded Chinese Communist Party had only thirty-two members in the entire Guangdong province, and none of the striking seamen held a membership. The support came, rather, from all "parties" in Canton, and a Hong Kong–Canton nexus was forged that would pave the way for more political protest.

The fifty-six-day seamen's strike came to an end when Ho Tung, a wealthy businessman and philanthropist, offered a large sum to pay for half of the seamen's lost salaries. The shipping companies then agreed to a salary increase of 15 to 30 percent. The final victory of the Chinese seamen apparently threw Governor Stubbs into despondency, as he reported to the Colonial Office: "We should hold Hong Kong for twenty years at the most."[9] Stubbs was even more despondent two years later, during the last year of his tenure, when another strike of even larger scope occurred. This was the famous Canton–Hong Kong General Strike of 1925, celebrated in all Chinese history books but scarcely mentioned in Western histories of Hong Kong.[10] The strike originated with the May Thirtieth incident in Shanghai in 1925, when a Sikh policeman killed and wounded more than thirty demonstrators. Demonstrations raged all the way from Shanghai to Canton, where some fifty people were murdered in what became known as the Shakee Massacre on June 23, 1925.

Tremors were felt in Hong Kong, where demonstrators and strikers took to the streets in sympathy. Seamen and dock workers were, again, the first to rise up, followed by students who boycotted classes, postal workers, barbers, waiters, and even the cleaning staff in Jardine's. The total number of strikers in late June numbered between 100,000 and 200,000 — or nearby half of the total work force, and one fourth of the entire population. As rumors of killings and deaths spread, between 130,000 and 140,000 people left Hong Kong for China, causing local rents to plummet.

The resentment of the lower classes against Governor Stubbs was palpable. Someone nicknamed him "Shit-tubs." Enraged, he petitioned London to send gunboats to Canton. When London refused, he tried to raise money to bribe the authorities in Beijing to intervene. When this failed, he resorted to chicanery in implicating the Tung Wah Hospital in "secretly advancing $50,000 to finance a coup."[11] Finally in October, after none of these measures succeeded, he left Hong Kong, abandoning the whole mess to be cleaned up by his successor, Cecil Clementi (1925–1930).

Called "an old fox" by one Chinese scholar, Clementi cleverly parlayed his way into revolutionary politics in Canton and sided with the right-wing

Nationalists (Guomindang) under Chiang Kai-shek. With Chiang's sudden purge of Chinese Communists in April 1927, the strike in Hong Kong lost the support of the leftists. Some of the business community's most eminent leaders actively intervened on behalf of the government, and once again this united front on the part of colonial bureaucrats and Chinese businessmen ended the strike.

Sir Cecil was a fluent speaker of Cantonese, an accomplished calligrapher, and a translator. Yet his immersion in classical Chinese literature and culture did not change his late-Victorian taste or colonial airs. Often these two sides—Orientalism and Victorianism—seemed to reinforce each other in his bearing. He supported the establishment of the first Department of Chinese at the University of Hong Kong in the early 1920s, but he appointed two arch-conservative teachers who saw themselves as loyal remnants from the Qing dynasty. The department did not introduce the study of modern Chinese language and literature until 1935, when the Chinese author Xu Dishan became chairman.

Governor Clementi was clearly aware that continuing segregation between the British and Chinese in Hong Kong was breeding misunderstanding, but he could do little in the 1920s to ameliorate the situation. The tumultuous events taking place on the mainland—the founding of the Chinese Communist Party in 1921, the first clash between the Communists and the Nationalists in 1927, the Northern Expedition of the Nationalist troops under Chiang Kai-shek, who established the Nanking government in 1928—did not create a ripple in Hong Kong society. It was as stratified as it had ever been. A visiting English writer, Paul Gillingham, observed that "one's place was fixed according to race, nationality, accent, and position." Clementi's limited effort to enlarge the Chinese membership in the Legislative Council and his appointment of Sir Shouson Chow as the first Chinese to the Executive Council in 1926 did not have much impact on the colony's political structure, and none on the stagnant complacency and provincial snobbery of its social life.

During this critical time, when Hong Kong was in a fog of reactionism, Lu Xun, the dean of modern Chinese writers, was invited to Hong Kong to give two speeches. On February 18 and 19, 1927, in the auditorium of the YMCA on Hollywood Road and Peel Street, Lu Xun delivered his address. He spoke in

Mandarin, with his paramour and later common-law wife, Xu Guangping, serving as his Cantonese interpreter. The titles of his two talks were clearly political: "Silent China" and "Old Tunes Are Over." The first was published in the local newspaper, but the second never appeared and was only later published in a volume of his collected essays. The reasons for its suppression are not hard to gauge, for Lu Xun in these two talks and in other essays on Hong Kong definitely imparted anticolonial messages in his cynical survey of Chinese history and his implicit equating of colonial Hong Kong with "semi-colonial" Shanghai.

In Shanghai society, Lu Xun said, the most powerful group consisted of foreigners, and close to them was "a circle of Chinese merchants and so-called scholars. The people outside were all coolies and lower-class slaves." Hong Kong is a small island, he said, but it is a miniature on which many places from China's present and future are vividly inscribed. "A few foreign overlords in the center, under whom are found a number of ingratiating 'high-class Chinese' and a blabbing group of enslaved followers. Besides them, there are only the silent and hard-working natives. Those who can endure will die in this foreign land, and those who can't escape to the barren mountains. The primitive aborigines are all our ancestors."[12]

Behind this cynical view we can detect a measure of loathing for his own compatriots that is typical of his writing. But in his Hong Kong speech Lu Xun was more forthcoming in his advice: Stop singing the "old tunes" of traditional China, which was a "servile culture" that could only perpetuate the obedience of the Chinese toward their masters. He urged his Hong Kong audience to get out of its protected cocoons and confront danger, for the only alternative to danger is loss of freedom—imprisonment. Thus he concluded: "There are two paths," security and freedom, "and it is clear which path is better."[13] Given the colonial government's promotion of peace and prosperity at all costs, such subversive words were tantamount to sedition.

It was Lu Xun's misfortune to visit Hong Kong during the reign of Governor Clementi. The two men were diametrically opposed in their attitudes toward classical Chinese culture. Lu Xun, the undisputed leader of the New Literature and New Culture Movement in China, minced no words in denouncing the kind of reactionary writing in archaic Chinese that Clementi favored. In his essay titled "On Hong Kong," Lu Xun quoted with sarcasm a speech "in the Cantonese dialect" by "Governor Jin," who was of course Sir Cecil.[14]

Lu Xun was also disgusted by what he saw and experienced on the journey from Canton to Hong Kong. He was searched by colonial Chinese policemen, who asked for and were given bribes. He later read a news item about Hong Kong: two Chinese men in Western suits were searched by a British police officer in Shek Tong Tsui (a brothel area). "One of the men spoke in English to the officer, but the latter ignored him and warned him by saying ***. Finally they ended up in the police station."[15] What irked Lu Xun was the expurgated words from the news report. Whatever the policeman said was clearly a reaction to the English one of the men spoke and perhaps to the suits they wore—both prerogatives of the master race and therefore inappropriate for these Chinese natives.

The famous writer George Bernard Shaw, who met Lu Xun in Shanghai, also visited Hong Kong a few years later, in 1933, and was equally bitter. Shaw was invited to give a speech at a welcoming party at the University of Hong Kong. After being honored and toasted by his British host, he made his famous remark to the HKU students: If you're not a "red revolutionary" at the age of twenty, you'll be a "hopeless fossil" by the age of fifty. He further urged the students: "Always argue with your teacher . . . Always learn things controversially." With his usual acerbic wit, he pushed the students to be on the alert about university education, for it harbors "a continued plot to teach you one side of a thing dogmatically." Apparently to Shaw's disappointment, the Chinese press paid scant attention to his visit and misunderstood his ironic and critical intent in its reporting. When a Western reporter asked Shaw about his impression of Hong Kong, he reportedly answered: "Hong Kong is a disgusting place!" Even Lu Xun himself, although he insinuated as much, was not so blatantly negative about the colony's reactionary atmosphere.

Hong Kong had by this time become a colonial backwater, its former preeminence overshadowed by the rising splendor of Shanghai. While Clementi managed to come to terms with the new leader of the Republic of China, Chiang Kai-shek, he was way behind China's other modern intellectual trends. The triumph of the Communist Revolution and the establishment of the People's Republic of China in 1949 just made the Hong Kong colonial government under Sir Alexander Grantham even more cautious, and another massive influx of refugees from the mainland worsened the city's social, economic, and ideological divisions. Throughout the 1950s, local "politics" was played strictly according to administrative rules.

Not until the 1970s, after another major riot in 1967, did the government finally respond to native unrest. Despite opposition from many Chinese members of the civil service bureaucracy and the Legislative Council, Governor Murray Maclehose (1971–1982) used his own legal powers to initiate new public housing and other social welfare policies. This odd situation—of a reform-minded governor who wished to implement programs for the Hong Kong people, especially the poor, finding his way initially blocked by the apathy of Hong Kong's Chinese upper class—can be understood only in the context of a long tradition of Chinese cultural conservatism, nourished by the collaborative politics of colonial rule.

Both legacies continued well into the 1990s, when Christopher Patten, the last governor of Hong Kong (1992–1997), pushed for direct elections and found himself opposed by this same Chinese elite, whose conservatism now wore a "patriotic" face as fervent supporters of Chinese sovereignty. True, some members of Legco—those of the Democratic Party—campaigned hard for direct elections, but they did not have the necessary grassroots backing. As the handover loomed, the Hong Kong people themselves seemed to give up any hope for a true democracy. The silence and apathy of the Chinese majority even today is, alas, another sad inheritance from Hong Kong's colonial past.

THE CHINESE BUSINESSMEN and government officials who opposed social and democratic reforms in the twentieth century were mostly born in Hong Kong or Shanghai but were Western-educated, either abroad or at the University of Hong Kong. They spoke elegant English but were not necessarily equally versed in Chinese language and culture. Though sophisticated in modern business and financial matters, they were barely conversant in either

Chinese or Western learning. Efficiency without vision seems to be the primary lesson learned from their encounters with the West.

But if we take a different perspective, Hong Kong has been an exciting place for another group of Chinese elites—fringe intellectuals who made extended sojourns to the colony without becoming fully enmeshed in its conservative web and who eventually had considerable impact on the mainland. Hong Kong, like Shanghai and other treaty ports on the China coast, belonged to the Pacific littoral—the area that, for better or worse, came into early contact with foreigners. As such, it provided a window for Western ideas and a stepping-stone for reformist and revolutionary action.

One of the earliest figures in this group, and the most renowned, is Sun Yat-sen, father of the republican revolution. Born in a village near Canton in 1866, he went to Hawaii with his brother and received his early education there. He returned to Hong Kong to attend the Government Central School (later called Queen's College), and he became one of the first students of the newly established College of Medicine for Chinese, the predecessor to the University of Hong Kong. This bilingual education marked Sun off from mainstream scholar-officials who worked their way up through civil service examinations.

Hong Kong was the ideal milieu for Sun because of its fringe position. He credited the city as the "fountain spring of my ideas," because of its orderly streets and buildings, its Western customs and hygiene, and its atmosphere of open discussion and opportunity. But despite his enthusiasm for the colony, working for the cause of revolution was not always easy there. Sun had to start his revolutionary work on the bottom rung of the Chinese community, by working through traditional lineage, clan, and regional loyalties. He had to fraternize in Cantonese with local merchants to raise funds, while seeking the political protection of Governor Lugard.

Lugard shared with his capable assistant and successor, Francis May, the conservative's distrust of all revolutionaries. While he allowed Sun a relatively free hand, Lugard also cautioned those more sympathetic to the revolutionary cause to stay within bounds, for fear that public enthusiasm for the revolution could spill over into antiforeign and anticolonial riots. And Hong Kong's few Chinese intellectuals were by no means in full ideological rapport with Sun, either. Their double loyalty to both China and Hong Kong made it difficult for them to espouse the radical change that a revolution augured.

Ho Kai was one of these intellectuals. He partially financed Sun's revolutionary newspaper, the *China Daily*, and tried to use his connections with the Hong Kong colonial government to help Sun when he could. But he stopped short of supporting a radical revolutionary republic, favoring the British model of constitutional monarchy instead. Ho was a local Hong Kong boy who made good, having been educated in British schools in the colony and in England, where he married an English woman. He served three terms on the Legislative Council, more than ten years on the Sanitary Committee, and five years on the Committee of Public Works. A justice of the peace for twenty-five years, he was finally knighted in 1912.

The historian John Carroll argues that Ho is a perfect case of double identity and dual loyalty to China and Hong Kong. As the only Chinese faculty member in the College of Medicine for Chinese, of which he was also the main founder, Ho shared his liberal ideas freely with his students, including the young Sun Yat-sen. Epitomizing the Westernized littoral Chinese, he opposed the prevailing motto in China (coined by Zhang Zhidong) that Chinese learning should still be the "essence" whereas Western learning could only serve as "utility." Ho argued that it was precisely China's traditional "essence" that needed to change, through universal education, so that the population would be prepared for parliamentary democracy. Above all, Ho believed that "commercialism was the way for China to achieve wealth and power, and that merchants should form the base of a new China." This was a striking statement, in view of the fact that the merchant class was not highly esteemed in the traditional Chinese hierarchy. Ho's argument was clearly based on his own privileged experience in Hong Kong. Ironically, his incipient nationalism made him no longer trustworthy, and he was eventually forced out of public service by Governor May.[16]

In comparison with Sun Yat-sen, Ho fits more predictably into the part of Hong Kong's political culture that did not and could not breed genuine revolutionary radicalism. Had he lived longer (he died in 1914), he probably would have been distressed by the chaotic parliamentary system in China's newly established republic. And in all likelihood he would have been denounced by Maoist revolutionaries as a comprador who sold out to British imperialists. Yet in Hong Kong, Ho was seen as a respectable man, if not a paragon of virtue, who established the tradition of collaborative politics that characterizes Hong Kong's political elite today. The only difference is that the direction of "dual loyalty" has now shifted to the motherland, China.

In 2006, in a belated commemoration, Hong Kong honored Dr. Sun Yat-sen with a museum housed in historic Kom Tong Hall at 7 Castle Road in Central. The two floors inside this renovated house, built in 1914, are filled with old photos, documents, and other valuable archival materials related to his life and activities in Hong Kong. Visitors can also follow the Sun Yat-sen Historical Trail through a maze of small streets and alleys in west Central and Sheung Wan, where thirteen markers point out various sites where he lived, went to school, was baptized as a Christian, and held meetings to plot insurrections in China (no less than six failed attempts). The fact that Sun was not always an honored son of Hong Kong makes it all the more ironic that Nationalist Chinese textbooks depict Hong Kong as the seedbed of the Chinese Revolution, because of Sun's long association with the colony.

Seedbed of revolution or conservative backwater? Hong Kong in the first half of the twentieth century was both at once—a city between worlds.

Double-decker trams, heading east toward Wan Chai and Shau Kei Wan, and west toward Sheung Wan and Kennedy Town.

3

The World of Wan Chai

Wan Chai (Small Harbor in Cantonese) is the most crowded and bustling area on Hong Kong island. For most Chinese locals, this is where the real action is. The gently gaudy, playful look of its most notable landmark, the magnificent Central Plaza tower, captures the indigenous energy of this area. Wan Chai is the only district in Hong Kong that prominently displays its insignia on major streets. It contains only four Chinese characters: Wan Chai, Health, Vitality.

Altogether there are eighteen districts in Hong Kong island, Kowloon, and the New Territories. Wan Chai stretches from the Tamar grounds at Admiralty (future site of the new government compound) to Causeway Bay (with its profusion of sailboats and yachts) to Happy Valley (home of Hong Kong's first racecourse). Touring the area is not as convenient as walking through Central and Sheung Wan because this is one of the most congested parts of the island. The center of human density is surely Times Square and the Sogo Department store in Causeway Bay, but the main thoroughfares of Wan Chai itself—Johnston, Hennessy, Gloucester, and Harcourt roads—are so heavy with automobile traffic that crossing the streets can be an adventure, especially when double-decker buses rush by at incredible speed. Some people maintain that Hong Kong bus drivers hold the world's record for skill and daring.

The most effortless and fascinating way to navigate through this urban jungle is to take the slow-moving tram—itself one of the oldest relics in the city and the world's only surviving double-decker tram service. The upper deck affords a great view, as the cars ramble their way from Central along Queen's Road East.

With a number of twists and turns, the tram skirts Victoria Park and the Tin Hau Temple (one of Hong Kong's oldest) on its way to North Point, Quarry Bay, and Shau Kei Wan at the eastern tip of the island. The ride is convenient, if not so comfortable, and the panorama of buildings and people moving by in slow motion gives one the feeling of traveling backward through time—a nostalgic antidote for the stomach-churning, competitive pace of the Central Business District.

A busy street in Wan Chai, viewed from the upper deck of the tram.

The electric tram started operation in 1904, and the click-clonk of the cars quickly became the soundtrack of a new, modern era. The novelist Eileen Chang once confessed that as a kid in Shanghai in the 1930s, she could fall asleep only while listening to this familiar sound. Later on, at the University of Hong Kong in 1941, she witnessed with great sorrow the surreal sight of a deserted tram car in the midst of Japanese gunfire. Trams had become a fixation in her own imagination, as they still are for most Hong Kong residents.

The first twenty-six tram cars acquired from England were single-deckers with a cross-bench and a passenger capacity of forty-eight. In typical colonial fashion, they were divided into three classes, but this was eventually abandoned. An open-air double-decker tram, seating thirty passengers above and thirty-two below, was introduced in 1912 to meet growing demand. The upper deck was covered in 1923. After 1949 Hong Kong began to construct its own tram cars, and in the early 1950s the tram lines were extended all the way from Kennedy Town on the western side of the island to North Point and Shau Kei Wan at the eastern tip. When drop-in coin boxes were installed in 1976, just one conductor per tram was needed.

Today, the Hong Kong Tramways operates a fleet of 163 double-decker cars that carry an average of 240,000 passengers every day. It provides the cheapest form of public transportation in Hong Kong. The tram runs on six routes, including a single-track circular route around Happy Valley. Two antique open-air cars (Nos. 28 and 128) are in demand mostly for sightseeing. But the days are long gone when the tram offered spectacular views along the waterfront and the bustling harbor.[1] The territory of present-day Wan Chai and Causeway Bay has been so enlarged by reclamation that the original Small Harbor and Copper Gong Bay (the Chinese name of Causeway Bay, referring to its shape) have all but disappeared.

Land reclamation in Admiralty, future site of a new government center.

By 1929 several major reclamation projects had added a total of 85.85 acres of land in this part of Hong Kong island. The first was initiated by Governor John Bowring (1854–1859) in 1855 to reclaim the marshland north of Happy

Valley known as Goose Neck (later named "Bowrington"). In the 1920s, the ambitious Praya East Reclamation Scheme created what has since become central Wan Chai (between Hennessy and Gloucester roads) by razing Morrison Hill and building a special railway to transport the soil for landfill.

Present-day Wan Chai offers a confusing mix of the old and the new. Messy construction sites can be seen at almost every turn, and the future of the district is uncertain. An ambitious developer has proposed a new mega-tower of fifty stories or higher right at the center of Wan Chai, but the project has met fierce local opposition. Especially those who grew up in Wan Chai seem determined to preserve a sense of the district's past, if not through the preservation of every old street and building, then through commemoration. A host of personal reminiscences have appeared in the last decade, written mostly by native writers who grew up here in the early 1950s. They conjure up a community of poverty and suffering, punctuated by occasional joy.

In 2004 a friend and I led a group of some seventy local walkers—self-styled *flâneurs*—along Queen's Road East on a ritual exploration of Wan Chai's past. Shortly thereafter, I led a smaller group of American scholars from a humanities conference along this memory trail. We stopped at the shops of several printers on Lee Tung Street who were then putting up a courageous fight to save their neighborhood from urban renewal. Protest slogans of their own creation were written on the buildings' walls. Preservationists had taken up the cause, making a modest proposal to preserve not the ramshackle buildings themselves but the community of its residents. They argued that to drive them away would eradicate the last traces of an old lifestyle. Their successive appeals and proposals to turn the area into a half-residential, half-commercial compound that would maintain the old communal lifestyle were duly considered by a variety of urban planning committees and finally rejected.

Revisiting the site one late afternoon in March 2007, I found Lee Tung Street deserted and shrouded in darkness—an eerie sight. Chinese pedestrians on Queen's Road East did not cast even a glance at this legendary printer's row, which was once responsible for printing announcements for the most significant events in their daily lives—wedding and funeral invitations, the red Lucky

Money envelopes for the lunar New Year, calendars, and so on. The printers had lost their battle and vacated the premises—a fate that threatens residents and small businesses on neighboring streets in the district.

On the south side of Queen's Road, the market area around Stone Nullah Lane is also threatened with demolition, but the battle for its preservation has not really begun. One building at the corner of Stone Nullah Lane and King Sing Street, known as the Blue House because of its blue walls, has become something of a focal point for cultural preservation in the entire area. Across the street, on a high fence protecting an already demolished building, a large poster by the Urban Renewal Authority contains four words in English: Rehabilitation, Redevelopment, Revitalization, Preservation. Signs like this can be found everywhere in Hong Kong these days. Perhaps by no coincidence is the word "Preservation" placed last. Yet the question raised by the three Rs—how to redevelop an old area so as to revitalize it for rehabilitation, without simply destroying it altogether—goes largely unanswered in Hong Kong.

A very short walk up Stone Nullah Lane toward Kennedy Road leads to a Daoist temple in honor of Pak Tai (North God) and the goddess Yuk Hui. The old temple, with a 140-year history, was preserved and nicely renovated in 2005. Perched on a quiet hillside, it maintains its Daoist serenity, seemingly oblivious to the noise and chaos below—as if to suggest that this is how things have always been in Wan Chai. A secluded mountain trail offers a breathtaking view of the high-rise buildings below. Every day, walkers of all ages make the steep ascent up tiny Wan Chai Gap Road that snakes its way to the top of the mountain. A fitness trail also leads to the penis-shaped outcropping known as Lover's Rock (Marriage Rock in Chinese).

Workers remove equipment from Lee Tung Street, formerly an old printers' row.

The hilly southern area of Wan Chai, along Kennedy and Bowen roads, is quiet and reclusive, in sharp contrast to the hubbub on the north side. We can well imagine why a century ago Europeans of the second rank, who could not afford the exclusive lifestyle on Victoria Peak, chose to make their homes here. In the late nineteenth century, the "Peakies" considered the Europeans in Wan Chai to be of lower social status than themselves, and the two groups rarely mingled outside of business. The wives in particular had little to do with one another. Today, this part of Wan Chai contains some of the district's most expensive and exclusive real estate.

The human landscape is much denser on the north side of Queen's Road East at the corner of Cross Street and Wan Chai Road, where a street bazaar thronged with vendors and shoppers—some with their cars parked nearby—inspired the local cultural critic Ma Kwok Ming to write a celebrated article describing the world of street vendors.[2] In Ma's eyes, they embody, in their primitive way, Hong Kong's free market at work. This common sight, found on nearly every crowded street, once offered literally a moveable feast, as food carts selling everything from fish balls to stinky bean curd arrived at every corner where a crowd might gather. But recently the police have imposed a registration system to "stabilize" this economy. Most of the mobile food stalls (*dai pai dong*) have been forced inside and turned into noodle-and-porridge shops, or are required by law to stay put in fixed spots on small back streets. The makeshift eateries now stand beside other street stalls selling dried shrimp and vegetables or bundles of cheap clothing, with real or fake name brands. To most Western visitors, the smell and appearance of these street bazaars can be off-putting, but they are the lifeblood of the locals. Those who move away for awhile or go abroad are often lured back to Hong Kong by a nostalgia of the senses—especially the familiar smells of the city's traditional food stalls and street markets.

In Ma's view, under the weight of modernization, these rows of stalls—sometimes double or triple thick—are the trenches in which small vendors are fighting their wars of survival. "The world of the street vendors is fast disappearing," Ma laments, "but from the grand viewing stand of culture, the cultural significance of the small vendors is much greater than any old historic building."[3] This lively street scene is a reminder of childhood for every local boy or girl who was sent by parents to buy food and other daily items for the family. This hardcore localism has also inspired a series of street-gang films (called *gu wah tsai*) and cop thrillers, which have done their part to buttress a sense of Wan Chai's unique identity.

A CENTURY AND A HALF AGO, Wan Chai and Causeway Bay (then known as East Point) were largely the turf of the two largest companies plying the opium trade: Dent & Company and Jardine & Matheson. Years before Hong Kong was colonized by the British, Lancelot Dent established himself as a taipan in Canton. From 1835 to 1839 he learned Chinese and frequently meddled in local politics on behalf of the British merchants, among whom he was the undisputed leader. When Commissioner Lin Zexu came to town to confiscate the merchants' opium and flush it into the sea, Dent was the one man he wanted to arrest. Dent's Chinese name, Diendi, entered Chinese history books as an arch villain who dared to oppose Lin's anti-opium policies and in so doing triggered the First Opium War.

Right after the British won the war and took possession of Hong Kong, Dent succeeded in his bid for land along the coast of Wan Chai. With its own ships, docks, and godowns, his new empire in Hong Kong flourished. According to one story, Dent built a lavish residence in a Chinese-style garden, which he called Spring Gardens. It was a huge compound, at least a block long. The length between its north and south gates became today's Spring Garden Lane, a small alleyway between Queen's Road East and Johnston Road in Wan Chai. From his garden house Dent could oversee his business enterprise and drive his carriage along Queen's Road to his office in Central. There are reasons to doubt this story, however, for Lancelot Dent did not stay in Hong Kong long enough to enjoy such luxury. He soon returned to England. Most likely it was Dent's relatives and offspring who stayed behind and built the compound. It was used as a temporary residence for the first two governors of Hong Kong before Government House was built.

By the early 1860s the opium trade was secondary to Dent's new commercial ventures—exporting tea and cotton from China and dealing in foreign and domestic silver. But despite this diversification, Dent & Company went bankrupt in 1867, making Jardine & Matheson the largest trading house in Hong Kong. This "princely hong," whose business interests soon extended to Yokohama, Japan, and to Shanghai, became a synonym of foreign trade in the Chinese popular imagination.

William Jardine was born in 1784 in Scotland. His position as a ship's doctor brought him to India and China, where he began to build an opium trading house with his partner, James Matheson, also a Scotsman but of a more intellectual bent. Matheson published Canton's first English-language newspaper and studied Chinese with the help of a dictionary written by the Reverend Robert Morrison. He was present for the flag-raising ceremony at Possession Point on January 26, 1841. Jardine and Matheson had full confidence in Hong Kong's future and began construction of the company's first warehouse on the waterfront only a month after the British landed.

Legend has it that William Jardine would sit on top of the hill known as Jardine's Lookout and, with his telescope, watch for approaching clippers. As soon as a ship appeared on the horizon, he would send out a fast boat to intercept the mail. Since there was no telegraph service, the advance information he got from the mail gave him a commercial advantage over his competitors, if only for a few hours. This is a wonderful story of capitalist ingenuity, but it is a myth. William Jardine left Canton in 1839 for England, having never set foot in Hong Kong. He died two years later.

In 1844 James Matheson moved the company's headquarters from Macau to Hong Kong. By the late 1850s, profits had reached a new peak and the company began to branch off into other businesses—shipping, insurance, and financial services. The pride of Jardine & Matheson was a sizable fleet of ships that brought opium from India to China and carried away tea and silk from China to England. Chinese goods bound for Britain were shipped via India to the Red Sea and Suez, where they were unloaded and transported by camels to Alexandria on the Mediterranean, and from there they traveled by water to

England. With so much coming and going of trading ships in Hong Kong, time was synchronized by the firing of a cannon at noon everyday on the Jardine compound.

The suits worn by company bosses were tailor-made in London and shipped to Hong Kong. Jardine & Matheson also imported a British chef, to compete with Dent's chef from France. The taipans in Hong Kong lived in splendid houses and were very well fed: "They drank claret with their breakfasts, beer with their midday tiffin, and in the evenings great quantities of claret, champagne and port . . . Alcohol seemed to be unlimited."[4] English merchants and diplomats all along the China coast ate in the same style and drank equally large quantities of liquor and wine.

View of Jardine & Matheson looking northwest from Causeway Bay, 1846 (Murdoch Bruce).

In 1872 Jardine & Matheson withdrew from the opium trade and diversified into textiles, real estate development, and tramways. At the time of James Matheson's death in 1878, the company was thriving. Its godowns and factories occupied three and a half acres centered on today's Paterson Street in Causeway Bay. The company's holdings included a sugar-refining plant and an ice company. In Central, Jardine's most prized possession was the Hong Kong and Kowloon Wharf and Godown Company, founded by taipan William Keswick in 1886. In 1898 it bought the Star Ferry from Dorabjee Nowrojee and later took over the tramway system.

The major building in Hong Kong bearing the Jardine name today is a modern fifty-two-story high-rise in Connaught Place, Central. When it was completed in 1972, it was the tallest building in Hong Kong and a landmark on the waterfront. With its 1,700 round windows, Jardine House evoked a flurry of nicknames. The Chinese called it "the house of a thousand orifices." Some members of the English-speaking expatriate community were more graphic: they called it "the house of a thousand arseholes," and not just in reference to the windows.

In 1979 the Hong Kong and Kowloon Wharf and Godown Company was seized in a hostile takeover by a Chinese newcomer, the shipping magnate Y. K. Pao, backed by the Hong Kong and Shanghai Banking Corporation, Jardine's former ally. In real estate, the market share of a major Jardine subsidiary, Hongkong Land, was threatened by another Chinese tycoon, Li Ka-shing, currently the king of Hong Kong developers and the ninth richest man in the world. Overpowered by these Chinese upstarts, the Jardine Matheson Group adopted a defensive strategy of extending its interests outside Hong Kong. In 1984 when Beijing and London were sealing the terms of their agreement to hand over Hong Kong to China, Jardine Matheson made the decision to move its registry to Bermuda. In 1990, for the first time, the Hong Kong office ceased to appear in the company's annual *Report and Account.*[5]

The past grandeur of Jardine & Matheson was glamorized in two popular novels by James Clavell. The hero of his *Tai-pan* is largely modeled after William Jardine but mixed with other personages. *Noble House*, set in the mid-1960s, recounts the company's fortunes under a new and modernized taipan who dares to disobey the company's traditions. Both are heavily romanticized accounts, with the hero in *Tai-pan* having a Chinese mistress and the "noble house" embroiled in all kinds of ignoble business intrigues and amorous affairs.

From the beginning, Wan Chai's development was plagued by feuds between the powerful merchant houses along the waterfront and the colonial government. In the 1850s when "Quack" Governor John Bowring wanted to build an entire new town (Bowrington) on the vast stretch of land between Central and Wan Chai, his scheme fell through because John Dent and members of the Legislative Council openly opposed the visionary and arrogant governor. While this squabble was taking place, the military forged ahead on their own and built army barracks and naval dockyards in the disputed area, thus blocking passage between the CBD and Wan Chai. The dockyards are gone now, though the area is still called Admiralty.

The proximity of military barracks and shipyards to Wan Chai meant that hordes of British soldiers and sailors brought their drinking and whoring to this part of town. Ship Street became a new red-light district, and in an era before antibiotics were available, almost half of the Hong Kong garrison suffered from syphilis. Along with drunken sailors and brothels came smuggling, burglary, extortion, and petty theft. In January 1918 a case of robbery on Gresson Street erupted into a shoot-out between robbers and police that lasted eighteen hours. Today, Gresson Street is one of the few alleys in this dilapidated area where a busy street bazaar still exists; a row of red-colored lights imparts a certain charm at night and seems to recall the street's wild past.

Wan Chai was again the site of fierce street fighting when Japanese troops invaded Hong Kong in 1941. They landed at North Point and Shau Kei Wan on December 18 and met with unexpected resistance from the Hong Kong Volunteer Defense Corps, a band of expatriates between fifty-five and seventy years of age organized by Colonel A. W. Hughes of the Union Insurance Company. On Christmas Day Governor Mark Young passed through the defensive lines and gave himself up to the Japanese commander in Wan Chai. He was taken by motorboat to Kowloon, where the formal ceremony of British surrender took place in the Peninsula Hotel. Thus began three and a half years of Japanese occupation.

The Japanese had begun to move into Hong Kong even before the war began, opening shops, hotels, and bars and turning Wan Chai into a Little Tokyo. During the occupation, the red-light district was reserved solely for the "rest and recreation" of Japanese soldiers. On Mount Cameron overlooking the town, the Japanese built a large war memorial in 1943 to honor their dead and celebrate the expansion of Japan's "Greater East Asia Co-Prosperity Sphere." But this slogan turned out to be a sham. In practice, the Japanese demonstrated a great deal of respect for their fellow imperialists, the British, but treated their fellow Asians in Hong Kong very badly. They even required the residents of Causeway Bay to bow at a cemetery where the dead horses of the Japanese cavalry were buried.

After the war, Japanese power took an economic turn, with a cluster of department stores at the center of Causeway Bay. Today, only Sogo remains, and its ownership is now in Chinese hands. Crossing the street in front of Sogo is an experience unmatched even by Times Square in New York City. The crowds are like a human tide that pushes you to the other shore—a physical experience that can be exasperating and exhilarating at the same time. If the Japanese were to invade today, their troops and horses would have no room to maneuver against this endless wave of humanity.

SINCE THE LATE 1950S, Wan Chai has been, in Western eyes, the world of Suzie Wong. The popularity of this story accounts for much of the area's attraction, if not notoriety, among tourists. The bar culture on which the story is based was a direct result of the Korean War, when bars and nightclubs opened to cater to American sailors and GIs. Richard Mason's famous novel of 1957, *The World of Suzie Wong*, which in 1960 was made into an even more popular movie starring Nancy Kwan and William Holden, captured the romanticized charm of this period in Wan Chai's history. The novel continues to be widely read, and the film is available on DVD in video stores everywhere. The popularity of this story surpasses another 1950s best-seller, *Love Is a Many-Splendored Thing* by Han Suyin, and indeed it eclipses every other novel or film that has ever been set in Hong Kong, of which there are quite a few. As a testament to its enduring influence, in spring 2006 the Hong Kong Ballet Company staged a dance version of Suzie Wong.

Richard Mason, an English writer, had no subject in mind when he came to Hong Kong in 1955 for a brief sojourn between assignments writing screenplays. On the recommendation of a friend, he stayed at the Luk Kwok (Six Nations) Hotel at the harbor front, near the Wan Chai pier. The old Luk Kwok (torn down in 1988) was then a popular pickup place used by prostitutes. As Guy Haydon said about the author, "Checking into a Hong Kong brothel is probably the most fortuitous decision Richard Mason ever made in his life."[6] As Mason himself recalled years later: "I went down the first night to have my *chow fan* [fried rice], and saw all these women at the bar and I realized that it was virtually a brothel. I was absolutely thrilled. At the time I had no idea at all, and thought it was just an ordinary hotel. But I thought 'This is fabulous, I've found it!' From that moment I knew I had the book. I thought that was unbelievable—like a gift from God."[7]

This latter-day recollection sounds equally unbelievable. Did this episode actually happen, or was it an urban legend concocted later for the media's consumption? One thing we can be sure of: the Luk Kwok Hotel where Mason stayed was a reputable place for social gatherings such as wedding receptions and meetings by writers. It was not "virtually a brothel." In the novel, Mason's hero Lomax passes up "the famous hotel called Luk Kwok" because

Nancy Kwan, dancing with a sailor as Suzie Wong in the 1960 film.

it is "obviously too expensive" and settles for the cheaper Nam Kok (Southern Country) hotel—a fictional creation—which reminds him of "some old family hotel in Bloomsbury." In the film version, this "family hotel" is made seedier by being next door to the bar where Suzie Wong solicits her customers. The new Luk Kwok Hotel that stands today at Gloucester Road still maintains an Old World look in its façade, but there is no downstairs bar where Mason presumably saw prostitutes pick up their customers and listened to the telling and retelling of their life stories.

Mason was no novice when he wrote *Suzie Wong*. He had published an earlier novel called *The Wind Cannot Read* (1947), which was inspired by his personal experience studying with a Japanese woman tutor at the School of Oriental and African Studies in London. "It was a love story of a young soldier learning Japanese in the time of the Japanese War who falls in love with his Japanese instructor." Mason wrote the screenplay with director David Lean for the film version (1947) starring Dirk Bogarde. He had written another novel called *The Shadow and the Peak* (1949) set in a Jamaican school, which was also made into a film titled *The Passionate Summer* (1958). He did a script for the film *A Town Called Alice* (1956) about women taken prisoner by the Japanese in Malaya. This huge commercial success came just before his trip to Hong Kong in search of new inspiration. "Everything about the Far East is so fascinating," Mason confessed. "I just want to write it all down and get it all into something, even if it was never published."[8]

As a writer of screenplays, Mason certainly had a subtle ear for dialogue. Some commentators maintain that Mason captured the bar girl's pidgin English perfectly. In the very beginning of the novel, as the hero encounters the heroine on the Star Ferry, Suzie Wong tries to disguise herself as a rich man's daughter. But when approached by Lomax, her first words, "No talk," instantly betray her lower-class background. The film version, with a script written by the veteran John Patrick (who also wrote *Love Is a Many-Splendored Thing*), has so dramatized the phrase that the Suzie Wong Fan Club calls itself "No Talk." This chance encounter on the ferry leads to romance when Lomax sees her again in the bar next to his hotel.

In the middle part of the novel, Mason must maintain a balance between Suzie's lower-class language and her noble heart. Since her linguistic abilities can no longer carry the full weight of her growing emotions, the story has to be told in the elegant English of the first-person narrator, the protagonist Lomax. This brilliant framing of the narrative, perhaps by necessity, also tilts her story into essentially his story, as her language is "quoted" from his memory. Since the first-person narrator is an amateur painter and artist, all native characters and scenes are viewed through his sensitive if naive eyes.

Some critics understandably find fault with the explicit orientalism of the novel, which turns a bar girl—a product of Western consumption—into an exotic creature that a Western hero could fall in love with. Mason cleverly reverses the tragic ending of the *Madame Butterfly* formula into a happy one, but it seems equally unrealistic. The Chinese world of Wan Chai becomes merely a backdrop for playing out an orientalist romantic fantasy.

What makes the novel and film still enjoyable today is the rich evocation of a Wan Chai that no longer exists. When Lomax enters the old part of Wan Chai in search of a hotel, he steps "into the teeming alleyways with the litter-filled gutters, the pavement vendors, the street-stalls, the excitement and bustle." Further along the quay, "shirtless, barefoot coolies were unloading junks, filing back and forth along the gangplanks like trails of ants." This thick description is as lively as it is authentic, and it takes a writer with a visual sensibility to capture the sight and sound of it all. "Across the road from the quay were narrow open-fronted shops, between which dark staircases led up to crowded tenement rooms; and along the pavement children played hopscotch whilst shoveling rice into their mouths from bowls."

A novel with such rich detail is ready-made for film. Under Richard Quine's direction, this scene was shot on location, in a real street market, where the crowded stalls of vendors sold all kinds of fresh vegetables and livestock, including a live snake. The location, some locals believe, is in the present area between Canal and Bowrington roads, where there was once a bridge over the canal called Goose Neck Bridge. Street life can still be found there, although most wet produce is housed inside a two-story building called Bowrington

Market. Underneath the highway bridge, one can still find old women squatting on the ground and performing a voodoo-like ritual called "Beat the Petty Men" (*da hsiu yan*), which Suzie resorted to against her bad clients. The old women give customers a piece of paper on which to write the names of those "petty" people they hate and then the women beat the papers with their shoes. In the film version, apparently Suzie does the beating herself, though not with her own high-heeled shoes.

Another memorable scene follows when Lomax checks into the Nam Kok Hotel. In the novel, his third-floor room has a balcony that commands an immense panorama: "On one side it looks over the rooftops of Wan Chai, behind which rose the skyscrapers of Hong Kong and the Peak, whilst in front was the harbor scattered with ships of every shape and size . . . And across the harbor, so close that I could count the windows of the Peninsula Hotel, was the waterfront of Kowloon, with a backdrop of tall bare hills stretching away into China." A beautiful view indeed, perfect for the studio of a foreign painter living in seedy Wan Chai. But one wonders how this cheap hotel could ever offer such a view to begin with. Is it constructed only for our artist-hero to look at? Is this immense panorama any different from the privileged view on top of Victoria Peak, where colonial masters used to dwell? The set-up recalls the balcony studio of another poor painter-hero played by Gene Kelly in the Hollywood film *An American in Paris* (1951), who also commands a magnificent urban view.

In the film version, as Robert Lomax/William Holden goes to the balcony, he not only looks out onto the marvelous panorama of the harbor but also down onto the rooftops of old tenement buildings, where children are playing alongside primitive shacks. These were indeed the real living conditions for many residents in Wan Chai throughout the 1950s, when the district was crowded with poor refugees and immigrants fleeing the mainland. The novel and the film were produced at a time before the colonial government decided to construct public housing. The reader who follows only the hero's romance with Suzie Wong may forget that Lomax, for the most part, has not severed his links with the colonial world of power and privilege. He socializes, if by necessity, with the

Anglo-American bankers and is the love object of a banker's daughter. To plunge into the real world of poverty in Wan Chai, as he tries to do at the end of the novel, would have taken more courage and devotion than the novel's happy ending seems able to offer.

WAN CHAI in the collective memory of its Chinese residents was a totally different place from the world of Suzie Wong. Local residents lived in their own sphere, separated from bars and brothels. The boundary line between the two was the Southorn Playground, a large open square (now rather small and compressed) located between Hennessy and Johnston roads. Even late at night, drunken sailors from the bars on Lockhart Road never stepped beyond the northern edge of the Playground, and local Chinese residents kept to the southern side. These two worlds of Wan Chai did not overlap, and that is still true today, even as the Western sphere slowly shrinks and the Chinese world expands.

In the early years, Wan Chai had a diverse population consisting of Portuguese from Macau, Indians, some Filipinos and Africans, British, and Americans. But the overwhelming majority of the population was Chinese. They were mainly shopkeepers, small businessmen, artisans, and coolies. Beginning in the early 1950s, the massive exodus of immigrants fleeing the Communist Revolution settled in areas like North Point (often called Shanghai Town), Kowloon, and Wan Chai. The colonial government let these refugees fend for themselves, and most had to sublet rooms and squeeze into already-crowded living quarters in old three-story tenements. Some even lived in shabby huts constructed on flat rooftops. A few of these old tenements still exist in dilapidated condition, but most have disappeared.

Crowded living spaces encouraged local youths to venture out into the neighborhood movie theaters, where they had their first taste of Hollywood films. Most of Hong Kong's first-run "movie palaces" were in this area—the Lido, Roxy, King's, Cathay, National, and Empire. They were all demolished in the 1970s. The most famous was the Lee Theater, built in 1925 by the family of Lee Hysan, a prominent opium merchant who became a millionaire by investing in real estate. Lee bought a small hill from Jardine & Matheson, flattened it, and built an amusement park called Lee Gardens. He was assassinated under mysterious circumstances in 1928, but the once-magnificent theater bearing his name had by then become a legend. It not only showed first-run Hollywood movies but staged Cantonese operas starring the most famous actresses. The theater was torn down in the 1980s and replaced by a high-rise office building bearing the name Lee Gardens.

In the postwar period, Wan Chai experienced a modest cultural renaissance. Three of the largest postwar Chinese newspapers—*Hong Kong Times*, *Ta Kung pao*, and *Wen Wei Pao*—all had their headquarters in Wan Chai, and several prominent writers among the new immigrants became editors of literary supplements in the local newspapers. The tradition was set by the famous poet Dai Wangshu (1905–1950), who arrived in Hong Kong in 1938. He stayed through the period of Japanese occupation and was briefly imprisoned by the Japanese military. Dai edited the literary page of the *Sing Tao Daily* for many years and contributed poems and translations of his own, including Baudelaire's *Les Fleurs du Mal* and an edition of Spanish Civil War songs. He opened a store for old books on the same Lee Tung Street where printer's row stood, but the shop soon closed for lack of business. He also hunted for old treasures in bookstores at Ladder Street and Hollywood Road in Central, where he bought precious editions of Shakespeare and Baudelaire for very little money.

Some of Dai's literary friends and colleagues from Shanghai, such as Mu Shiying, Shi Zhecun, Xu Xu, and Ye Lingfeng, all Chinese modernists, followed him to Hong Kong. Xu and Ye stayed in the colony until their deaths. In the late 1940s, a host of other Chinese writers—including famous leftist writers like Mao Dun, Guo Moruo, and Xia Yan—passed through Hong Kong and left their literary and personal imprint. They sometimes congregated in the two-hundred-seat auditorium inside the old Luk Kwok Hotel for literary assemblies. Richard Mason obviously had no inkling of this Hong Kong equivalent of the Harlem Renaissance, since he knew no Chinese and never bothered to gain any knowledge of modern Chinese literature.

Hong Kong's new literary and artistic coterie assembles elsewhere today. One place is the Hong Kong Arts Center on the north side of Gloucester Road. A narrow building occupying limited space, it is the center of art exhibitions, experimental performances, and avant-garde films. Next to the Arts Center is the Academy of Performing Arts, whose departments of music, art, dance, and film have been the training ground for a new generation of creative talent. In some ways, Wan Chai has become the "Central District" of Hong Kong's new culture. This view is probably endorsed only by the writers and artists themselves, but Dai Wangshu and other immigrants certainly set a precedent. A younger generation of recently settled or native-born writers have fashioned their own literary voices in fiction, poetry, and essays published in a few small literary journals. Even a casual glance at these works leaves the impression that they are unlike anything written by English colonials before or since. There is none of the exotica or decadence usually found in English writings. Instead, the Chinese works are anchored on home ground and written in the style of social realism, sometimes coupled with experimental techniques.

The Pussy Cat in Wan Chai.

The father figure of this first native generation is surely Liu Yichang, a refugee writer from Shanghai who, following in the footsteps of Dai Wangshu, became editor of the literary supplement of the Sing Tao Evening News, where he published his own works as well as those of younger writers he discovered. These included Ye Si (Leung Ping-kwan), Xi Xi, and many others who continue to write today about living in Wan Chai. One writer recalled that when he was a boy, he first saw the English sign for a bar called Pussy Cat and had to check his dictionary for a definition.

Today, the hectic, messy urban jungle of Wan Chai can still inspire. For Western readers, the world of old Wan Chai may be vaguely Dickensian, with its labyrinth of streets and alleys bustling with all kinds of licit and illicit activity, and peopled with rogues and thieves alongside writers, artisans, street vendors, and craftsmen. These imaginative possibilities have never occurred to local politicians or developers, except perhaps to a few cultural preservationists who have just begun efforts to mount exhibitions and other publication projects for a reconstructed cultural history of the entire Wan Chai area.

HORSE-RACING is the one thing that both the Western and Chinese population of Hong Kong have participated in with great enthusiasm from colonial times down to the present day. There are now two racecourses: the old one in Happy Valley and the new one in Sha Tin in the New Territories, opened in 1978. The season lasts from September to June, with meetings divided between Happy Valley on Wednesday evenings and Sha Tin on Saturday afternoons.

The famous racecourse in Happy Valley, first built in 1846, was the center of colonial recreation. Austin Coates, in his book *China Races*, describes a journey to Happy Valley in a typical racing day in old colonial times: "A journey to Happy Valley was a country excursion. One took a picnic lunch. The varied conveyances—traps and gig, an occasional carriage, and chairs swiftly borne by trotting coolies—made their way out of town along the peaceful waterfront road, past Spring Gardens and the sleepy village of Wanchai, following the exact line of the present Queen's Road East and the Wanchai Road, turning into the Valley exactly as today, and making for the matshed grand-

stand, which was exactly where the grandstand of the Royal Hong Kong Jockey Club is now situated."[9] Nowadays this journey is no longer a country excursion but a short trip by automobile or tram, which goes along approximately the same roads but through the urban hubbub of Wan Chai and Causeway Bay.

According to Coates, Happy Valley was the only conceivable place to build a racecourse on Hong Kong island (despite its location down the hill from the cemetery) because it was not far away from Victoria City and was sparsely populated. After removing some local Chinese farmers and draining the stagnant water out of their rice fields, the British formally opened the course in 1846, only five years after taking possession of the island. The place looked deserted most of the year, but during the February racing week it suddenly came alive with thousands of attendees. Military bands played, and everyone that counted in colonial society was dressed to the hilt and sitting in the grandstand. "Everyone, of every hue and nationality, attended, even those not particularly interested in racing. The ladies, *de rigueur,* had to have new dresses—five, because they wore a different one each day."[10]

Making a living in the narrow alleyways and streets of Wan Chai.

Wong Nei Chong in the 1840s, soon to be renamed Happy Valley.

In the beginning, there were no professional jockeys, just amateurs, including many British officers, but the sport had its monetary trappings. Only the rich could afford to buy horses in Australia, the Philippines, and China and import them to their stables in Hong Kong, and only the super-rich, such as the Jardines and the Dents, had their own stables. The races gradually turned into a bitter social rivalry as these two competitive families vied for victories. In one memorable race held on Wednesday, February 23, 1867, the two horses owned by the Dents finally beat the Jardines' pony, but the triumph was short-lived. The Dents' real fortune collapsed the following October, leaving Jardine as the major trading house in Hong Kong.

A spirit of friendly competition was eventually restored chiefly through the good offices of Sir Paul Chater, an Armenian banker from Calcutta who was hailed upon his death in 1926 as "the greatest man Hongkong has known." Chater masterminded the formation of the Hong Kong Jockey Club, which he ran for thirty-four years and which admitted Chinese members in 1926—the only European racing club that ever did. By this time financial power in Hong Kong had gradually shifted to Chinese businessmen, and the colonial government found it necessary to appease these local elites after an unprecedented general strike the year before nearly toppled the colonial regime. Memberships in the pro-forma Legislative and Executive Councils were not enough. Non-Europeans seeking to climb Hong Kong's social ladder also wanted to become members of the Board of Stewards in the Jockey Club. And they gave as good as they got: the Chinese members, along with Chater, Hormusjee Mody (a

"LEAP YEAR," WINNER OF THE HONG KONG DERBY, AND A STRING OF WINNERS FROM MR. JOHN PEEL'S STABLES

Top: Leap Year, the winner of the Hong Kong Derby. Bottom: General view of the course in Happy Valley (*The Graphic,* June 2, 1888).

Parsee from Bombay), and Ellis Kadoorie (a Jew from Baghdad), enriched the club's coffers with their huge contributions.

The British colonial masters stood only to gain from this game, as they soon discovered. In 1949, when Governor Grantham was confronted with more than one million refugees from China living in squatters' huts, he found a perfect source of funds for building urgently needed hospitals, schools, and housing: the turnover of more than three million dollars at the racetrack every Saturday. At the suggestion of Sir Arthur Morse, who was chairman concurrently of the HSBC and the Board of Stewards of the Jockey Club, it was decided that the Jockey Club should in principle turn over a third of its proceeds for "civic and social undertakings" that the government deemed worthy of support. In the first year, the donated figure ran to five and a half million dollars.

Many projects and buildings throughout the city now bear the name of the Jockey Club. When the Hong Kong University of Science and Technology—which the locals call "The Rolls Royce of universities"—was first built in the late 1980s, at least half of the seed money came from the Jockey Club. Hence the joke that started floating around: there are two governments in Hong Kong, the official one and the real one, which is the Jockey Club.

Today, the horse-racing season is year-long except for a break during July and August. It retains its social significance for the rich and famous, but the average Hong Kong racing enthusiast is interested in just one thing—betting—since racing is the only form of legal gambling in the city. Betting booths can be found throughout the island and Kowloon. Nearly all the newspapers have a horse-racing section and print extra pages on race days, and the trains make special stops at the Sha Tin station on Saturdays. In 1994 the Happy Valley racecourse was expanded, and the magnificent club house with its fine restaurants and other amenities have become one of the favored places for social gatherings among Hong Kong's elite.

The entire horse-racing scene has entered into the world of Western popular fiction. In John le Carré's spy novel *The Honorable Schoolboy*, which is partly set in Hong Kong in the early 1970s, we find the following description of Happy Valley: "The grass at Happy Valley Racecourse must be the most valuable crop on earth. There was very little of it. A narrow ring ran round the edge of what looked like a London borough recreation ground which sun and feet have beaten into dirt." But the astute eyes of le Carré, who made a research visit to Hong Kong himself, did not miss the rest of the scenery. At this particular junction in the novel's plot, the English spy hero Jerry Westerby stands outside the racecourse and looks from a distance at a Chinese tycoon, Drake Ko, picking up his European mistress right after a race that his horse won. This is how le Carré saw Happy Valley on both its sunny and its shadowy sides: "The place was less a valley than a fire-bowl—glistening white stadium one side, brown hills the other—while ahead of Jerry and to his left lurked the other Hong Kong: a card-house Manhattan of grey skyscraper slums crammed so tight they seemed to lean on one another in the heat." If le Carré were to visit the new racecourse in Sha Tin and look around, he would find many more, and much taller, "grey skyscraper slums" in this satellite city.

FROM CAUSEWAY BAY the tram passes along King's Road to North Point, Quarry Bay, and Shau Kei Wan. These areas are not tourist destinations but have become increasingly important for work and residence. The most famous of the three is North Point. In postwar years North Point was quickly built up, as refugees first from Shanghai and later from Fukien province in China made their home here. The Shanghai refugees in the late 1940s and early 1950s included some of the most prominent figures and families, who became Hong Kong's future elite. But the Little Shanghai community in North Point also comprised middle-class and poor families living in temporary, poorly constructed buildings that reflected their sense of impermanence. Alienated in Hong Kong, they formed their own ghettos in North Point—a home away from home and an outpost of a Shanghai that had already vanished.

The Shanghai refugees despised Hong Kong. Rebecca Pan, a famous singer who appeared in two of Wong Kar-wai's films, recalls that when she first arrived in North Point from Shanghai in 1951, she thought Hong Kong was a rustic fishing port, whose local population was totally ignorant of the sophisticated lifestyle she had enjoyed in her former city. Thus the Shanghaiese had to set up in North Point all of the things they missed from home, from Western-style coffee houses to fashion boutiques. An amusement park built on King's Road, called Ritz, was comparable perhaps to Shanghai's Rio Rita, complete with swimming pool, night club, skating rink, bar, dance hall, and restaurant. Its opening celebration in 1946 was officiated by four famous female stars of Shanghai's film world.

Patrons from Shanghai who missed the famous Russian soup and cakes in Shanghai's legendary DD's could make do with similar restaurants like Queen's and Windsor's in North Point. Those who missed home cooking frequented the Four-Five-Six and other shops that specialized in authentic Shanghai foodstuffs and other products, and where customers and owners conversed in Shanghaiese. Cosmopolitan Shanghai conquered North Point in a few years and set a new standard for hairstyles among the ladies and for Western suits among Chinese men. Suddenly, Shanghai tailors and beauty parlors were much in demand everywhere in Hong Kong. This is how a local historian described the Shanghai barbershop: "Staffed by dapper elderly barbers, their windows screened by lace-net curtains and emblazoned with the word 'Shanghai,' the interior décor—and the choice of hairstyles offered—haven't changed much in forty years . . . These barbershops are an enduring reminder of the time when Shanghai represented all that was smart, fashionable and modern in China."[11]

The new émigrés looked down on the less sophisticated Cantonese population of Hong Kong, who in turn labeled North Point as a "lost territory"—a cynical reference to the Communist-occupied areas in China during the Second World War. But the two language groups did not come to an outright clash. And there were attempts at reconciliation, most notably in a number of popular comedies made by Shanghai refugees themselves (two scripted by Eileen Chang), with such Chinese titles as *South-North Harmony* or *South and North Are One Family*, in which the quarrelling neighbors speaking Cantonese and Shanghaiese finally attain peace and happiness together. (The English titles of these films are more dramatic: *The Greatest Civil War on Earth*, and *The Greatest Wedding on Earth.*)

But many mainland-owned and leftist-supported businesses did indeed exist in North Point in the 1950s and 1960s, and in 1967 a department store called Wah Fung, owned by "Red Chinese," was surrounded by police as bombs were thrown from its windows. This outbreak of urban guerilla warfare was quickly quenched, but it left a bad taste on both sides. Because the British colonials never forgave North Point for its dalliance with Communism, in subsequent decades the area failed to develop into a prosperous district like Wan Chai and Causeway Bay to the west or Taikoo Shing farther east. As the first wave of Shanghai refugees—especially the rich ones—moved out of North Point and dispersed to more prosperous areas of the island, a second wave of Fukienese immigrants, who were poorer and not so cosmopolitan, began arriving in the 1960s. Many were overseas Chinese from Indonesia who had been displaced in both Southeast Asia and China and had found their way to Hong Kong. Little Shanghai gradually became Little Fukien.

A poignant reminder of a time when this part of Hong Kong resembled a suburb of Shanghai can be found in director Wong Kar-wai's films *Days of Being Wild* (1992) and *In the Mood for Love* (2001). Its atmosphere of nostalgia is evoked not only by home décor and women's clothing, such as the sleek long gowns—called *qipao* in Shanghai and *cheung sam* in Hong Kong—worn by the star, Maggie Cheung, but by the husky Shanghai accent and the sophistication embodied in singer Rebecca Pan, whose fading beauty epitomizes perfectly the splendor of a bygone era. In the first film, Pan plays basically herself, a former singer from Shanghai; in the second, she becomes a landlady from Shanghai who is stranded in Hong Kong. Though not specified, the place of her residence in both films seems to be either Happy Valley or North Point.

The areas east of North Point—Quarry Bay and Taikoo Shing—are fast developing into a mini-CBD, where some of the communication giants such as PCCW and publishing companies such as the Ming Pao enterprises and the English-language newspaper the *South China Morning Post* are headquartered. A century and a half ago, Hakka stonemasons began settling around Quarry Bay soon after the British arrived and opened quarries in the hillsides nearby—hence the

English name. Older residents still refer to the area as Tsat Tsz Mui or Seven Sisters, since according to local legend seven sisters who felt very close to one another once lived there. When one of them died, the other sisters made a pact and all killed themselves. A goddess took pity on them and turned their dead bodies into seven granite stones on the seashore.

The next stop on the tram is Taikoo. This word was originally the Chinese name for the shipping and trading company Butterfield and Swire, now subsumed under the giant Swire Group that controls a major share in Cathay Pacific airlines. The company once had a dockyard and a sugar refinery in Taikoo Shing (hence the street Tong Chong or Sugar Factory Street). Both have disappeared. Where they once stood is the modern Taikoo Place, with its trendy restaurants offering burgers and coffee or Thai and Indian curries.

The Hong Kong Film Archive in Sai Wan Ho, just a tram stop to the east, is a small building containing one of the world's largest collections of Hong Kong's historical films, with frequent showings throughout the year. Today Sai Wan Ho is undergoing a new phase of development, as newcomers who have found work nearby are transforming this part of Hong Kong island into a Little SoHo. An old "memory lane" near Tai On Street has become a popular destination for architecture students who wish to learn about the use of functional space in tightly packed food stalls, small shops, and eateries.

And just a couple of tram stops away from Sai Wan Ho is Shau Kei Wan (Rice Basket Bay), the end of the tram line. This bustling town used to be a fishing village with a thousand residents. The bay—so called because it resembled a rice basket—is also known as Aldrich Bay, named after an officer of the Royal Engineers stationed here in the early years. The Chinese translation of "Aldrich" becomes "Love of Order," which is not a bad name for the tight upper-lipped British colonial servant. German missionaries began to settle here after the 1860s; Basel Road is named after the German Protestant Mission from Basel.

Shau Kei Wan's Main Street East (or Tung Tai Gai) used to be right at the seaside, and fishermen moored their boats there. With some effort, you can still locate their small temple of Tin Hau, now hidden behind the high-rises.

The street comes alive in the evening when cars line up on both sides, and people flock to its many restaurants and noodle shops for late-night *dim sum*. As a local journalist remarked recently: "Many times I have walked down [this street] to observe the old shops that sell fishing tools, Chinese biscuits in huge glass jars and little stalls selling plastic toys. On my way back home, I often take the labyrinthine underground tunnel and imagine myself coming back from a visit to another time."[12]

Fishing family in Shau Kei Wan, 1926.

From Shau Kei Wan, the No. 9 bus travels along some of Hong Kong's most scenic hilly roads to the village of Shek O on the southeastern shore. Its sandy beach and the bungalows on the cliffs overlooking the sea offer the kind of nature-loving lifestyle increasingly favored by young expats who want to escape the busy crowds in Central and withdraw into one of the few "primitive" areas remaining on Hong Kong island. From Shek O it is a short drive along the coast to Stanley, another favorite beach spot on the southern tip of the island. Stanley too has become fashionable with the international set, especially on weekends when the bars and restaurants fill up with the sound of live rock music.

Many of these young sophisticates are only vaguely aware of the old Stanley Prison not far away, where British residents were interned by the Japanese during the Second World War. These men and women were removed from their comfortable homes on the Peak and put through a humiliating ordeal at the hands of the occupiers—an ignoble chapter in British imperial history now mostly forgotten. To get a postcolonial perspective on their view from the top of British colonial life, we now return to Central and ascend by tram to Victoria Peak.

Waterfall in Cheung Kong Garden, Central.

4

Views from the Peak

At 1,811 feet above sea level, Victoria Peak is the highest point on Hong Kong island and the former Crown colony's rarest "jewel." Since near the end of the nineteenth century, an address on the Peak has been the most exalted status symbol the city had to offer. Today, the Peak is also a favorite lookout for sightseers, who reach it by taking the Peak cable tram at its terminal on Garden Street in Central.

A leisurely walk to the Peak tram terminal in Central might begin at the corner of Queen's Road and Ice House Street, where the old Ice House pier used to stand. Ice for a subtropical colony? The anomaly is not as absurd as it sounds, for ice was considered a daily necessity in British households, for both comfort and food storage. The Hong Kong Ice Company, established in 1845, imported this natural commodity all the way from Boston, Massachusetts. It was kept cool in the basement of a property on Queen's Road previously used for coal storage. In return for free rent, the government required that the company provide ice for hospitals at low cost.[1]

In the 1860s the Hong Kong Ice Company ran into competition from a new business, Dairy Farm Ice and Cold Storage, which offered man-made ice. As the demand for milk and other dairy products increased, Dairy Farm (a subsidiary of Jardine & Matheson) finally took over the entire ice business in Hong Kong. Its storage site was the odd-looking building on sloping Wyndham Street, at the intersection with Gleanealy. This rounded building remains one of the few genuine architectural relics from Hong Kong's early colonial days, and today it houses an organization for alternative art, the Fringe Club. From Ice

The old ice house on Wyndham Street, now home of the Fringe Club.

House Street, a turn onto Battery Path leads up the hill to a handful of other colonial buildings whose future under the Hong Kong's postcolonial government is far from certain: Murray Barracks, St. John's Cathedral, and the French Mission (now the Supreme Court).

The Peak tram, originally a small funicular railway, took three years to build. When completed in 1888, it was considered a marvel of engineering and the first of its kind in Asia. The plan germinated with two enterprising businessmen, Phineas Kyrie and William K. Hughes, who in 1881 applied to the Hong Kong government for a permit. The leading English newspaper of the time, the *Hongkong Telegraph*, reported on May 30, 1888: "The Peak Tramways commenced operations this morning, the first car leaving St. John's Place punctually at 8 O'clock . . . A few passengers, ladies included, availed themselves of the opportunity to enjoy a ramble over the breezy hills in the morning—an extremely healthy diversion."[2] On its first day of operation, a total of eight hundred passengers went for the ride, and in its first year almost 150,000 riders took the tram to the top.

The steam engine that powered the cable was replaced in 1926 by an electric motor. In 1956 the old wood cars were retired and lightweight metal cars, with a seating capacity of 62 passengers, were put into operation. In her vivid description of the Peak tram in the first (1988) edition of *Hong Kong: Epilogue to an Empire*, Jan Morris gave high praise to "British technique, for everything was made in England, put together by Scottish engineers, and run by British employees—drivers, brakesmen, conductors, and all." The "shapes of its trams crawling so daringly up and down" presents "an image of imperial accomplishment in the benighted East."[3] Morris's paean to British ingenuity was out of date within the year, however, for the company that completely revamped and modernized the tram in 1989 was Swiss. A new track was constructed, controls were computerized, and two-compartment cars that could accommodate a total of 120 passengers were installed—one traveling down and another counterbalancing it on the way up. (A third spare car is kept on reserve in a shed near Kennedy Road station.) Today, more than four million people ride the Peak tram annually, for an average of 11,000 per day.

The Peak Tower at Victoria Gap.

The car ascends on a steep slope with varying gradient and two pronounced curves, a total distance of about ⅔ of a mile. The ride itself, which takes about five minutes, can be more fun than its destination. The terminus of the tram is a new "shopping and leisure complex" called the Peak Tower at Victoria Gap, about 492 feet below the summit. Visitors are herded like cattle through the levels of this garish mall, past a Bruce Lee wax figure at Madame Tussaud's, before they can ascend to the terrace and lookout platforms. Local families who bring their children to the Peak for Sunday outings complain of the steep prices for food in the restaurants and cafés of the Peak Galleria nearby. And while a circular trail, shaded by rocks and trees, offers an hour of leisurely walk around the area, all in all the atmosphere on the Peak is hardly conducive to nostalgia. Almost nothing is left to help visitors recall the colonial flavor of the past, now that race and class barriers have finally broken down. Even the governor's lodge, which was damaged by a typhoon in 1874 and rebuilt in 1902 as "the largest and handsomest building on the Peak," was demolished in 1946 after being heavily damaged during the Second World War.

Still, the views from the trail and the viewing platform can be breathtaking on days when the Peak is not fogged over and the pollution level is low (only about fifty-three days per year). On a typical day, the harbor and Kowloon peninsula appear much grayer and fuzzier than they were only a decade ago, but they are still visible. On the island side, daytime visitors can pick out the more prominent steel-and-glass skyscrapers such as the Bank of China building, The Center, the IFC, and Central Plaza. And at night, when the lights of the city cut through the obscuring smog, the harbor erupts in a panorama of color and movement. But the distant hills of the New Territories, once majestic on the horizon, are almost always invisible, shrouded in a gray-brown haze of pollution—part of the high price extracted by the Hong Kong miracle.

Before the Peak tram was built, the "Peakies" were carried up and down the steep hill in bamboo sedan chairs held up by teams of two or four Chinese "chairmen." Every Peak house had its chair shed, "the Hong Kong equivalent of a coach-house." This form of transportation was considered cheaper than horses, and the colonists seemed not to mind the human debasement it entailed. Two Russian travelers made the following observation: "On more than one occasion a poor coolie (a porter) received a beating from a passing dandy for not moving out of the way in time or simply because the latter wanted to make use of his cane."[4] Some early residents liked this old mode of transportation so much that they objected to the construction of the modern cable cars, and sedan chairs continued to be used for several years after the tram was opened. A brief news item in the *Peak Pioneer and Magazine Gap and Mount Austin Advertiser* in 1892 reported that "in a half

The view from the Peak, afternoon and evening.

gale that visited Cloudland [the Peak] recently, the chair coolies' matshed was blown away." The matshed was never rebuilt, and a café was constructed on the site in 1900.

For half a century, until 1940, Peak tram cars were divided into three classes: first class for mostly Western passengers, second class for soldiers and policemen, and third class for the servants of Peak residents. The two front seats of first class were reserved for use by Governor Richard MacDonald, who built a summer lodge on the Peak in 1868, and his successors. The rest of the local Chinese population was barred from the tram and the Peak itself. Between 1904 and 1930, a Peak Ordinance decreed that the Peak was reserved for the exclusive residence of Europeans and government officials.

Victoria Peak is still prime residential real estate for Hong Kong's rich and powerful, regardless of race, as long as they can afford to buy the multi-million-dollar homes and condos there. As of January 2007, according to a report by ABC News, the Peak was the site of the most expensive piece of residential real estate in the world. The government's auction of a piece of land at 12 Mount Kellett Road brought US$231 million from Sun Hung Kai Properties—134 percent of the opening bid, or $5,417 per square foot. Hong Kong now is the world's third most expensive city to live in, after London and Monaco, at an average cost of $2,008 per square foot, which means that $1 million buys a living space of about 50 x 10 feet. And the Peak is the most sought-after low-density neighborhood in all of Hong Kong. Very few if any properties go on the market in a typical year.[5]

For our purposes, however, sightseeing and real estate prices are of secondary importance. A visit to the Peak affords an opportunity for historical reflection — a vantage point from which we can gain some critical perspective on Hong Kong's colonial past.

EUROPEANS BEGAN to move uphill to the Peak near the end of the nineteenth century. A typical rationale for their exclusive right of residence is provided in the following statement written in 1906 by Dr. James Cantlie (most probably the same doctor who taught Sun Yat-sen at the Hong Kong

College of Medicine and who rescued him from kidnapping in 1896): "When the Chinese began to swarm into the colony, the Europeans were gradually driven to the higher levels of the city . . . As the years passed, the encroachment of these undesirable neighbors became so acute, that other places of the colony were sought after as suitable residences for Europeans. At first dwellings were erected on the lower levels some miles or two out of the city; but as these proved 'feverish,' refuge was sought on the higher altitudes. The example set by one or two of the wiser men began to bear fruit, and now the main bulk of the foreign community dwell on the peak."[6] This statement, typical of its time, revealed a besieged mentality: the Chinese were undesirables, and the Peak was the white man's last bastion of defense. But the main reason for their "refuge" was seclusion and comfort. The air at higher altitudes was cooler and healthier, homes were not so crowded, and the view was commanding.

Victoria Peak around the beginning of the twentieth century.

A massive literature of early Western impressions of Hong Kong, written mostly in English, is available for the historically minded and has been quoted by countless Western commentators on Hong Kong. Thus a veritable mythology has grown up over the past century in which life on the Peak epitomized the pinnacle of British colonial wealth and power. Yet a critical look at these writings reveals that they seldom, if ever, contained any self-reflection or self-criticism. To the contrary, as the early colonial writers looked down on Hong Kong's exotic landscape from their exalted position, they expressed an abundance of self-righteousness about the "white man's burden." In their eyes, Hong Kong was beautiful but primitive, not a suitable place for Western living, except inside their comfortable homes, where they were "protected" from contamination and could cultivate a respectable late-Victorian lifestyle. Their comfort came, of course, at the expense of the silent Chinese servants who catered to their every whim.

This familiar picture of colonial life could be found in all British colonies, of course. Yet compared with India, Hong Kong's case may have been worse, not only because the vast majority of the Chinese population, servants, coolies, and other "natives" were illiterate and never spoke out about themselves but also because the "high society" of nineteenth-century Hong Kong was exceedingly small, consisting mostly of career officials and social climbers who would have enjoyed only middling status at home in Great Britain. But in Hong Kong, these Brits were able to create an enormous gulf between themselves and the rest of the population, with only a thin layer of Chinese elite in between. Thus the voices available to us from the past belonged almost entirely to a few hundred European residents (mostly Peakies), a handful of travelers, and three English-language newspapers—*Friend of China* in the early years, *China Mail*, and *Hongkong Telegraph*, whose rivalry and opposing views provided some reading amusement for the Western community.[7]

A British colonist writing under the pseudonym of Betty at the turn of the century said that Hong Kong at that time had a population of 283,905, of whom 274,543 were Chinese. But as far as she was concerned, "the population consists only of William and about three hundred more, none of whom is Chinese." At least Betty was honest. She was also forthright in reporting that colonial society in Hong Kong was itself divided into two hierarchies: the Peak, "wherein live the elect," and the lower levels (which today is called the Mid-Levels), such as the hillsides in the southern Wan Chai and Central, "inhabited by the great business population . . . The Peak looks down on everything and everybody. The lower levels look up to the Peak, while Kowloon is supremely indifferent to both."[8]

This English woman, writing in an epistolary form for the *China Mail*, was apparently still single when she arrived in 1903 and met the man called William: "I cannot make up my mind to be a Mrs. Taipan [living on the Peak] . . . or a Mrs. Service [living at the lower levels]. In the first case, you have lots of money, and can walk about with your nose in the air like a high-born aristocrat and live like a hot-house flower; while in the second case you have a very good time and are only slightly patronized by the Taipans." But it was easier to be a Mrs. Service, she concluded, since her William was so employed. In these few frivolous sentences, Betty encapsulates the common fate of English women in the colony—a privileged minority of idle hot-house flowers who decorated colonial high society.

If Betty had stepped out from her comfortable turn-of-the-century home and taken an investigatory tour of the Chinese community, she would have been horrified. Cholera was rampant, and the infant mortality rate was extremely high. On October 26, 1901, the *Hongkong Telegraph* reported that only 72 out of every 1,000 Chinese born in the colony survived until their first birthday. This figure was no doubt exaggerated, but the reality of poverty, malnutrition, disease, and infant mortality was appalling.[9]

Quite a few personal accounts were written by women like Betty, literate Victorians whose vision of the world proved extremely narrow. Since most of them had accompanied their husbands to this far-away island, life consisted entirely of dinners, picnics, afternoon teas, social gatherings, and dances. Autumn was the "dancing season," and St. Andrew's Ball was the great event. Social activities also revolved around clubs—from the Royal Hong Kong Golf Club to the Ladies Recreational Club. Members drank in the club house and gossiped. In the afternoons, some of the ladies preferred to be carried down the hill in their wicker sedan chairs for promenades in the fine new Botanical Gardens, where they would "sit and read in the fresh air, still in their chairs, looking

BALL IN THE CITY HALL ON ST. ANDREW'S DAY

PANORAMA OF THE TOWN OF VICTORIA, HONGKONG, AS SEEN FROM THE HARBOUR

WITH THE CHINA SQUADRON IN THE EAST—AT HONGKONG

Top: Ball in City Hall on St. Andrew's Day. Bottom: Panorama of the town of Victoria, Hong Kong (*The Graphic,* February 26, 1887).

across the harbor while their chairmen [chair-carrying coolies] sat gossiping on the grass beside them." And in the evening, "with luck, there might be a play to see."[10]

Peakies rode through town on rickshaws, sedan chairs, and horse-drawn carriages. In 1901 there were 1,175 licensed rickshaws in Hong Kong, 556 licensed sedan chairs, and 7 gharries (four-wheeled horse-drawn carriages). Tram service began in Central in 1904, and the motorcar made its appearance in Hong Kong around the same time, though it was greeted with a great deal of negative comment. A decade later, automobiles had come into such wide use that the clock tower on Pedder Street had to be pulled down to make way for new streets. When suitable roads were constructed up to Victoria Peak after the Second World War, Rolls Royces and other fine motorcars were used as the major means of transportation for the residential elite.

Before the early twentieth century, many European men in Hong Kong were single because of the scarcity of unmarried women in the colony; they lived in comfort in bachelor establishments. The Reverend E. J. Hardy, who spent over three years as chaplain to the British forces in Hong Kong in the 1900s, disapproved of this state of affairs, considering it "unnatural": "The poor fellows are starved at heart, however, replete in stomach, and each starts a dog for companion. Alas! Some of them go to the dogs in other ways. A ten-thousand-miles-away-from-home feeling has many temptations connected with it."[11] One such temptation was provided by Chinese prostitutes, who offered perhaps the only social contact between white men and Chinese women. For European prostitutes, one would have to go to Flower Street or Lyndhurst Terrace in Central. Venereal disease became so rampant that a clinic had to be set up in Tsim Sha Tsui in Kowloon, next to the army barracks (constructed in 1892). The clinic was later moved, and the place where it stood became a small street called Lock — referring, in British slang, to prostitutes who "put in the lock" after contracting venereal disease.

A typical pastime for men was heavy drinking. An early resident in 1844 had the following description: "The number of low tippling houses [bars] is large, and spirits are very cheap. Everyday people may be seen reeling about under a burning sun, scarce able to stand, and the result is all attributed to the climate. Parties from 50 to 100 are occasionally allowed to land from the ships in the harbour, with leave of absence for two days, during which they are not an hour sober; and in all probability the great mortality in the army has some connection with the same cause." This typical sight seems to have continued

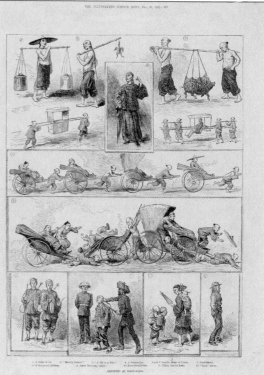

Sketches of Hong Kong life (*Illustrated London News*, December 12, 1882).

throughout the next century, particularly in the bar district in Wan Chai. The early resident advised more exercises. And, indeed, polo was popular throughout the year, as was cricket, though not as popular as in India, where the natives made it a national sport. Hunting in the New Territories was another physical activity that suited British taste, as well as horse-racing in Happy Valley, although the latter was less a sport than a social event.[12]

WITH ALL THESE PLEASURES and dissipations, one wonders how the Europeans in Hong Kong had the time or energy to do any work. Yet these accounts never fail to credit the early colonists for their mammoth achievement in transforming "a plutonic island of inviting sterility" into "one of the most pleasant cities of the earth." One early commentator went so far as to say that "the grand aqueducts and roads which cross the mountains of Hong Kong are worthy to be compared with some of the monumental works of ancient Rome."[13] Such hyperbole fails to mention how the government found the monetary resources to build such "grand aqueducts and roads" and make Hong Kong a most "pleasant" city to live in (for the colonial residents), or who supplied the back-breaking labor. There is little if any description of how business was transacted and money was made.

A valuable study by Christopher Munn explains that for nearly a century, between 1845 and 1941, the Hong Kong government drew a large revenue from granting monopoly licenses on the retail sale and processing of opium. In the period between 1845 and 1885, the opium monopoly, which the government auctioned off to the highest bidder, accounted for between 4 and 22 percent of annual revenue. As late as 1910 the government was still receiving $1,183,200, or the equivalent of 17 percent of its annual revenue, from this source. When the Hong Kong government took over the opium monopoly itself in 1914 as part of British imperial policy to eventually suppress the narcotic's use, its opium revenue soared, reaching $8.5 million in 1918—a benefit of opium suppression measures elsewhere and the wars in China. These revenues paid the salaries of Hong Kong's growing band of civil servants and helped maintain their comfortable lifestyle on the Peak.

Writing in 1922, Dorothy Dix wondered openly how a few white men could still control the faceless Chinese majority: "You plunge into the Chinese city and see the Chinese, thousands upon thousands, and hundred of thousands of them, and you begin to realize that the foreign part of the city is just a fringe on the native part, and you come face to face with the insoluble mystery of race—of how, wherever he is, the white man somehow dominates the situation."[14] This remark puts her in a league with H. Rider Haggard, the British imperialist whose adventure novels, set in Africa, always glorified the white heroes who conquered both nature and natives across this "dark continent." Hong Kong was too small for such exploits, but still one has to wonder, along with Dix, how the white men somehow managed "to dominate the situation." Most accounts left the details unexplained.

A government-sponsored publicity pamphlet published in 1924 gave full credit to British administration: "Hong Kong is a splendid example of what can be accomplished by British energy and capital, associated with the courage and restraint that go hand-in-hand with British colonization. Eighty-two years of patient administration by nineteen governors and eleven administrators have brought Hong Kong into the front rank of the world's commerce."[15] An adjective used here to describe colonial administration is "patient," which seems to imply either good-natured tolerance of inferiors or long-term arduousness.

But in fact, most of the governors and their associates blundered or groped their way through their tenures. Even a British sympathizer like Jan Morris admits that in the colony's early years "the senior administrators of Hong Kong were randomly selected" and government was run "by a mixed assortment of army men, ships' officers and miscellaneous adventurers, often wandering up from Australia in search of fortunes."[16] At its best, British administration can account for only a small part of the Hong Kong legend. The rest is more complicated.

In the many accounts of British pluck and enterprise, hardly anything is said about the labor of Chinese coolies. An 1845 letter from a resident provided some rare statistics: the cost of coolie labor "is nominally low. For one dollar, which at present is equivalent to 4s. 4d. sterling, you can secure the service of seven coolies for a day, or four masons, or three carpenters; an European laborer, however, if he could stand the heat, would be much cheaper [sic] at higher wages." In these early years, European laborers were probably hard to find, especially those who could stand the heat; whether they would be "cheaper" at higher wages is anyone's guess. By the end of the century, the demand for coolie labor was insatiable, and the traffic was run by brokers. Several Western observers have compared it to the African slave trade.[17]

When English newspapers paid any attention to the Chinese labor force, it

Dock workers in Hong Kong at the turn of the twentieth century.

was mostly limited to reporting the capture of Chinese thieves and bandits and to descriptions of their punishment. A notice on the *Hongkong Daily Press* announced on January 23, 1872, that "the public flogging of eighteen prisoners will take place at the whipping post, this day, at 3:30 " The whipping post was located half-way up Wyndham Street near the present On Lan Street. Solomon Bard, who compiled a number of newspaper excerpts like these, commented that "members of the English Club (predecessor of the Hong Kong Club), which was located at the bottom of Wyndham Street, would have had an excellent view of the flogging from the upper balcony." In addition to legal floggings, Chinese were frequently beaten in the streets. According to an eye-witness account: "You cannot be two minutes in a Hong Kong street without seeing Europeans striking coolies with their canes or umbrellas."[18]

The occasional hints of insurrection did occur. In 1857 a notorious case of bread poisoning received wide press coverage: After eating their breakfast on January 15, some four hundred Britons were taken mysteriously and seriously ill. Apparently the bread was found "heavily dosed with arsenic," and "the most respected baker of the island"—a certain Cheong Ah Lum, actually a Chinese merchant, who was responsible for supplying bread to the Britons—was suspected to be the criminal. He was put on trial but acquitted for lack of sufficient evidence.[19] The case would not have become so notorious had it not been for the fact that Lady Bowring, the wife of the governor, also "became delirious and was forced to withdraw to England where she died." James Pope-Hennessy, the grandson of another later governor, described the case as an indirect consequence of the British predilection for heavy breakfast, which consisted of sausages, fried eggs and bacon, kippers, finnan haddock, strong tea, and of course toast. English breakfast was "one of the first prerequisites of normal life which Victorians introduced into their colonial territories," the younger Hennessy commented in an amusing 1969 book called *Half-Crown Colony.*[20] In any case, the person responsible for the bread poisoning was never found. But Ah Lum lost his business as a result.

The Reverend James Legge, who had learned Chinese and translated the Chinese Classics into English, was one of the very few Englishmen who ventured into the Chinese world and made friends with the Chinese. In a parting speech given in Hong Kong's City Hall on November 2, 1872, he summarized his impressions this way: "I will only say that during my many years of residence here, my intercourse was quite as much with the people as with their books. Several hours of every day were spent in visiting them from house to house, and shop to shop, conversing with them on all subjects, and trying to get them to converse with me on one subject [Christianity] . . . I could say that, excepting the brothels, there was hardly a house in Victoria and the villages in which I had not repeatedly been, and where I was not known as a friend."[21] He then goes on to envision a future for Hong Kong:

> When I try to pierce into the future, I see a railway from Kowloon to Canton, and branch lines connected with it. I see this island the natural outlet to all Europe, and by the Pacific lines to the United States. I see itself the home of a happy population, three times more numerous than the present, and foreigner and Chinese dwelling together in mutual appreciation. I see its harbor a forest of smoking funnels with hardly a white-winged sailing vessel among them; opium a phantom of the past. The emigration of the poor goes on from it on principles approved and guarded by the Chinese and other governments, while the enterprise and integrity of its merchants, the kindness, forbearance, and purity of all its inhabitants are spoken of with delight from Peking to Hainan, from the furthest west of Szechuan to the borders of the Eastern sea.[22]

This is the most positive and idealistic view ever expressed by a non-Chinese about Hong Kong and its people in the nineteenth century. Today, Legge's utopian vision has largely been realized, although he could not have imagined the effect of pollution from this "forest of smoking funnels." It was rare to find such words as "kindness, forbearance, and purity" used to describe all of Hong Kong's inhabitants.

BARBARA-SUE WHITE spent considerable time and energy searching the archives for her collection of largely colonial writings, fittingly titled *Hong Kong: Somewhere Between Heaven and Earth*. That volume (from which some of the quotations in this chapter are taken) provides telling glimpses of what life on the Peak was like. But as White acknowledged, "Not every piece included is or even aspires to be great writing," and indeed most are not. We cannot help wondering why the literary value of these selections proved so puny. True, the majority of them are memoirs and travelogues, chosen because "they capture the spirit of an age." Still, when compared with English colonial writings on India, or Dutch colonial writings on Indonesia, these specimens from Hong Kong express an extremely truncated vision.

One of the better writers among them is Stella Benson, who in the 1930s was married to the last inspector of customs in China, James O'Gorman Anderson (father of two distinguished historians, Perry and Benedict Anderson). Benson may be considered an early feminist, with both essays and fiction to her credit and several volumes of diaries containing her impressions of Hong Kong. Benson was an outspoken critic of prostitution, legal or illegal, and was one of the very few Western women who ventured into the low-class brothels of Yau Ma Tei, in Kowloon, to report on the horrible conditions there. Having spent some time in California before marrying Anderson, she was also known as an independent woman who resisted the snobbishness Hong Kong's high-society women—a group presided over by Bella Woolf, sister-in-law of the novelist Virginia Woolf and wife of Lord Southorn, the colonial secretary under Governor Cecil Clementi.

Bella Woolf's Peak perspective comes through very clearly in both Benson's satirical portrait of her and in Woolf's own stories. She mostly wrote trivial tales about domestic life within her circle—such as getting one's Chinese servants to borrow a spoonful of castor oil. Mrs. Kettlewell, a character in one of her stories, was so "busy wondering whether the cook had cheated her over that last leg of lamb" that she never had time to look at the magnificent view from her house on the Peak. Woolf gave a glimpse of what that view was like: "Each house had a row of steps up to the front door, a small patch of garden and then a paved piece of terrace ending in a wall. Over the wall was a view that took your breath away, a stretch of sea and islands and headlands shimmering on fine days in a magic woof of turquoise and green."[23]

Mary Poynter, author of *Around the Shores of Asia* published in 1921, offered this description of the colonial hospitality she enjoyed on the Peak: "We lunched on one side of the Peak with wide views of islands and far glimpses of the China Sea in the distance, and tea was served to us in a garden at the other side overlooking the mainland of Kowloon, that looked blue and impressive if somewhat barren of vegetation."[24] Why, one wonders, did Kowloon look blue and "barren of vegetation"? In the early twentieth century, hills on the mainland of Kowloon—what is now known as the New Territories—must have been covered with lush forests and dotted with villages of Chinese settlers whose earliest traces of immigration to the peninsula and some offshore islands could be traced back thousands of years.[25] Since the British took over the peninsula in 1860, barracks for soldiers and a few summer houses for Europeans had been built. When the Kowloon-Canton Railway opened in 1910, some Europeans moved to Kowloon, though not in large numbers. But viewed from an English garden on the Peak, over an afternoon cup of tea, distant Kowloon was barren and devoid of civilization—like the so-called "barren rock" of Hong Kong island before the British came.

The colonials' self-imposed segregation confirmed Rudyard Kipling's famous line: "East is East, and West is West, and never the twain shall meet." Kipling himself visited Hong Kong in the 1890s and even spent one night cruising the bars (and possibly brothels) to see what life was really like. Still, it sometimes took outsiders—other writers from England—to see through the artifice and foppish hypocrisy of this little Victorian society on a colonial hill.

W. Somerset Maugham wrote a short novel titled *The Painted Veil*, set in Hong Kong and China in the 1920s. In the preface Maugham offered some revealing self-explanations that shed light on the colonial mentality in Hong Kong at the time: "I had originally called my hero and heroine Lane, a common enough name, but it appeared that there were people of that name in Hong Kong. They brought an action, which the proprietors of the magazine in which my novel was serialized settled for two hundred and fifty pounds, and I changed the name to Fane. Then the Assistant Colonial Secretary, thinking himself libeled, threatened to institute proceedings. It seemed to me strange that the temporary occupant of so insignificant a post should think himself aimed at, but in order to save trouble I changed Hong Kong to an imaginary colony of Tching-Yen."

Perhaps Maugham's fictional portrait of Walter and Kitty Fane bore too strik-ing a resemblance to some real personages, or perhaps its story of Kitty's adultery with a colonial official was too familiar for comfort. In the novel, the British couple come to Hong Kong because Walter is employed in the colonial service as a bacteriologist. They meet a fictional assistant colonial secretary, Charles Townsend, who lives with his wife on the Peak "with a wide window over the sea." The Townsends' drawing room where they receive Kitty is spacious and "furnished as with every other drawing room she had been in at Hong Kong in a comfortable and homely style." Townsend is a charming man, impeccably dressed down to cufflinks and waistcoat buttons from Cartier's. On his sun-burned face, "the little trim curly mustache which did not conceal his full red lips" was, for Kitty, irresistible. He "played tennis and polo and golf" and "kept racing ponies." This sardonic portrait of a colonial official is typical of Maugham. As the plot unfolds, Townsend is revealed to be a scoundrel, "the most vain and fatuous ass that it's ever been my bad luck to run across," said Kitty, the remorseful heroine at the end of their affair.

However, it is not in Hong Kong but in a cholera-ridden Chinese town some sixty miles north, Mei-tan-fu, that the heroine finds redemption. Her husband, having discovered her affair with Townsend, punishes her by forcing her to ac-company him on this suicide mission. Kitty survives the cholera, but as soon as she returns to Hong Kong she finds herself plunging right back into the affair with Townsend. When Kitty finally leaves Hong Kong, she feels relieved as her ship departs from the harbor. What happened "seemed to have happened in an-other world."

Obviously, in Maugham's eyes, Hong Kong provided no space for self-re-flection, since the characters all lived behind a "painted veil." But the Hong Kong of Maugham's portrait is itself a painted veil, as fluffy and ephemeral as the characters it enshrouds. We know from Jeffrey Meyers's biography that Maugham traveled for four months in China in 1919–1920; he was, according to Meyers, the first among British writers to write about China in a travel book, *On a Chinese Screen*, and in a play, *East of Suez* (both published in 1922). On his way to China and back, he stayed in Hong Kong and "enjoyed the spectacular view of the harbor from Victoria Peak."[26] It does not take much reflection to realize that the novel's central setting and focus—the purgatorio of the protagonists' moral trial and redemption—is China, not Hong Kong. The colony merely provides a story-frame—or two frames, one at the beginning and one near the end of the novel—that shuts off this colonial world from the world of cholera and suffering in China, just as the shuttered frames of the windows and bolted doors in colonial houses on the Peak shut off the real world down below. As if to further underscore the point that the novel has nothing to do with Hong Kong, in the most recent screen adaptation of the novel (2007), the director simply changed the Hong Kong setting altogether and substituted Shanghai instead.

Meyers faults Maugham for not rising to the authenticity of Thomas Mann (*Death in Venice*) and Albert Camus (*The Plague*) in describing the cholera epidemic that was sweeping China. What I would fault him for is not knowing or caring that, downhill from the Peak where he was visiting, thousands of Chinese had likewise died of the plague in 1894. In Maugham's fictional quest for life's meaning, Hong Kong clearly did not qualify as the "heart of darkness." He does not delve into the horrors of the human psyche like Conrad, or into the existential condition of real people, but rather chooses to remain on the surface of the story. In that respect he is just another in a long line of British colonial writers who showed no interest in the plight of Hong Kong's Chinese population. For many Western writers who visited Hong Kong, the colony provided, at best, material for a travelogue or an occasional glimpse. Such writings perpetuated the image of a "borrowed place" on "borrowed time"—of Hong Kong as a temporary stopover for unsettled sojourners who could see only its superficialities and who ignored its unfathomable multitude.

THE GREAT MODERNIST POET W. H. Auden, along with his companion, Christopher Isherwood, also passed through the colony on their way to China, and in 1939 they published a joint book of impressions in both poetry and prose called *Journey to a War*. Auden wrote a poem entitled "Hong Kong"—not an inspired piece of work, and certainly uncharacteristic of modern poetry, of which Auden was an acknowledged master. Yet it captured the self-absorption of the British colonists he encountered in Hong Kong:

> The leading characters are wise and witty;
> Substantial men of birth and education
> With wide experience of administration,
> They know the manners of a modern city.

On the "Late Victorian Hill" where these men reside, "Only the servants enter unexpected." The juxtaposition of masters and servants creates a perfect stage for the colonists' willful ignorance of China's war with Japan, being fought off-stage "like the slamming of a distant door." The poem ends with what reads like a message: "For what we are, we have ourselves to blame." Whether intentional or ironic, the ending leaves us with some nagging questions that Auden refuses to answer. What went wrong? How did these "wise and witty" characters manage to turn a deaf ear to the distant thunder on the mainland?

Also in the late 1930s, on the eve of the Japanese invasion of Hong Kong, a woman writer and journalist, Emily Hahn, moved to the city with her new British husband, Charles Boxer. Her autobiographical account, *China to Me* (1944), recounts her previous experience in Shanghai, where she lived openly with her Chinese lover, Shao Xunmei, a decadent and rich dandy educated at Oxford. She came to Hong Kong mostly to be with Boxer, and the new couple found the colony pleasant but boring. A short paragraph describes what life was like on the Peak during the years when the mainland was already occupied by Japanese military forces:

> Nobody among those British ever gave China a thought. You could
> go through the day, from the eleven o'clock drink in the Grips
> through lunch at someone's house and tea somewhere else down
> to dinner, stately on the Peak with plenty of cut glass and damask
> linen and heavy silver, and nobody would talk of the war in China
> except as a far-off exotic manifestation of the natives . . . It was much
> the existence I would have been leading in London, save for the

fact that with a few exceptions the people we saw were not as amusing as those we could have dug up elsewhere. I didn't mind it as much as I would have under different circumstances. I enjoyed it. But after a few months I was homesick for China.[27]

This sheltered, comfortable life on the Peak finally came to an end on December 8, 1941, when Japanese forces attacked Hong Kong. Two days before, on December 6, Happy Valley was still filled with crowds watching the horse races. Dances and parties had been held as usual at the Peninsula Hotel and other places, though Governor Mark Young was conspicuously absent. On the night of December 7, Emily Hahn's husband, who was in charge of intelligence, did not sleep at all, because he was busy listening to the radio broadcast from Tokyo. At 4:45 A.M., the news that Japan had declared war against Great Britain and the United States was finally confirmed. And at 8 A.M., thirty-six Japanese planes bombed the airfield even before the British defenders had time to sound the alarm. Five days later, Kowloon and the New Territories fell into Japanese hands.

Hong Kong island was expected to last three months, but it held on for less than three weeks. Some scattered forces in Wan Chai and Repulse Bay put up a valiant but hopeless defense. On December 23, two days before Christmas, about fifty British and Canadian prisoners who had been captured in the neighborhood of the Repulse Bay Hotel were brutally slaughtered: some had their arms sliced off, others were decapitated or bayoneted.

As Philip Snow vividly describes this experience in *The Fall of Hong Kong*, the Peakies at first refused to leave.[28] Some even "appealed to the Japanese conquerors for the right to be interned in the familiar surroundings of the Peak." But they were quickly brought down to earth, both physically and symbolically. The 2,500 British and other Allied nationals were first packed into seedy Chinese boarding houses that had once doubled as brothels and were then imprisoned in a permanent camp at Stanley. Their accommodations consisted of unfurnished rooms, each housing eight or nine people. Food was rationed to a minimum, and the worst quarters were given to the Peakies in order to intentionally humiliate them. Most of the prison guards were Sikhs who had served in the old Hong Kong police force, and now they had their chance to air old grievances. "The whole spectacle was enacted in front of an audience drawn from the colony's former subject communities." A little ditty by a nameless author began to circulate:

> Rock-a-bye, Taipan, on the Peak's Top.
> While your bluff holds, the fortress won't drop;
> But when your bluff's called, the fortress will fall
> And down will come Taipan, vested interests and all!

As Snow points out, the British in Hong Kong got off more lightly than their compatriots in Southeast Asia. "The keynote of their treatment was humiliation rather than brutality for the sake of it." But the prisoners suffered nevertheless, precisely because they were so unused to "local" conditions, including rice and other victuals. Without servants and luxuries, some of the "pillars of [the] pre-war community" began to break down under the strain, while "humbler men and women displayed unexpected strengths."[29]

Charles Boxer was put in the prison camp at Stanley, and Emily Hahn's efforts to give aid to her husband make far more interesting reading than most British memoirs of camp life. But still, one wonders why this harrowing experience of incarceration failed to produce any literature of enduring worth. No work produced in the Stanley camp is comparable to A. G. Ballard's *Empire of the Sun*, which describes the author's experience as a boy in a Japanese camp near Shanghai. Nor can we find any fiction like James Clavell's *King Rat*, which was based on his imprisonment in Singapore. There is no *Bridge over the River Kwai*, real or imagined, in Hong Kong either. Was life on the Peak so comfortable and pampered that it permanently stultified any creative impulse, even after the comfort and pampering were gone?

IF COLONIAL HONG KONG did not produce a literature worthy of a Conrad, Camus, or Mann, it did manage to inspire a string of best-selling novels dealing with the themes of commerce, romance, adventure, and spying. These include Robert Elegant's *Dynasty* (1977), James Clavell's *Tai-pan* (1966) and *Noble House* (1984), Richard Mason's *The World of Suzie Wong* (1959), Han Suyin's *Love Is a Many-Splendored Thing* (1952), Timothy Mo's *The Monkey King* (1978) and *An Insular Possession* (1987), Christopher New's *A Change of Flag* (2000) and *The Chinese Box* (2000), Robert Ludlum's *The Bourne Supremacy* (1986), Paul Theroux's *Kowloon Tong* (1998), and John le Carré's *The Honorable Schoolboy* (1977). Most of these novels were made into Hollywood movies, to which we may also add *A Countess from Hong Kong* (1967), *Ferry to Hong Kong* (1959), *A Soldier of Fortune* (1955), and many others.

One could argue that Hong Kong is the perfect setting for these thrillers and romances, and the city does not need any high-brow writing in English or any other Western language to make its residents proud. After all, the argument goes, Chinese natives do not read English, the English themselves look up only to their own literary masters in London, and the old colonists had little practical use for the classical pursuits of Oxford and Cambridge. As Bella Woolf said of her heroine, Mrs. Kettlewell: "She had no use for poetry, either Shakespeare's or any other."[30]

This sentiment is echoed in a poem written by another late Victorian in Hong Kong who wrote under the pen name of Dolly; the first and last stanzas go as follows:

> Away with books! Nor let in Pleasure's train,
> One single elevating thought remain;
> What boots it, though in ignorance we live?
> The human mind was made for naught but gain.
> So we can boast that we in Hongkong here,
> Are far without vain Learning's futile sphere;
> And count, where "ignorance is bliss," that we
> Are doubly happy in the larger share.[31]

One could make the case that the "ignorance for gain" mentality evoked in this bit of doggerel still prevails in Hong Kong today. Humanistic learning is looked down upon by many as a useless pursuit. In contemporary Hong Kong, all is image, and the government would not have it any other way. For a long time, the Hong Kong Tourism Board featured a photograph of a junk as its official emblem, in order to attract tourists with the oriental exoticism of this faraway island. This boat still puts up its faded orange sails and floats slowly around the harbor, giving tourists a free ride and a chance to snap some pictures.

Two films will serve to bring our survey of Western images of Hong Kong up to 1997, the year when Britain turned over its former colony to the People's Republic of China. The first is a 1955 adaptation of Han Suyin's autobiographical novel, *Love Is a Many-Splendored Thing*, directed by Henry King with screenplay by John Patrick (who also adapted *The World of Suzie Wong*). The book and movie are not typical representations of colonial views from the Peak, in part because Han was not a white colonial Peakie. She was Eurasian. What makes the film (as distinct from the novel) so representative of the era is its glamorous portraiture and locations. In real life, Han felt in love with an Englishman, but in the film version he is transformed into an American journalist played, once again, by William Holden—the amateur painter Robert Lomax transformed into Mark Elliot the war correspondent, who dies on the Korean front. Holden's characterization is always the same, whether he flirts with Suzie Wong in a dingy Wan Chai hotel or courts Dr. Han Suyin somewhere in the Mid-Levels.

The noble Eurasian heroine in the film works in a hospital that looks suspiciously like the main building of the University of Hong Kong, a red-brick two-story edifice in late Victorian style (called Luk You Tong in Chinese). Presumably she lived in the hospital dormitory, and he stayed at the Foreign Correspondent Club on Conduit Road (now moved to Wyndham Street, next door to the Fringe Club). To make the story—especially the final ending—more dramatic and appealing, the lovers have their tryst under a tree on top of a hill that is supposedly somewhere on the Peak. (Actually, these scenes were shot on the side of a canyon near Los Angeles.) Why would they go up the hill and not down, since Han Suyin is portrayed as a medical doctor who considers herself Chinese and cares deeply for Chinese children? It is as if only on the

Peak and nowhere else could they find the "many-splendored thing" of true love.

Thus, despite the political correctness (at the time) of its overt messages, the film version, if not the entire novel itself, perpetuates a glamorized view of Hong Kong from the Peak. There is not a single reference to Kowloon and the New Territories, not to mention the bars of Wan Chai. The lovers meet in a party filled with racist white men and women, where Dr. Han's dignity as a Eurasian woman really stands out. Mark Elliot is a good-mannered gentleman, noble and chaste to the core, who courts her with singular devotion. He shows up at her hospital to give her a ride and then takes her to dine at a famous tourist spot, the floating restaurant in Aberdeen. They go for a swim in Repulse Bay and visit her friends in a secluded but scenic house nearby. Every location is so beautiful and tasteful that the real chaos and commotion of Hong Kong are lost. Even *The World of Suzie Wong* provides scenes of the street market and children playing around the roof sheds of old tenements.

Thus when Elliot is suddenly summoned to the war from their love nest in a Macau hotel, all contemporary relevance—the international politics of the Cold War, the civil war in China, Hong Kong's own unstable status after the Communist victory on the mainland, and the massive waves of refugees—is obliterated. When his love letters from Korea finally arrive in her hands, it is too late. Mark Elliot is already dead.

In view of Han Suyin's blatant endorsement of Mao's Revolution later on, it is surprising that she did not paint a more revealing portrait of Hong Kong itself—if not a more scathing exposé of life at the top. The story, in both film and fiction, betrays the limitations of Han's experience and her sheltered view from the Peak. In one episode, when the heroine takes a plane to visit her family in China, the traditional surroundings and value system offer a sharp contrast to her Westernized world in Hong Kong. But unlike Maugham's Chinese village in *The Painted Veil*, Han's hometown offers no attractions, and we are only too glad when the heroine returns to her American lover in the colony. Elliot, like Han's English lover in real life, is a married man whose wife in Singapore ignores his pleas for divorce. Whether or not this is based on fact, the film's plot makes an unwitting counterpoint to the adultery story in *The Painted Veil*. What is finally "unveiled" is neither moral corruption in colonial Hong Kong nor moral redemption in plague-laden or war-torn China but the sentiments of star-crossed lovers in the exotic Orient.

Our final sample of Western images of Hong Kong is not entirely of colonial making. The film *Chinese Box* (1997) directed by a Chinese-American, Wayne Wang (who later made *The Joy Luck Club*), gives a vivid though lopsided portrait of colonial life on the eve of the "transfer" (the term preferred by the British) of Hong Kong to China. The story and screenplay were written by Wang in collaboration with veteran screenwriter Jean-Claude Carriere, a Frenchman, the English novelist Paul Theroux, and Larry Gross, an old Hollywood hand. (It was not based on the novel by Christopher New under the same name.) The film stars the British actor Jeremy Irons and the Chinese actress Gong Li, with a supporting cast drawn from Hong Kong. The comedian Michael Hui plays Gong Li's Chinese paramour, and the beautiful Maggie Cheung plays a former prostitute with a scarred face. The language is English, with only a sprinkling of Cantonese and Mandarin thrown in.

Though shot entirely on location in Hong Kong by a director who had previous experience making a local film, *Chinese Box* is for all practical purposes a colonial film geared to Western audiences. It chooses to view Hong Kong from the angle of its protagonist, an English photojournalist named John, who has spent over a decade in Hong Kong. As portrayed by the pale-faced Jeremy Irons, John suffers from a rare form of leukemia that gives him only a few months to live. The metaphor for British colonialism is too obvious to miss. But aside from his terminal disease, what else does he suffer from? What does it mean to be the "last colonist" to witness this historic event? Does he draw any final lessons from a decade of living in Hong Kong and writing about its economy and politics?

The answer is supplied easily in the middle of the film: no! Hong Kong has become even more inscrutable to Westerners as its colonial history draws to an end. Hand-held camera shots convey a sense of *cinéma verité*, but the mood is romantic: John falls hopelessly in love with Vivian, a high-society woman

(Gong Li), who leads a double life as a high-class prostitute. Why is Hong Kong, in the eyes of white men, always cast in the role of prostitutes? Indeed, in this case, two prostitutes! Since *The World of Suzie Wong*—perhaps even before— this racist formula rarely changes.

To be sure, the white male protagonist is made more vulnerable by his un- requited love and his terminal illness. John does not live on the Peak but in a rundown apartment in the old part of Central, near the Mid-Levels escalator and next to the old Central Market, where he befriends an aging local vendor. He is so bored with Hong Kong's social life that the suicide of a human rights activist at a New Year's Eve party he attends does not even affect him. His heart is already filled with Vivian, the mysterious woman who lives with, but cannot marry, a local Chinese businessman. Her paramour is the embodiment of a new species of Hong Kong entrepreneur who wants to get richer after the Chinese takeover. The film's political message is blurred, however, by the wishy-washy attitude of Vivian. In a long sequence, she watches an old film starring Marlene Dietrich (*Morocco*, 1930) and imitates her gestures. It seems to suggest Vivian's own lack of heart and will to decide her own fate—until it is too late.

Vivian's brief romance with John is finally consummated shortly before he goes to a bench along Victoria Harbor to die. Does John feel fulfilled during his last months in Hong Kong? His final letter, written in unbelievably elegant Chinese characters, makes clear that he is grateful for her love, but it contains nothing else. Before dying, he also tries to do his last good deed for the scarred prostitute, Jean, by bringing her to the man she claims was her former lover— a heartless Brit who does not even recognize her. This rejection scene takes place in Statue Square, against the background of the Legco building, where on the evening of June 30 demonstrators took over the balcony and shouted slogans for democracy. The historic incident is duly captured, newsreel-style, by a hand-held camera and tagged onto the romantic story. It makes little sense ex- cept to provide some "realistic" background for Jean's own disillusionment.

She grasps John's video camera and tries to tell her own story, in a scene that is intended to help viewers appreciate the complexities of Hong Kong's colonial past. Her facial scar is clearly a symbol of a ravaged city whose loyalty to Britain—to the point of committing suicide for the sake of her master—is now repaid with cold rebuff and disdain. The implied political point seems to be that Great Britain should not abandon her former subjects with such heartlessness. But it is already too late for the tender-hearted colonial protagonist to rescue his two "colonized" women. *Chinese Box* is a travesty of a story that brings no critical reflection to bear on a century and a half of colonial rule. Its intricate design merely opens up to emptiness.

Of course, not all Westerners are travelers or sojourners, and not all creative writing in English about Hong Kong is orientalist or carries the "white man's burden." A small crop of works written in English about contemporary life in Hong Kong have appeared since 1997, all published locally, that are enjoying a growing reputation. The most famous among them is Xu Xi (also known as S. Komala and Sussy Chako), who has published three novels and two short story collections. In comparing the works of these writers with the colonial writings discussed above, one is immediately struck by a much more intimate knowledge of Hong Kong itself. Clearly the angle of perception is at least "half-native" in both characterization and location.

For instance, in Xu Xi's *History's Fiction* (2005), a collection of short stories organized with a historical frame (a retrospective chronology going back from the 1990s to the 1960s), the characters are ordinary people who are mostly local but also cosmopolitan. They seem to reflect the author's own background as a Hong Kong–born Chinese-Indonesian who now divides her time between Hong Kong, New York, and New Zealand. Her characters speak both Chinese (Cantonese or Mandarin) and English and negotiate between them with ease: "He had lapsed into Mandarin, but she held her tongue. Why argue anymore that reality was lived in Cantonese?" "She insisted he make love to her in Cantonese, *Gwongdong wah*. When he wanted to tease, he would speak Mandarin all evening, and she would laugh, holding her hands over her ears, saying *mouh yahn sik teng*—no one 'knows how to hear,' no one comprehends."

As the title of the collection clearly suggests, history and fiction are combined, and some of the most important events, such as the 1967 Star Ferry riots, the

1989 Tiananmen Square massacre, and the 1997 handover, lend color and authenticity to the narrative. The scope of vision is certainly more global than colonial, and a strong modern feminist perspective has replaced the Victorian view from the Peak. Xu Xi, unlike most of the writers or film-makers discussed above, feels no nostalgia for the old colonial era in Hong Kong either in sentiment or as intentional irony.

Another recent collection of stories by Mathew Harrison, an Oxford-educated British writer who spent twenty years in Hong Kong, is simply titled *Queen's Road Central and Other Stories*. Published locally by a small press in Wan Chai in 2006, the book went through three printings in three months, which perhaps testifies to its growing, though still limited, readership. Not one of its eight stories, bearing such location-grounded titles as "Queen's Road Central," "Admirality," "Queen's Road East," "Pedder Street," "Hennessy Road," and so on (all on Hong Kong island), is set on Victoria Peak.

Billed by the Hong Kong Tourism Board as the "last authentic sailing junk in Hong Kong," the *Duk Ling* makes a regular appearance in Victoria Harbor.

The bird market in Mong Kok.

5

Kowloon, Past and Present

The peninsula of Kowloon (Nine Dragons) is linked to Hong Kong island by three cross-harbor tunnels, which provide access by automobile, bus, and subway. Before the tunnels were constructed in the 1970s, the only way to cross the harbor was by boat. The Star Ferry began regular service from Central to Kowloon peninsula in 1888, and eventually it offered service to Wan Chai and Hung Hom. Even today, with so many transportation options in Hong Kong, a trip on the Star Ferry is an adventure.

Both the upper and lower decks offer stunning views of the harbor skyline, especially after 8 P.M., when the spectacular *lumière* display on the Hong Kong side of the harbor comes to life. This orchestrated spectacle of moving and changing neon lights was the seminal achievement of chief executive Tung Chee-hwa's administration. It cost the Hong Kong government millions to design and install, but for a new government determined to maintain the former colony's position as a shopping and tourist paradise, the investment was well worthwhile. If ever a single sight has attained iconic status in the minds of Hong Kong's visitors—a sight imprinted on numerous postcards and commercials—it is the skyline of Victoria Harbor at night. And for millions of local residents, this confection, created for commercial consumption, is a normal part of their daily lives.

The harbor view can also be enjoyed while taking a leisurely stroll along the Star Promenade facing the harbor on the Kowloon side. This tourist attraction was concocted by the government to showcase Hong Kong's film industry—which was once the third largest in the world, after the United States and India. The promenade is a shameless copy of the "hand-print" trail of famous movie

The famous Hong Kong skyline, viewed from Tsim Sha Tsui, at the tip of Kowloon peninsula.

stars in front of Grauman's Chinese Theatre in Hollywood. (Luckily, the exotic-looking theater itself was not duplicated.) Yet few tourists or local pedestrians pay any attention to the names and fingerprints of Hong Kong movie stars, past and present. They would rather watch the promotional vignettes on a giant screen at the end of the promenade. But despite these touches of vulgarity, a walk along the waterfront is worthwhile, if only to watch the skyline on the opposite side and enjoy the sea breeze. The skyline is also spectacular from the expensive harbor-front restaurants and cafés in nearby hotels.

THE TIP OF KOWLOON peninsula is called Tsim Sha Tsui, literally Sharp Sandy Mouth. It was also known as Heung Po Tau, or Fragrant Quay, named after the incense trees grown in the New Territories that were transported to Hong Kong's "fragrant harbor." Sparsely populated with villagers when

Kowloon was ceded to England in 1860, Tsim Sha Tsui is now one of the most congested areas in the entire peninsula. It is also the most "heteroglosic": on any street corner one is likely to hear Cantonese, Mandarin, English in at least four different accents (British, American, Australian, Indian), along with several European languages and Indian dialects. The area boasts the largest concentration of Indian residents of any district in Hong Kong.

Just one of Tsim Sha Tsui's many high-fashion malls.

Visually, this part of Kowloon, perhaps more than any other, epitomizes Koolhaas's image of a "generic city" in its random mixture of buildings and streets without any semblance of a center or an urban plan, all of it geared to blatant consumerism. After getting off the ferry at Tsim Sha Tsui, passengers are immediately flanked by malls, shops, and hotels. Ocean City Mall is (as the name suggests) a small city in itself, filled with hundreds of shops conveniently connected to Ocean Terminal (the landing site for passenger ships and other ferries) and several hotels. Most hotels in the area have their own shopping malls, which are interconnected in an endless underground maze.

But alongside its crass commercialism, Tsim Sha Tsui is also an important venue for "high culture." The old railway station that once stood here was demolished in 1974 to make way for a large complex of buildings at the choicest site facing the harbor. The flagship building, Hong Kong's Cultural Center, is indeed shaped somewhat like a ship and sits near the edge of the water. Yet on its harbor side—overlooking one of the signature urban skylines in the world—the building has not a single window. Requiring more than a decade to build, the final product, opened in 1989 with Prince Charles and Princess Diana officiating the ceremony, is surely one of the ugliest contemporary buildings in this city or any other. And indeed it could be anywhere—it has nothing whatsoever to do with its urban context in Kowloon or Hong Kong or China.

To make things worse, the acoustics of the 2,019-seat concert hall are among the worst in the region, although it boasts the largest Austrian pipe organ in Asia. It is currently the home of the Hong Kong Philharmonic Orchestra, with its new musical director, the renowned Dutch maestro Edo de Waart. The Grand Theater upstairs, with 1,734 seats in three tiers, was designed for performances of "large-scale opera," ballet, and musicals, although visiting opera companies at the Hong Kong Arts Festival, held every spring, have found its stage not wide or deep enough.

The buildings next to the Cultural Center—the Hong Kong Museum of Art and the Hong Kong Space Museum—are equally characterless. In Koolhaas's model, these three structures occupy a "junk-space," the residue of what colonial modernization leaves on the place, or "what remains after modernization has run its course or, more precisely, what coagulates while modernization is taking place, its fall-out."[1] Naturally, this "culture complex" was designed by a bureaucracy, the Hong Kong government's Architecture Department. Since 2000 it has been run by the Department of Leisure and Cultural Services.

The art museum was originally housed in City Hall and was moved to these premises in 1991. Its mission is "to preserve the cultural heritage of China and

promote art with a local focus." Despite its many exhibitions mounted with care, the museum has not attracted the expected number of visitors; yet when a famous painting by Picasso was on display elsewhere in the city, long waiting lines formed to view it. This contrast led some local commentators to remark that Hong Kong is among the least heritage-conscious cities in Asia. But it probably also had something to do with Hong Kong consumers' appetite for name brands.

As if to compensate for the city's flagrant loss of a historical site, the clock tower from the demolished railway station was saved and incorporated into the design of the Cultural Center complex. The old station had been constructed in 1913–1916 after the completion of the Kowloon-Canton Railway (KCR) in 1910. The clock tower was built in 1921. As with its counterpart on the Star Ferry pier across the harbor (now demolished), the four faces of the clock had for a long time governed the lives of Kowloon residents. A bell sounding out the hours was silenced only once—during the three and a half years of Japanese occupation.

The Star Ferry teminal in Tsim Sha Tsui, with the old railroad clock tower and windowless Cultural Center in the background.

43

When the Kowloon railway station was relocated to Hung Hom in 1974, only the silent tower was left behind, to offer a mere reflection of history—a decoration intended for tourist consumption, like the lit-up harbor skyline.

On the street opposite the Cultural Center stands the Peninsula Hotel, first opened in 1928, one of the oldest hotels and certainly the most illustrious in the city. The H-shaped seven-story wing (in front of a thirty-story modern addition) still conveys a certain Old World charm. In its famed high-ceilinged lobby, high tea is still served every afternoon. In the era before the invention of cell phones, the venerable colonial custom of "name-calling" added excitement, as bus boys passed among the tables while ringing bells and holding up signs with names of the guests wanted on the telephone. To sit in the lobby for tea was to exhibit one's social status and be seen.

On June 30, 1997, all of the hotel's dining room seats and the rooms upstairs were taken—in fact, reserved far in advance—by old-timers and tourists to celebrate, or commemorate, the last day of British colonialism in Hong Kong. Half a century before, on Christmas Day 1941, Governor Mark Young had come to the hotel to sign the formal papers of surrender to Japan's invading forces. Today, the hotel's corridors are filled with Japanese tourists, whose guidebooks no doubt contain similar references to this historic moment.

KOWLOON HAS A MUCH LONGER recorded history than Hong Kong. Early maps from the Ming and Qing dynasties consigned all of what would become Kowloon and the New Territories to Xin'an county. The name "Nine Dragons" presumably once referred to low mountain ranges in the area that looked vaguely like dragons. According to one legend, the last emperor of the Song dynasty, pursued by the invading Mongol army, retreated to this area, where he lived in a mountain cave. Looking at his new surroundings, he counted eight dragon-like hills—but then corrected himself: no, in fact there are nine dragons, including the emperor himself. According to a different legend, recorded in a Qing dynasty guidebook, the name comes from nine brothers, all fishermen and good swimmers, who on one moonlit night jumped into the sea and turned into nine dragons.

In the early nineteenth century, British opium ships used Kowloon's harbor to pick up fresh water and supplies. On July 7, 1839, a party of drunken sailors got into a fight with local villagers on Tsim Sha Tsui, and a Chinese by the name of Lin Weixi died. Commissioner Lin Zexu demanded that the British give up the culprit, but Admiral Charles Elliot refused. Tension mounted, and a long-simmering conflict over the opium trade finally exploded into open warfare. From their military stronghold in Kowloon, the Chinese forces were able to use their guns to repel the first wave of invading British ships on September 4. Much encouraged, Commissioner Lin ordered two more cannon forts installed in Kowloon to prepare for a long siege. But China suffered a quick and humiliating defeat, and as a result the British claimed possession of Hong Kong island in 1841.

The British Fort Victoria on Kowloon, 1841 (Thomas Allom).

The British formally acquired Kowloon peninsula as a result of the so-called Second Opium War. But the Convention of Peking signed in 1860 merely legalized what had been an informal arrangement with local Chinese officials for a long-standing British presence there. Gunboat diplomacy obviously worked, but it also gave the gunboat commanders considerable power over diplomats. Since Kowloon was acquired presumably for strategic reasons, there were contending claims between the British commanders and Governor Hercules Robinson and his civilian government as to the use of this new piece of land. The military insisted on building army barracks, in the area that is now Kowloon Park. Only years later was the governor able to obtain portions of the land for commercial and residential purposes.

The eastern side of Kowloon Park borders the district's major thoroughfare, Nathan Road, which runs northward to Boundary Street at the northern edge in Mong Kok. Governor Mathew Nathan (1904–1907), for whom it is named, had a large hand in building the road and planting trees along both sides. Boundary Street was once the most significant geographical signpost in Kowloon. Before 1898, when the British leased the New Territories from China for a period of ninety-nine years, Boundary Street, with its wooden fences, marked the border between China and the British colony. A few checkpoints were open for passage between sunrise and sunset. After 1898 this street became a boundary in name only, and in the early twentieth century the area between Boundary Street and Lion Rock to the north was designated New Kowloon. The name New Territories was retained for the countryside beyond Lion Rock.

Kowloon (including New Kowloon) is physically smaller than Hong Kong island, but it has a much larger population. As of July 1, 2005, 1,264,300 people lived on Hong Kong island, while 2,070,000 lived in Kowloon and 3,597,800 lived in the New Territories and islands.[2] But these population figures tell only part of the story. The physical, even visceral, sensation of walking through the human density in Kowloon must be experienced to be believed. This is particularly true in the three areas on the south side of the peninsula—Tsim Sha Tsui, Yau Ma Tei, and Mong Kok, which form one official district known as Yau Tsim Mong. Reportedly, film director Ridley Scott was inspired to recreate this crowd scene at the beginning of his famous science-fiction thriller *Blade Runner*.

Except for really adventurous types, most Western tourists do not go beyond Tsim Sha Tsui. Consequently, they miss the real Hong Kong that the locals consider home—greater Kowloon. In sharp contrast to Hong Kong island, with its cosmopolitan atmosphere derived from a colonial past, Kowloon peninsula is almost totally Chinese. Residents of Kowloon still adhere to traditional family values, much more so than do their chic counterparts in the Central Business District or in Taipei and Shanghai. The deeper one moves into the northern part of the peninsula, the more one gets in touch with the sight and smell of an indigenous world where only Cantonese is spoken.

A shop in Kowloon selling traditional Chinese foods and herbal remedies.

A long walk along Nathan Road (or two subway stops from Tsim Sha Tsui) leads to Yau Ma Tei, one of the oldest areas in Kowloon. The Chinese characters refer to the place (*tei*) where once the fishermen repainted their boats with oil (*yau*) and repaired their hemp ropes (*ma*). A sign of the place's early origin is the Tin Hau (Goddess of Heaven) Temple, which was built in the early nineteenth century to protect fishing people.

Skinning frogs' legs in a Mong Kok wet market.

At night Temple Street transforms into a carnival, with booths and stalls selling folk art products and local artists singing folk songs and Cantonese operas, and fortune-tellers with different skills—palm reading, cards, incense—vying with street vendors for tourist attention. The street was immortalized in the popular movie *Everlasting Love* (1993), about a beautiful blind singer and her love affair with a talented composer. But the old romantic atmosphere portrayed in the film is largely lost today, taken over by noisy bazaars packed with booths selling cheap goods to swarms of customers. Shoppers for precious stones are drawn to the Jade Market, while cinema lovers head for the Broadway Cinematheque, which has a bookstore café called Kubrick, named after the American director, a cult figure among local cineastes. Inspired by its prototype in Paris, the cinematheque started out screening art films exclusively, but now shows mainstream films as well in order to keep the projectors running.

Most Hong Kong tourists and customers who can afford it do their shopping in the expensive malls in Central, Admiralty, or Tsim Sha Tsui, but the turf of bargain-hunters and young customers is Mong Kok (Prosperity Corner). The shops here are more lively and prosperous than in Yau Ma Tei, in part because this is the most densely populated district in all of Hong Kong. Crowds are so thick that some of the main streets are designated pedestrian-only. Vendors of video products, stereo systems, and other electronic ware near the Mong Kok subway station make a deafening din with their loudspeakers announcing new sales. It takes a courageous customer to brave the human tide through the street stalls and go inside the multistory buildings to peruse the many products offered there at modest prices.

Shops selling items of the same stock, such as electronics or Hi-fi equipment, are often housed in one building, so that customers can ascend the various floors to browse and haggle with the seasoned shop clerks and find the cheapest prices for models to their liking. The shops in Mong Kok are so small and congested that one must squeeze one's way through humans and machines, all packed within a few square feet of space. A similar experience can be had by eating in Mong Kok's street-corner noodle shops, where the kitchens are right in front and strangers eat at the same table. The locals consider it a "must" for a weekend outing.

Mong Kok is famous for its Chinese bookstores, which offer cheap editions in simplified characters imported from the mainland, together with legal or illegal video copies of old and new films. Most of these bookstores are hidden in obscure corners on the second or third floors of buildings and are not easy to find. Like everything else in Hong Kong, there is always a shady side to the bright spectacle along Kowloon Harbor, and to venture into these dark corners to shop for what one needs and desires, at notably variant prices, is part of the excitement of living here. Mong Kok prospers precisely because it offers locals so many hidden corners for exploration.

A crowded pedestrian street market in Mong Kok.

THE NEIGHBORHOOD JUST NORTH of Boundary Street is Kowloon Tong, which is the next stop by train, or three stops by subway, from Mong Kok. It is a major transfer station linking the railway to the subway. In the 1930s this area was envisioned as a "garden city" for higher-income residents, and some streets carry the names of English rural towns—Hereford and Suffolk, Devon and Durham, Hampshire and Wilshire, even Oxford—in an attempt to conjure up the pastoral gentility of the English countryside. But the project failed, and only a few garden-style townhouses can now be found along these streets.

East of Kowloon Tong is Kowloon City, where once stood a walled compound—an old "city" that was first constructed in 1847 and served as the Chinese administrative center for the whole area during its precolonial era (before 1898). In the course of negotiations for the lease of the New Territories, the Qing government was taken aback by the British demand for a much larger extension than expected, and it wanted to preserve a semblance of Chinese sovereignty inside this area. Eager to obtain the lease, Britain agreed that "within the city of Kowloon the Chinese officials now stationed there shall continue to exercise jurisdiction except so far as may be inconsistent with the military requirements for the defense of Hong Kong." The British prime minister in London, Lord Salisbury (for whom a major road in Kowloon is named) also declared that "the walled city of Kowloon was to remain within Chinese jurisdiction and the Kowloon landing stage was to be reserved for the use of Chinese ships, including men-of-war."[3]

However, some fudging in the details of the arrangement led to contending views about sovereignty. Hampered by knowing so few details of the agreement, Lord Salisbury declared that "in conformity with the ordinary rules of military prudence that all strategic considerations should be so revised that if an accident we cannot foresee takes place we should not be exposed to any danger or disadvantage." An "accident" did occur in April 1899: when a company of British militia and police went to the New Territories to prepare for the takeover, they met armed resistance by the local residents in Tai Po. Three more companies were dispatched and the rebellion was duly suppressed. This incident provided the needed excuse, and British rule was unilaterally imposed on the walled city on December 27, 1899. The British quickly drove away the few Chinese officials and considered the city "integrated with the colony."

But a succession of Chinese governments—from the Qing to the Nationalist to the PRC—protested this high-handed move. Thus the issue of sovereignty was left in limbo or "marooned," and the 2.7 acre site became a "free zone"—a free-for-all place where Triad gangsters, drug addicts and dealers, and other suspicious elements mixed with regular residents. It also attracted a few Westerners who sought adventure and gambling, especially after 1872, when all gambling except for horse-racing was banned in Hong Kong. In that year, a notorious incident—a personal duel—took place on the drill grounds in front of the city gate. The Spanish consul in Hong Kong, M. L. Checa, challenged the Peru consul at Macau to a duel of pistols and wounded him. Both were later fined HK$200.

Despite official contentions to the contrary, the walled city remained a heavily populated de facto Chinese hub, with thriving commercial activities in the area immediately outside the city walls, especially on Nga Tsin Wai Road—now lined with Cantonese, Thai, and Vietnamese restaurants. The street's name refers to a walled village in front of the city wall believed to be the oldest in the entire Kowloon peninsula. The whole area was linked to a pier (now defunct) on its northwestern side, Sham Shui Po or Deep Water Port (still one of the most densely populated areas in Kowloon today), where goods were received and transported to shops and markets. Like their counterparts on Hong Kong island, the local Kowloon elite had their own philanthropic programs for establishing schools and hospitals. These were formalized in 1904 with the establishment of the Lok Sin Tong (Good Deed Hall). One hospital, built in 1911, was later combined with two others on the Hong Kong side to form the famous Tung Wah San Yuen—the three-hospital group that also served as a Chinese civic center. One can well imagine its former glory before the area fell into administrative neglect and gradual decline.

In the 1930s the population inside the walled city increased to more than 2,000, and the residents began to assert their rights against government pressure to raze their dwellings. These efforts received sporadic support from the Nationalist government in China, which was busy with its own problems. During their occupation of Hong Kong, the Japanese tore down the walls and used the stones to construct the nearby airport extension. From the 1960s to the 1980s, Kowloon Walled City had some 8,300 buildings and 31,408 residents, who managed to squeeze into less than three acres of land. There were a thousand shops, eighty-seven illegal dentists, and seventy-four doctors. The cheap

Kowloon Walled City in the 1980s, and the gate to Kowloon Walled City Park, opened in 1996 on the site.

dentists were especially in demand. The buildings were so close-knit that their balconies were linked together to form aerial alleyways. The climactic shootout in the *Long Arm of the Law* (1987) was filmed here. The movie was hailed by cinema buffs not only for its realistic location but for the tricky shots made within alleyways barely wide enough for one person to pass.

Kowloon Walled City was demolished in 1987, and on its grounds now stands Kowloon Walled City Park, first opened in 1996. It features pavilions and ponds, trees and shrubs, all planted with exquisite care to make the park look like an early Qing dynasty garden. In one corner is a renovated building resembling a *yamen*, which displays the history of the walled city and a scale model of the village in the mid-nineteenth century. The stone remnants of the original south and east gates are preserved on the grounds.

The park provides a new way of dealing with the past—by destroying it and then building a beautiful make-believe model to attract tourists. On a recent visit one afternoon, I found only a few old people sitting and chatting in the pavilions. They seem to have taken possession of the park, as they have done with numerous other public parks throughout the territory. On the humid, sunlit grounds, caught in an early spring heat, a few younger pedestrians walked hurriedly past, apparently taking a short cut to the busy streets beyond.

Today, the old Kowloon Walled City remains alive only in legend. Architects consider it a world-class example of "parasitic living," a mode of life adopted by poor people who clung to a small enclosed area and grew spontaneously like wild plants, yet despite the chaos formed a self-sufficient world. Their power to sustain life under such crowded conditions seems beyond belief. Some architectural theorists even consider Kowloon City to be something of a structural symbol: present-day Kowloon is like the old Kowloon Walled City writ large— now much modernized and magnified, and without its walls, but exhibiting the same energy and dynamism of an utterly chaotic but self-sufficient world locked into itself, almost in spite of its modern development.

Several blocks south of Kowloon Walled City Park, not far from the old Kai Tak airport (now closed), is a small park almost hidden in a noisy corner at the western tip of Sung Wong Toi (Sung Emperor Tablet) Road. Both the park and the road are named after the last emperor of the Song dynasty (1127–1279). In the park, a stone tablet commemorates the legend surrounding the death of the last Song emperor. The tablet has been moved several times, but the legend never varies: the last emperor, a young boy of twelve, was carried by his loyal minister as they both jumped from a rock into the sea and drowned. No one is exactly sure where the suicide occurred, but Kowloon City took on a special aura through this act of royal patronage. The story has become part of a Kowloon folk tradition, told again and again, perhaps to counter the "master narrative" of British acquisition.

THE URBAN LANDSCAPE in Kowloon underwent a drastic transformation in the twentieth century, thanks to a series of modernization projects that began with the construction of the Kowloon-Canton Railway in 1910. A master plan devised by Patrick Abercrombie in 1946 recommended that in the next fifty years Kowloon peninsula should be the central focus of urban development in the greater Hong Kong region, and that more land should be reclaimed. Part of the reclaimed area was used to expand the Kai Tak airport into Victoria Harbor. A popular pastime for young couples after the Second World War was to have a drink at a rooftop bar while watching planes fly by right in front of their eyes and land on the narrow airstrip. Pilots and passengers alike claimed that flying into Hong Kong was one of the most exciting experiences to be had in an airplane.

The 1970s was a crucial decade in the history of Kowloon's development, thanks largely to the long tenure and unstinting efforts of Governor Murray Maclehose (1971–1982). He reversed the colonial policy of sending major revenues to London and instead used taxes to fund local construction projects. In order to accommodate the large number of immigrants from China, Maclehose launched a ten-year plan for public housing, which transformed Kowloon into a forest of residential towers. The first harbor tunnel was also completed in 1972, followed by two more. The new railway station in Hung Hom, replacing the old one in Tsim Sha Tsui, was completed in 1974, and a modern subway system with electric trains began operation in the early 1980s.

All these projects of urban construction and renewal became necessary because as early as 1953 the population of greater Hong Kong had already increased to 2.3 million, of which 250,000 lived in wooden shacks. On Christmas Eve of that year a fire broke out in the poverty-stricken Shek Kip Mei area of New Kowloon, leaving 58,000 homeless. In view of the danger posed by fires in this and in other squatter areas, the government launched a massive public housing and resettlement program there.

Flying low over Kowloon, a plane heads to the Kai Tak International Airport in Victoria Harbor, shortly before it closed in 1998.

The Mark I Resettlement Blocks, constructed with great speed, were all six stories high. Each one, according to Hugh Baker, contained "384 rooms measuring 12 feet 6 inches by 9 feet 6 inches and housed over 2,000 people who shared 36 communal flush latrines and 12 water standpipes." Housing blocks built after 1964 were higher, from eight to sixteen stories, with lifts serving the top ten floors, private lavatories, and electric power. These flats allowed "35 square feet per occupant over the age of 10, an increase of 11 square feet over the earlier minimum." Of course, real occupancy far exceeded this allocated minimum, as more and more people squeezed into each flat. Rents were very low and the estates were managed and maintained professionally. The program obviously met a deep-felt need, since by 1983 "more than 40 percent of the population was in permanent, government-built accommodation."[4]

The Shek Kip Mei Low-Cost Housing Estate, built in phases starting in the 1950s on the site of the burnt-down shanties, comprised twenty-six buildings, each with an official capacity of 2,500 residents. Each housing block was six stories high with an exterior corridor linking all the units on each floor. The size of a unit was only 300 square feet (24–28 square meters) and was supposed to house five people (but actually more). On each floor there was only one communal sanitary facility, and family cooking had to be done outside, right on the

Shek Kip Mei
housing project,
awaiting demolition
in 2006.

corridors, since the cubicle-sized units had no space for kitchens. This new living arrangement was not much different from that in the traditional Chinese tenement, except for more modern fire-proof materials (cement and concrete).

In a detailed critical study of Shek Kip Mei, Alan Smart has argued that the project proved too costly and failed to achieve the government's original goal of creating "an urban landscape free of squatters and their accompanying prospects of social disorder . . . while producing a healthy flow of land-leased revenues."[5] Yet what Smart failed to address was the human dimension, for the Shek Kip Mei project succeeded quite admirably in creating both a new form of modern living and a continuation of the old.

On a recent visit in late 2006 I found only empty rows of dilapidated buildings, since all the old blocks built in the 1950s have been officially condemned and vacated for demolition. The long corridors looked especially deserted—yet haunted by memories of their recent past. One can well imagine what life was like some forty years ago when the new occupants began to move in from their much shabbier squatter homes. The long exterior corridors, designed with maximum functionality, must have provided a vital link to all the residents, where they established old and new social contacts in spite of—or because of—their small and compressed living quarters. A closely-knit neighborhood feeling, a sense of continuity with their old lifestyle, must have been maintained. This new "life-world" may have been a necessary byproduct of Hong Kong's population pressure, but it seems contrary to the pervasive *anomie*, alienation, and social unrest one finds in poor urban neighborhoods of some American and European cities.

True, the new housing projects did not eliminate crime and juvenile delinquency, which merely found a new home base. In fact, these housing blocks became a key setting for many Hong Kong movies. Fruit Chan's cult film *Made in Hong Kong* (1997) focuses on the lives of poor errant youths who fought, loved, and died in drab-looking public housing estates like Skek Kip Mei. Yet despite the human tragedies depicted in films like this, their central theme is still family living and neighborhood interaction on an everyday level (including the frequent and inevitable squabbles). *Made in Hong Kong* makes an interesting case for comparison with the Hollywood film *Rebel without a Cause* (1955, starring James Dean), where the sense of family connection and urban space is notably different.

By 1971, the population in Kowloon and the New Territories had reached 3 million, and by 2006 it exceeded 5.5 million. Even low-rise public housing compounds like Shek Kip Mei proved insufficient and were replaced by much taller residential towers shooting up like mushrooms after a rain. This marked another transition to a new phase of urban development, "new towns" and "satellite cities" (which will be described in Chapters 6 and 7). Greater Kowloon today has become a sprawling metropolis unto itself, with its own centers and suburbs. The government seems intent on erasing all traces of the old poverty and in developing some former squatter areas in the outskirts (such as Kuan Tong and Tseung Kwan O) into ultra-modern industrial parks, and others (such as Tiu Keng Leng, the site of perhaps the most famous post-1949 squatter area) into even more massive housing compounds. Even Mong Kok—the most densely populated area in Kowloon—is being subjected to urban renewal. A new shopping plaza now stands right at its center, next to the subway station.

Shopping malls are ubiquitous in Kowloon. They come in all sizes and shapes, but unlike the malls in American suburbs, which are usually reached by car, those in Kowloon are connected to housing projects through a labyrinth of underground or above-ground stairways and corridors. Some malls are built on top of railway and subway stations, to eliminate any need for additional transportation. One can ascend the escalators from the station to the mall in a few minutes and shop around in the mall before descending the escalators to the

Festival Walk
shopping mall in
Kowloon Tong.

subway or railway station. The whole process of movement and consumption can be undertaken entirely indoors, in modern air-conditioned spaces without regard to whether it is raining or shining outside. On any Sunday the crowds are so thick in the major malls that a shopper can barely edge through.

Festival Walk in Kowloon Tong is the most modern and attractive of them all. The mall's Chinese name literally means Another City. It begins at the Kowloon Tong railway and subway station and leads to the campus of City University via a narrow passageway. For the university's thirty-thousand students, going to school requires passing through this palace of consumerism every day. To live and study in Kowloon is a totally different experience from small-town college life in rural Vermont or Devonshire.

Yet it was precisely in this modern jungle of Kowloon that local artists have recently found new spaces for doing their work—by renting at moderate prices some of the old public buildings and factories that have fallen into disuse. The Central Cattle Depot in To Kwa Wan, a slaughterhouse in the interior of Kowloon, which was first established in 1908, has been recently renovated into an artists' village of fourteen independent buildings, complete with workshops, studios, and exhibition spaces. The village has become a new cultural depot for young artists and avant-garde art groups such as Zuni, Artist Commune, 1a Space, and the Cattle Depot Academy.

Among the volunteer faculty of the Cattle Depot Academy are some of the most active personalities in Hong Kong's cultural scene: the dramaturgist and choreographer Danny Yung, the director and critic Mathias Woo, and the broadcaster-publisher-critic Leung Man To—arguably Hong Kong's most famous public intellectual who also heads the Cattle Depot project—to name just a few. Their central mission is to challenge everything that the establishment stands for—commercialism, urban development, bureaucracy—by offering fresh alternatives for the young and free-spirited. Cattle Depot is a Chinese counterpart to the English-speaking Fringe Club in Hong Kong, whose logo is "Arts+People."

FEW TOURISTS OR OUTSIDERS would ever set foot in an area like To Kwa Wan and go into an art studio at Cattle Depot, yet in most of the world's metropolises, some of the most daring experiments in art take place in the least likely places. Greater Kowloon has always been a center of Chinese culture, both traditional and modern, elite and popular, as opposed to the "foreign" culture of Hong Kong island. For, unlike North Point, where most of the cosmopolitan immigrants from Shanghai first settled, Kowloon since the early 1950s has been the home of intellectual refugees from China's provinces who spoke a variety of local dialects or dialect-accented Mandarin but no English. When former professors from well-established mainland universities lost their positions after the Communist Revolution and had to find temporary teaching posts, the doors of the colonial and elitist University of Hong Kong were closed to them. But Kowloon, with its motley group of small colleges and high schools, offered these Chinese scholars jobs, and its cheaper housing and more traditional environment were familiar and welcoming.

Among the new refugees from China were a few high-minded intellectuals who in 1950 set up a small college in two rented tenement buildings on Kweilin Street in Sham Shui Po, one of the poorest areas in Kowloon. In the beginning there were only eight faculty members, including the distinguished historian Qian Mu, founder and president, and Tang Junyi, renowned Confucian philosopher, and initially about thirty students, all refugees from China. Qian and Tang lived in two rooms on the third floor, while other rooms were used as classrooms and dormitories. Downstairs on the ground floor was a textile factory, a restaurant, and a dance hall. Smells from the kitchen and the raucous sounds of dance music apparently did not dampen the scholarly pursuits upstairs. Later on Tang was joined by Mou Zongsan and Xu Fuguan, two other Confucian philosophers.

Thus was the "Spirit of New Asia" born, which called for a revival of Chinese culture by renewing the humanistic essence in the Confucian tradition. This brand of Neo-Confucianism was intended to meet the challenge posed by a "third wave" of foreign influence in China—Marxism and Communism. The first wave was Buddhism from India in the third century AD, and the second wave was Christianity from the West in the seventeenth to nineteenth centuries. A manifesto signed by the professors and their students specifically opposed the anti-Confucian ideology of Maoist China.

After the first few years of hardship, New Asia College received a grant from the Yale-in-China program and began to attract local and international attention. Several generations of students trained at New Asia became renowned scholars and intellectual leaders. Among the first class of its graduates was Professor Yu Ying-shih, an internationally known scholar of Chinese history who later taught at Harvard, Yale, and Princeton universities, and the 2006 recipient of the Kluge Prize at the Library of Congress (reputedly the humanities counterpart of the Nobel Prize). Professor Tu Wei-ming, another leading scholar of Confucianism at Harvard, also took private lessons with Tang Junyi and his colleague Mou Zongsan.

The presence of New Asia College offered not only an educational alternative to the English-based University of Hong Kong but provided a needed source of intellectual solace for many refugee intellectuals from mainland China. Like anti-Nazi German intellectuals who migrated to America and settled in Hollywood in the 1930s, they had found both a political and a spiritual haven in this glitzy commercial town. Yet the colonial government paid scant attention to these distinguished intellectual exiles. Hong Kong had only one public university, HKU, where classes were taught in English. The colonial government had hoped to introduce a Chinese curriculum into HKU's extension program, but the initiative was voted down by the university's board of trustees.

Thus, a large number of small colleges, all private or church-sponsored, sprang up to fill this gap in the higher education of a growing Chinese population.

By that time, New Asia had already established quite a reputation, with a distinct intellectual tradition of its own. After moving to a new campus on Farm Road in the Ma Tau Wai area, it merged with two other colleges to form the Chinese University of Hong Kong (the name was recommended by Professor Qien Mu himself). Established and funded by the government in 1963, this new university adopted both Chinese and English as its teaching languages. Meanwhile, in response to the 1966 outbreak of the Cultural Revolution on the mainland, nationalism was on the rise in Hong Kong, together with an incipient radicalism among students, particularly in the newly established CUHK. With two thriving public universities and a plethora of small private colleges, this "colonial back water" became a truly exciting place to be in the 1960s.

The political climate in Hong Kong and Kowloon in these Cold War years was by no means serene. One did not need to be a spy to sense the atmosphere of intrigue. Intellectuals, dueling with their separate newspapers and publications, used the region as an open battleground for contending ideas and ideologies. The colonial government benignly ignored the political ideologues from both left and right, so long as they did not openly disrupt social stability.

The leftists, followers of the People's Republic, rallied around two major newspapers (*Ta Kung Pao* and *Wen Wei Pao*), a movie studio, several bookstores, and a handful of department stores selling "national products." Their major source of support was the workers' unions. Leftist activism reached its climax in a large-scale riot in 1967. The "rightists"—followers of the Nationalist or Guomindang Party in Taiwan—also began to build up their propaganda machine through newspapers (*Hong Kong Times*), magazines, and other publishing outlets. Many former Nationalist troops who were stranded in Hong Kong lived among the poor squatters of Tiu Keng Leng, an area in the eastern outskirts of Kowloon. They displayed their blatant anti-Communist sentiments every year on October 10, the national day of the Republic of China, with a sea of Nationalist flags on the rooftops of their shabby abodes. The Tiu Keng Leng area was the site of several fires and other natural disasters before it was finally torn down in the 1970s.

The American government, via its consulate in Hong Kong, joined in the ideological fray. The United States Information Service, with funds from the undercover CIA, published a journal *World Today* that became probably the most widely circulated intellectual monthly from the 1950s to the 1970s. Another important journal, *The Chinese Student Weekly*, edited sometimes by graduates from New Asia College, represented the spiritual awakening of Hong Kong's own generation of young intellectuals. The journal had a special film review section, and one of its frequent contributors was John Woo. Its short stories and translations were avidly consumed by a young readership too poor to go shopping.

These activists are now near retirement age or dead, and that very exciting era is long past. Still, the post-handover quest for a "Hong Kong identity" aroused waves of nostalgia for this earlier time, and several locals who grew up in postwar Kowloon produced a spate of writings to explore their personal history. In his novel *Natural Creation: Vivid and Virtual* (2005), Dung Kei-cheung charted the course of three generations of his own ancestors, beginning with his grandparents who crossed the border from China to settle in a remote village in the New Territories. His father set up a machine workshop in the Kowloon Walled City area, and the young protagonists, including the author's alter ego, went through schooling and puberty all over Kowloon. In one episode, the hero, Little Dung, is brought by his priest teacher to a high hill "overlooking the whole of Kowloon"—an intended contrast to the view from the Peak on the other side.

Another artistic rendition of Kowloon is found in a 1972 novelette called *Intersection* (*Duidao*) by Lau Yee Cheung (Liu Yichang), originally from Shanghai, who is arguably Hong Kong's most respected senior writer. The story, which was a source of inspiration for Wong Kar-wai's film *In the Mood for Love* (2001), takes place in Kowloon. Unlike its more glamorous movie version, Lau's original story has only two characters—the middle-aged Shanghai man who lives in North Point and a young native woman who lives in an old building near Nathan Road. They are total strangers whose paths cross in a narrative structure shaped like tête-bêche stamps. The novel focuses as much on the realistic setting of Kowloon as on their individual psyches. In its structure, if not content and language, the story reads like a modest variation of Joyce's *Ulysses*. But the Kowloon in Lau's fiction is less mythic and even poorer than Joyce's Dublin. (Lau was one of the early modernists in Hong Kong who admired Joyce.)

The time of the story is the 1970s, when the middle-aged hero takes the No. 102 tunnel bus to Kowloon and spends an afternoon in Yau Ma Tei and Mong Kok; the young heroine does the same. The two happen to sit together in a movie theater, and her image somehow enters into his dreams at night. This is certainly not in the same league as the encounter of Stephen Dedalus and Leopold Bloom on a Dublin bridge, but it is a valuable if unpretentious portrait of postwar Kowloon nonetheless.

The novel is a far cry from the film version, which openly acknowledged its debt to Lau but moved the setting to North Point in Hong Kong, where Wong Kar-wai traced his own Shanghai ancestry. The mood conjured up by *In the Mood for Love* was perhaps too glamorized to be authentic. In films made back in the 1950s and 1960s by Cathay and Shaw Brothers, we did not see sophisticated actresses like Maggie Cheung change into more than a dozen sexy gowns over the course of the movie. On the contrary, in the classic film *Father Takes a Bride* (*Xiao ernu*, 1963), scripted by Eileen Chang, the plain-looking young heroine gets on a Kowloon bus only to have her skirt caught in the claws of crabs carried by a male passenger.

POVERTY AND CROWDED LIVING conditions were not the exclusive experience of Chinese residents. Many Indian immigrants to Hong Kong shared the same fate. Today, the city's Indian minority is concentrated in Kowloon, mainly in the Tsim Sha Tsui area, and segregated from the Chinese population. Indians came to Hong Kong with the British. When Captain Belcher landed in January 1841, his troops included 2,700 Indian soldiers and four Indian merchants. They were the predecessors of the two principal groups of Indians to settle in Hong Kong. Those from poorer backgrounds worked in colonial service as policemen and soldiers; the more venturesome or well-to-do became businessmen.

The early Hong Kong police force, comprised largely of Indians and Sikhs, guarded and administered prisons. Sikh soldiers came from a tribe in northern India who, during the 1857 revolt, had fought on the British side. Their loyalty earned the trust of the colonials, who transported them to other locations to serve as guards. Prior to the Second World War, about 60 percent of the entire police force in Hong Kong were Sikhs. To keep a certain balance, the colonial government also recruited Bohra Muslims from Punjab. A Muslim garrison was stationed in Kowloon in 1860; the local Chinese referred to them as "Moluo," and a street in old Central, named after the Muslim Lascars, is sometimes called Moluo Street. A small mosque was erected on Shelley Street, not far from Lascar Row in Central, and a larger mosque, called Jamia Masjid Islamic Center, was built on Nathan Road in 1896, an imposing white edifice that still stands today.

From the very beginning of Hong Kong's colonial history, the Indians—especially the Parsees from Bombay—made great contributions in trade and banking. A Parsee taipan, Sir Jamsetjee Jeejeebhoy, the first Indian so knighted, was on friendly trading terms with Robert Jardine. The Sassoons, Jews from Bombay, expanded their fortunes to both Shanghai and Hong Kong. Members of the family—Albert, Arthur, Frederick—all served on the boards of banks, including the founding committee of the Hong Kong and Shanghai Bank in 1864. The legendary businessman David Sassoon of Shanghai made occasional appearances in Hong Kong, especially during horse-racing season. Prominent Indian leaders took a strong interest in this sport, and the two Indians who made the greatest contributions to the development of Hong Kong—Sir Paul Chater and Sir Hormusjee N. Mody—were linked by this shared entertainment.

After his arrival from India in 1864, Chater—who was born in Calcutta of Armenian Christian parents—was the principal mover and shaker not only in establishing the Jockey Club but in reclaiming the land that became the CBD, building Nathan Road, developing the port on Kowloon peninsula, and leasing the New Territories. He collected artwork and owned a valuable collection of the early paintings of Victoria Harbor by George Chinnery, which was recently exhibited in the Hong Kong Museum of Art. A member of both the Legislative

Council and, for forty-two years, the Governor's Executive Council, Chater was always at the center of Hong Kong's public affairs. When he died in 1926 at the age of eighty-two, he was hailed as "the greatest man Hong Kong has known"; the local English press summarized his contributions this way: "A biography of Sir Paul Chater would be a history of Hong Kong."[6]

Chater's friend and business associate, Sir Hormusjee N. Mody, was a Parsee from Bombay who joined Chater in setting up one of the most successful brokerage firms in Hong Kong's history, a predecessor of the Hong Kong Stock Exchange. Chater persuaded the gentle Mody not only to serve as the first chairman of the Jockey Club but to become the largest donor of funds to establish the University of Hong Kong.

The first Sindhi firm in Hong Kong was established by Dharnamal Chellaram of Hyderabad in 1894, as a branch of his company headquartered in Cairo. By the 1920s the firm, which dealt with local arts and goods, had expanded to twenty-seven branches around the world. The founder quoted the British colonial motto to his own advantage: "The sun never sets on Chellarams." The foremost Sindhi family in Hong Kong today is the Harilelas, who came in the 1930s from China, where the family business went bad due to economic depression. Upon arriving in Hong Kong, they squeezed into a small house at Portland Street in Kowloon. After years of hardship, the two young sons, Harry and George, finally landed a contract to make military uniforms for British and American soldiers after the war. In the 1950s they went into the tailoring trade, and at its peak the family business included thirty-two tailor shops and six hundred tailors. In the 1960s and 1970s they ventured into the hotel business and made more millions. Despite their immense fortune, the six brothers and their families still live together in two three-story buildings in Kowloon.

The largely silent Indian minority in Kowloon is scarcely noticed by the Chinese majority. Its representation in films by Chinese film-makers is spotty and the treatment is mostly biased and negative. For example, in *Chungking Express* (1994; the Chinese title is more appropriate, *Chungking Jungle*), directed by Wong Kar-wai, the name "Chungking" comes from Chungking

Chungking Mansion.

Mansion, a commercial building near the bottom of Nathan Road where Indian merchants congregate and sell cheap products. In the first part of the movie, the Chinese heroine, wearing dark glasses and a blonde wig, walks into this Indian jungle for some clandestine transactions, only to be duped by the Indians she has hired. A hand-held camera follows her for an energetic sequence while she chases her Indian associates. The film proved immensely popular, especially in Japan, and this old building with its dark corridors and rundown shops has now become a mecca for film aficionados and tourists.

ALTHOUGH WESTERNERS also lived in Kowloon, they left few literary records about the place, certainly not as much as they wrote about Hong Kong. One of the few valuable English memoirs is *Gweilo: Memories of a Hong*

Kong Childhood (2004) by Martin Booth, in which he recalls with fondness his life as a young boy living in Kowloon in the early 1950s. His family of *gweilos* (the vaguely pejorative Cantonese slang for foreigners) lived in a small hotel called Four Seas near Prince Edward Road, and he attended a school nearby called Kowloon Junior. As one of the very few English boys who broke away from the colonial fold, the young Martin walked freely on Kowloon's streets and ate at the dingy *dai pai dongs* in Mong Kok, where he met all kinds of Chinese. In his view, Kowloon "was to Hong Kong what the Casbah was to Algiers." Like most Chinese children in Kowloon of that time, the young Martin seldom set foot on Hong Kong island, although his father worked in the dockyard across the harbor.

Especially in the Tsim Sha Tsui area, Kowloon's streets were a danger zone of pickpockets and thieves. The young Martin seemed to have no fear, and no sooner had his mother warned him about the Walled City than he ventured into it the next day and talked to a drug dealer who spoke pidgin English. Rickshaws were everywhere, and "coolies carried extraordinarily heavy loads on bamboo poles over their shoulders . . . whilst the Hakka women wore hats with black cloth fringes like curtains hanging on a rim," and "people ran like hell across the street through fast-moving traffic to shake off the demons they believed were perpetually following them." Unlicensed street hawkers sold sweetmeats, sugar cane, melon seeds and *wah mui* or plums soaked for several days in sea water then dried in the sun. Still others "carried braziers on poles, selling roasted peanuts or chestnuts, slices of hot roast pork with the crackled skin still on the meat, cut from a whole pig such as I had seen cooking in the Ho Man Tin squatter area." Such vivid and detailed evocations of the sights, sounds, and smells of Kowloon tell us that we are in an authentic world, away from the supercilious life on the Peak. In the more popular genre of Western fiction, Kowloon often takes on an ugly face. Robert Ludlum's best-selling novel *Bourne Supremacy* (1986) is set in Kowloon (though the movie adaptation moves the setting and action to Europe). The novel opens with a murder in a Tsim Sha Tsui bar—a typical Western tourist hangout, like the bars in Wan Chai—but the avenging hero stays in the luxurious Regent Hotel (now the

InterContinental) at Salisbury Road. His rendezvous with a Triad boss (faked by a British spy) takes place in Mong Kok, and a secret arms dealer hides in a shipyard in a West Kowloon container terminal. The realism of the novel is based on the author's brief sojourn (perhaps only one extended trip) in Hong Kong. These settings, vividly described, become the background for a neocolonial glorification of its American protagonist, Jason Bourne. A Vietnam veteran, he lords over every Chinese in sight, including the poor driver from the hotel, in order to hunt down his nemesis. The novel even carries the chase across the border into Shenzhen.

Paul Theroux's novel *Kowloon Tong* (1997) has a surer grasp of both setting and character from an experienced master of travel writing. Like *Chinese Box* (a screenplay he helped script and which also inspired him to write this novel), the story in Kowloon Tong is set on the eve of the handover. The novel describes "two last-ditch Brits existing in a fusty time-warp" who "become belatedly aware that their time is running out." Theroux, like most Western writers about Hong Kong, seems fascinated by Hong Kong as a "borrowed place" on "borrowed time," and his two principal characters, mother and son, are struggling to come to terms with this unavoidable shift.

The mother, Betty Mullard, has spent nearly half her life living near the Peak, with outings to gamble at the races in Happy Valley and Sha Tin. But her son, Bunt, who runs the family's clothing factory, Imperial Stitching, in Kowloon Tong, has a secret: he frequents a bar called Pussy Cat near his office where he goes for lunch and whoring: "They were afternoon and early evening affairs, in the hours between work and home, his factory and his mother." As observed by the experienced and omniscient narrator, "This was not Wan Chai or Tsim Sha Tsui, the ridiculous clubs haunted by local gweilos and tourists, over-priced, hurry up, mister, only tree-thousand." No, this was Kowloon Tong, a respected Chinese residential area that Theroux's novel, with its relocated Pussy Cat bar and desperate afternoon whoring, gave a bad name!

True to formula, the family house in the novel is on the Peak, and Bunt normally drives his Rover to work. Also true to formula, he falls for a Chinese woman, in this case Mei-ling, a girl who works in his office. Bunt wants to take her back to London and marry her; his mother does not agree. The family business is finally sold to Hung, a Chinese businessman with mafia and Chinese military connections who forces these two diehard colonials out of Hong Kong. To sign the final deal, they go to a Chinese restaurant that Hung and the Chinese army owns, and there Betty reveals her true self: "Nothing personal," Betty said, "but we don't touch Chinese food. Never did. All the grease, all the glue. And it's always so wet. Makes me want to spew."

For half a century she has not eaten any Chinese food? Is this meant as satire? Does the novel have nothing to add at this historic moment, except to depict the persistence of a Brit's eating habits and racist attitudes? It turns out that Bunt is a weakling, a mama's boy still, at the age of forty-three. His portrait is remarkably similar to that of John in *Chinese Box*. But in *Kowloon Tong*, there is not even a note of elegy—only fear and rampant anti-Communism. Somewhere along the plot line, before "the wrecking ball swung sideways from the crane, hit the Imperial Stitching and punched it from the roof of the building," Kowloon Tong gets short-changed by being made a symbol of the last British holdout in Hong Kong.

So much for Western images of Kowloon.

One of many statues lining hillside paths above the Sha Tin railway station.

6

New Territories, Ancient Traditions

In 1970 I took my first teaching position as a beginning instructor at the newly founded Chinese University of Hong Kong. It was built in a hilly area called Ma Liu Shui, or Water for the Horses. I lived on campus in Sha Tin, which was still a village in the New Territories, and fell in love with the surrounding countryside. In my spare hours, especially on weekends, I would go mountain climbing or camping on one of the offshore islands, which seemed barely populated. Or I would go picnicking or boating with students at Tolo Harbor at the foot of the university campus. I would also visit the market fairs in nearby villages to buy food and other daily necessities.

At one booth in the market, a pile of plates made of primitive porcelain with the simple design of a fish hand-painted in blue caught my eye. I bought the whole set of a dozen plates and brought them to America two years later. I kept them in my kitchen for over two decades, until they were broken one by one. There are still plenty of painted plates available in the supermarkets of Hong Kong, but somehow they no longer hold any attraction for me. My original plates were inexpensive but looked authentic. The imitations are just cheap mechanical reproductions.

In 1970 the only fast and convenient form of transportation between Kowloon and the New Territories was the train. The buses took much longer. The compartments of the old trains were divided into three classes: the single first-class compartment was reserved mostly for foreigners, including those few Western visitors who were allowed to enter China; the several third-class compartments were used by local villagers, who often carried live fish and chickens on board. The handful of second-class compartments were left for average passengers like myself. Often I peeked with a sense of longing at the privileged "foreign dignitaries," especially those from African countries, in the first-class compartment who had just returned from China, where I was born but could not return. A famous poet from Taiwan, Yu Kwang-chung, who also taught at Chinese University in the 1970s, would take the train to the end of the line and stand at an outpost to look at the other side through binoculars. The experience inspired him to write several poems about his longing for China. Thus, at least for my generation of old-timers, the New Territories held a special meaning because of their proximity and intimate connection to our motherland.

This is how I remember the New Territories: a world of rustic beauty stretching out between Hong Kong and China, an expanse of rugged green landscape dotted here and there with villages and mountainside temples. But in the 1970s the colonial government initiated a New Town Program with the goal of building three major "satellite cities": Sha Tin, Tsuen Wan, and Tuen Mun. These satellite cities were soon followed by others, and in less than twenty years the New Territories, like neighboring Kowloon, was transformed into a jungle of high-rise housing compounds.

The village of Sha Tin, which in Chinese means Sandy Fields, became one of these satellite cities, designed on a vertical model inspired by the theories of Le Corbusier. In his essay "The Radiant City" ("La Ville Radieuse") the French Modernist architect argued that future cities could house more population with vertical skyscrapers linked by elevated corridors and platforms containing gardens and playgrounds. This utopian vision never caught on in Europe, but it became a reality in Hong Kong for entirely practical reasons: to accommodate an exploding population on very little space.

More housing seems to have solved the problem of population growth, at least temporarily, but increased commercialism has all but destroyed the old rural lifestyle. Some remnants of traditional villages still exist, overshadowed by skyscrapers. Pai Tau Village near the Sha Tin railway station, for instance, is reduced to a row of traditional-looking houses with a street sign in front. One has to go farther north to find authentic remains of the old "walled villages" of the New Territories.

According to official figures, the New Territories and islands have a total land area of 377 square miles, almost six times the size of Hong Kong island and Kowloon combined. Its total population of over 3.5 million in 2005 represented half of the entire population of the Hong Kong SAR. When the British took over the area in 1898, there were 423 Chinese villages, of which 255 belonged to five principal clans: the Tang, Liu, Hau, Man, and Pang. The colonial government set up a municipal office in Tai Po and took control of all the lands, releasing those belonging to indigenous clans under a Block Crown Lease arrangement. The British divided the area into eight districts and over forty sub-districts and organized a system for collecting taxes. This administrative structure has remained, with slight modification, down to the present day, except that in 1986 Kwai Chung, originally a part of Tsuen Wan, was made into a new district, thus bringing the total number to nine.[1]

Pai Tau Village, Sha Tin.

In 1902 the British completed a tunnel under Lion Rock, and for quite some time the highway that ran through it, Tai Po Road, provided the only passageway from Kowloon through the New Territories to the border. Another major road linking Kowloon to the western territories was built between 1911 and 1920. A popular Chinese novel with leftist leanings written in the late 1940s, called *Biography of a Shrimp Kid* (*Ha kau chuen*), describes the experience of its picaresque young hero as he moves from the brothels in Wan Chai to Kowloon on his journey of return to China. Near the end of the novel, as Shrimp Kid climbs on foot to the top of Lion Rock and waves goodbye to his companions, he seems overjoyed to have crossed the border into the New Territories, on his way home.

Today, with two new tunnels under Lion Rock completed in 1972 and 1978, it takes only half an hour by train to travel from Sha Tin to the Chinese border in Lo Wu, where Hong Kongers carrying permanent resident cards can go through the electronic control booths in about a minute. The New Territories has become one almost continuous web of suburbs between Kowloon and Shenzhen, connected by the Kowloon-Canton Railway and by a subway line that link Kowloon to Lo Wu in the north and Tuen Mun in the west. In addition, bus and minibus lines form a matrix of convenient transportation crisscrossing the area.

The New Town Program has worked to a certain extent, but it created problems of its own. Interior congestion—too many people squeezed into too small a horizontal space—was one. And the residents of these housing compounds still had to get to work elsewhere, so more systems of transportation were needed. To provide for their daily needs in food, clothing, education, and recreation, more schools, libraries, cinemas, playgrounds, and shopping malls were built nearby. And to promote local self-government, town halls, district offices, and other public buildings were constructed. Each of these new cities or towns gradually formed a world of its own, but lacking individual characteristics, since they were all built in the same way—with H- or Y-shaped high-rises of thirty-five stories or more, each one a clone of the one before.

The New Town Plaza in Sha Tin, developed in 1984 by Sun Hung Kai Properties (which now owns more than twenty malls all over Hong Kong), provided an early prototype. Divided into three phases of development, this

Cookie-cutter high-rise residences, towering above the 200-year-old Sam Tung Uk walled village, a national monument restored as a museum in the 1980s.

complex quickly became the biggest shopping mall in the New Territories, boasting "the world's highest rate of population flow," according to its developer. On Sundays it is nearly impossible to negotiate one's way through the crowds. A musical fountain in the center of the main hall was removed to create more space for pedestrians. This nine-level hall (built during phase 1) is connected to the Sha Tin railway station. Inside, one can visit cinemas and restaurants in the basement and on level 1, a modern supermarket and other practical facilities on level 2, various fashion boutiques and cosmetic shops on levels 3–5, electronics stores on level 6, a roof garden on level 7, and more restaurants on levels 6–8.

The mall is connected to the Royal Park Hotel and several housing compounds. The adjacent Sha Tin Town Hall provides a 1,300-seat auditorium for concerts and other performances, along with a 250-seat Cultural Activities Hall, lecture and conference rooms, and dance and music studios. Next to the Town Hall is the Sha Tin Public Library and a public park, with a Chinese pavilion and azalea garden. A vernacular version of Le Corbusier's futuristic city, the interlaced human community of Sha Tin was planned with functionality in mind, offering residents everything they need for everyday living.

In 1998 I lived in the Royal Park Hotel for six months and adopted the lifestyle of its residents. I could walk from the hotel through the connecting mall corridors to the nearest Shanghai restaurant in five minutes. It was next door to a bookstore and a cinema multiplex, and the supermarket was only a hundred feet away. Late at night, I saw old residents from nearby housing compounds taking leisurely walks in the mall as though they were strolling down Main Street in smalltown USA, and housewives walking to buy groceries—all in their casual homewear. The mall's corridors and escalators led directly to the surrounding housing compounds, whose gates were guarded and locked at midnight. Once, when a friend living there met me at the gate late at night, he was wearing his pajamas, and no one paid any attention. In a sense, the shear density of humanity in these planned living environments has served to "domesticate" the cold rationality of Le Corbusier's visionary design.

In a recent public interview, Ho Lik Tien, a director of Sun Hung Kai Properties, reminisced that the New Town Plaza first opened just two months after the 1984 signing of the Sino-British agreement to hand over greater Hong Kong to China in 1997. The opening of a large new mall, he claimed, helped appease people's anxieties about Hong Kong's uncertain future. Be that as it may, this model mall was consciously designed as a public arena and not merely as a commercial space. Or, looked at another way, it was essentially a commercial investment that brought public spaces into its ever-expanding fold. By linking living so closely with shopping, it squeezed the public and private domains into one boundaryless arena. In Hong Kong, the mall comes to residents, rather than the other way around. Its tentacles reach into every corner of personal life; it is the very center of urban living. As Ho rightly points out, the mall has become a second home, or even a psychological and practical extension of one's home, which in the high-rise residential towers of the New Territories is usually quite small.

EXCEPT FOR OLD-TIMERS, most people in Hong Kong find it hard to imagine the traditional rural landscape of the New Territories, or the lives of the people who once lived there. But Western anthropologists in the field of Chinese studies have made careers out of doing just that. Because mainland China was closed to outsiders during the last half century, a number of academics from England and America made the villages in the New Territories the focus of their field work. The religious rituals, clan organizations, and social and economic structures of Sha Tau Kok, Sheung Shui, Fanling, Yuen Long, Kam Tin, Tai Po, Tai O, and Cheung Chau became the subject of a spate of scholarly monographs that uncovered valuable information about the area. Some overenthusiastic writers seemed to view the New Territories as a synonym for "traditional China," depicting the lives and customs of local villagers as representative of a mainland culture that had existed unchanged for a thousand years. That was not the case, but this chapter nevertheless owes a great debt to the many efforts of Western scholars to understand the folkways of the New Territories.

The first human habitation in the area can be traced to the Neolithic age around 6,500 years ago. The earliest inhabitants were hunters and fishers who lived on the sandy shores of the gulfs and bays of Tuen Mun, Lantau, Cheung

Chau, and surrounding islands. But they disappeared during the next three millennia, and humans did not reemerge until about 3,500 years ago. Archaeologists reached these conclusions based in part on prehistoric colored pottery that was unearthed in the 1990s during the construction of the new Chek Lap Kok airport on Lantau Island. More than a hundred prehistoric sites have been located throughout the greater Hong Kong region.

Ancient gravesites have been discovered in the northern border of the New Territories, including one in Sham Shui Po (Kowloon) that anthropologists assign to the Han dynasty (206 BC–220 AD). As Buddhism spread through China during the next three centuries, legends emerged about a few strange monks who traveled as far south as Canton, and around the beginning of the fifth century, during the Jin dynasty, a Buddhist temple was built in Tuen Mun. The earliest official record of habitation in the New Territories has been dated to 736 AD, when the Tang dynasty garrisoned a force of two thousand soldiers in Tuen Mun. By that time the town was already an outpost of Canton, a busy port of entry for Arab merchants, Buddhist monks, and overseas Chinese traders who were doing a flourishing business in Southeast Asia.

The fishers who lived at the shores or on boats were called Tankas or "Egg people"—a term that has nothing to do with eggs but refers to a group of primitive seafaring people who were, according to one legend, descendants of a bandit named Lo Tsuen. When Lo and his henchmen were defeated by the Jin army around 403 AD, they retreated to a place called Lo Ting south of Canton, where they escaped into the high seas. Over the years, so the legend goes, not only did their offspring become fishers but they started to look and act like fish. The women wore only a breast cape after marriage; otherwise the people were naked, arranged their hair in braids, and were able to dive underwater and live there for three or four months. This legend served as the basis for an extraordinary exhibition in Hong Kong in 1997, on the eve of the handover, which embellished the myth into a pseudo-genealogy of the Hong Kong people. The exhibition displayed a series of carefully fabricated historical records claiming to show that Lo Tsuen was a half-human half-fish creature whose entire tribe was massacred by the invading Mongol army.

Sizable migration into the greater Hong Kong region can be traced to the Song dynasty (960–1279). The Cantonese came first and occupied the fertile plains on the west side. They were known as Puntis or indigenous people. But settlers also came from elsewhere in the Chinese hinterland. Following the Mongol invasion of China in 1276, a new wave of immigrants from the provinces began to settle in the northern part of the New Territories. Most of them were Han Chinese, who were engaged primarily in farming. After the Han-led Ming dynasty (1368–1644) overthrew the Mongols, the entire Hong Kong area was reassigned to Xin'an county. The locals made their living by refining salt, making pottery, farming tea, and harvesting the fragrant tree that gave Hong Kong its name. The Tai Po area was one of the most important centers of pearl fishing and pearl production in the entire Guangdong province down to the mid-sixteenth century. But the trade declined as the oyster supply in nearby seas became exhausted.

Tai Po's most prominent Punti clan was the Tang family from Jiangsi, who also settled in Kam Tin near Yuen Long and in Long Yau Tou near Fanling. They were followed in turn by the Haus, the Mans, the Lius, and the Pangs. The Hakkas or "guest people," mainly from Meixian in Guangdong but also from Fukien and Jiangsi provinces, arrived later, during the early Qing dynasty (1644–1911), and occupied the hillier and smaller patches of land to the east, such as Sha Tin and Sai Kung. Immigration was slowed in the 1660s by the Qing's scorched-earth policy of forced withdrawal from all coastal areas due to the continued threat of pirates. After the ban on the coast was lifted in 1669, the Hakkas moved in en masse, reaching a population of 239,000 in 1818 and occupying 315 of the 366 villages throughout the New Territories.

The Hakka "guest people" and the Punti "indigenous people" did not mix well initially, and clan wars were frequent. Over the years the Hakkas preserved their distinctive clothing, cuisine, and dialect. Many of the women still wear cane hats with a black cloth fringe at the perimeter that looks like a curtain. The Hakkas never followed the custom of foot binding because, so the legend goes, their women had to do all the work in the fields. Hakka food is also distinctive. Salted chicken, roast intestines, and pork with preserved vegetables can be had in any Hakka restaurant in Hong Kong. A more authentic Hakka cuisine can be found in Tai Po Market and other towns in the New Territories. Being perpetual "guests," the Hakkas are also quite mobile. James L. Watson, a Harvard anthropologist, has observed one such village very closely for several decades. On a visit in the early 1990s, in the years just before the handover, he discovered that almost all of the able-bodied villagers had emigrated to England!

Hakka women, wearing black-fringed hats, breaking stone for road construction in the 1930s.

The clans of the New Territories preserved careful records of their ancestors and kept various accounts, both oral and written, of their clan organization, religion, temples, marriages, burial rituals, educational system, and above all customary laws of inheritance, according to which only male offspring were beneficiaries. In 1993 Christine Loh tried to introduce a new amendment in the Legislative Council to restore gender equality so that indigenous women of the New Territories would be entitled to inherit land legally. Her move was vigorously opposed by all the clan elders who, through their deputies in the Heung Yee Guk (village council), staged demonstrations and even petitioned the government in Beijing—all in the name of anticolonial nationalism. It became a media event and sparked a year-long debate about old Chinese customs versus modern gender equality. The bill was finally passed in June the next year.

Inside Lo Wai walled village.

According to official Chinese records, in 1688 there were nineteen walled villages (*wai tsuen*) in the New Territories and twenty-nine in 1819. Most of them no longer exist, but a few are remarkably intact. One such site in Fanling, called Lo Wai or Old Walls, is the oldest walled village in Hong Kong and has been declared a public monument. It is now deserted, and the desolate atmosphere inside its dilapidated walls recalls the thirteenth century, when members of the Tang clan moved here from Kam Tin. Its entrance is through a side wall rather than the front, and the steps leading up to it are turned ninety degrees, presumably to fend off evil spirits, who can travel only in straight lines. The thick walls are built with large bricks, and gun-holes are strategically placed for self-defense. Nearby is the Tang Chung Ling ancestral hall, built in the early sixteenth century with three halls and two courtyards, and a Tin Hau temple.

Further north in Sheung Shui (Up River) is Wai Loi Tsuen or Village inside Walls. The Liu clan came originally from Fukien province during the thirteenth-century Yuan dynasty but did not settle in the village until the seventeenth century.[2] The pentagonal village has not only walls but a moat, built in 1646–1647, to defend against pirates. Most of the iron gates and walls of the village are intact. Inside, the village was originally divided into four small districts reserved for clan families according to their lineage: the families of the eldest son lived in the north district, those of the second in the east and west, and the third in the south. The Liu clan boasts an illustrious ancestry, having no fewer than forty-seven members who passed the imperial civil service examination — a great achievement for such a small village.

Not far away is the ancestral hall Liu Man Shek Tong or the Hall of 10,000 *shi*, so called because a remote ancestor and his four sons all became high officials in the Song dynasty (960–1279), each earning 2,000 *shi* of grain, thus making a total of 10,000 *shi*. This clan hall, first built in 1751, has three sections with the ancestral shrine placed at the innermost section. The hall was used as a school from 1932 to 1974 and was restored to its original condition in 1985.

The domicile of the Tang clan in Kam Tin village in Yuen Long, called Kit King Wai or Fortune Walls, is a more typical walled village. First built in the fifteenth century, it is still relatively well preserved. The walls are constructed of brick, some as thick as one meter in width, and are provided with observation towers and small gun-holes. The whole village has only one iron gate for entry and is surrounded by a small canal for defense. Inside, the streets and houses are neatly laid out in a four-square shape with a central street leading to an ancestral hall for the whole clan. Village shrines honor local gods, and public "study houses" serve as educational centers for children.

The marketplace was crucial to traditional economic and social life everywhere in China. In the eighteenth century, Shenzhen, now on the other side of the border into China, was the distribution center for the New Territories. The other four major markets—at Yuen Long, Sha Tau Kok, Tai Po, and Sheung Shui—were submarkets. Market days were regulated to promote an exchange of goods between towns. One village's market would convene on every third, sixth, and ninth day of a ten-day cycle, whereas a nearby town would open its market on the second, fifth, and eighth day, and so on. But virtually every village of any size had a morning and evening market that sold perishable vegetables, meat, fish, and other foods on a daily basis, so that the women could use fresh foods for every meal. In addition to produce, these open-air bazaars of-

Luen Wo Market in Fanling.

fered services for sale, including letter-writing, fortune-telling, and match-making. Near the market was also a Tin Hau or Man Mo Temple, next to which was a village office where villagers settled their disputes under the supervision of elders and through appeals to the deities.

Strictly speaking, there were two kinds of markets: market bazaar (*hui cheung*, from an ancient word *hui* meaning "ruins") and market street (*gai shi*, a more modern-sounding word). The former was a large open space specifically desig-nated for periodic market activities, with stalls and displays often under the shades of trees. The market street was originally an alleyway lined with shops that were open every day; the stalls and displays were usually at the end of the alley or near a well. The market in Fanling, opened in 1951, was a good example of both types combined. Built by the Pang clan together with other merchants in the area, the

Luen Wo Hui or United Market, was located on a market street (called naturally Luen Wo To). Inside was an open courtyard bazaar where villagers displayed their produce, but fish, meat, and vegetables were sold in regular booths. The Luen Wo Market was the largest in the New Territories in the postwar period but now has fallen into disuse.

A much older market in Yuen Long, built by the Tang clan, has a history dating back to the Ming dynasty. Originally an open-air market, it expanded into the main streets of Sai Ping Wan village. It took place every third day in a ten-day cycle. The market originally had four streets lined with two-story brick buildings in which shops of all kinds were housed, and a small river for loading and unloading goods. Located centrally was a two-hundred-year-old temple and a pawnshop, the oldest extant in Hong Kong. Built with high brick walls, it had a front office, living quarters for employees, and a back warehouse to store pawned goods. The alleyways were enlarged into streets in the bigger towns, and the term "town well" (*shi jing*) became a generic term for the concerns of the local community, much as the phrase "grassroots" is used today. One can still find these two-story market buildings—an urban form of the village *gai shi*—everywhere in Hong Kong. Many residents go there for fresh meat and vegetables and to have a cheap meal in a gruel or noodle stand nearby.

The market town nearest to Kowloon is Tai Po, which is easily reachable by train. The village name has a legend of its own: the Chinese characters meant "big strides," since the area was a dense forest infested with wild animals. There was a popular saying, "Take big strides, otherwise the tigers and snakes will get you!" The character "stride" was somehow changed to "slope," presumably referring to its hilly landscape.

The old Tai Po Market was built in the Ming dynasty to commemorate a local son whose filial act was more than exemplary. As local legend has it, this young man, named Tang, who lived in the sixteenth century, had to rescue his father from pirates. He presented himself to the pirate chief and pleaded: "If you keep my father, it will mean that I and my brother will have no father, and my father will have no sons. If you free my father and keep me instead, then at least my younger brother will have a father, and my father will have at least one son. Besides, my father is an old man who cannot work as well as I do, because I am young and strong." Much moved, the pirates granted his wish; the father was hustled ashore and the pirate ship sailed away. The filial son on board was filled with grief and cried: "I will never serve these wicked men." With that, he jumped into the ocean and was drowned. His body washed up at Tai Po and was buried nearby. His clansmen built a temple near his grave.[3]

In the eighteenth century two descendants of the Tang family petitioned the government to buy enough land around the temple to make a market. Shops were constructed and leased out, with the proceeds going to the upkeep of the temple. The temple has since been destroyed, but the grave remains. The Tang family controlled the market, which was barred to other merchants. Several lawsuits ensued. Finally, the Tang family won the case, and a stone with an inscription to that effect was put up in the Tin Hau temple, which can still be seen. The competitor built a new Tai Po Market.

In April 1899, after the New Territories were legally leased to Britain, a British warship landed at Tai Po, where the sailors ran into unexpected resistance from the local population. Several thousand men armed with muskets, mortars, small cannon, and "jingals" tried to fend off the well-equipped soldiers of the Hong Kong Regiment (about five hundred men from a regiment of the Indian Army). The villagers were defeated, with small casualties on both sides. The rebels retreated westward toward Kam Tin, and the next day 2,600 men put up a final stand at Sheung Tsuen and were again defeated. The official takeover ceremony was duly held on April 16.

A proclamation was issued to the inhabitants by Governor Henry Blake (1898–1903), promising that "your commercial and landed interests will be safeguarded, and your usages and good customs will not in any way be interfered with."[4] Tai Po was made the administrative center of the entire New Territories, and a special magistrate office was set up in a red-brick building, constructed in 1907. This is one of the few historical buildings preserved in the city. A local self-government body, the Heung Yee Guk or village council, was installed, which was not that different from the old council of elders.

THE MOST POPULAR religious celebration in the New Territories is the Da-jiu festival. The term in Cantonese refers to the ritual of offering thanks to the gods and spirits of ancestors and asking for their blessing for future prosperity and peace. It is also partly a ghost-busting festival to exorcise evil spirits. The ceremonies, officiated by Daoist priests, consist of setting up the ritual stand and display, burning incense, reciting the canons, and chanting ritual hymns, often accompanied by candles, music, and dancing. It is important that every one of the gods living in the village and surrounding countryside attend the ceremonies—indeed, they occupy seats of honor. Processions of men go to shrines and temples to collect the animist, ancestral, Buddhist, and Daoist gods. Each village and township has its own Da-jiu festival, and the intervals vary—annually, biannually, or once every decade. Especially those given every ten years, such as the one at Kam Tin village, require elaborate preparation. High bamboo façades decorated with colorful banners and painted images of deities are erected for the occasion, and lion dances are performed.

In recent years, the Da-jiu festival that has received much media attention and attracted large crowds of onlookers and tourists is the one at Cheung Chau island. It is held every year in the early part of the fourth month according to the lunar calendar (May or June) and lasts three days. Since the eighteenth century, Cheung Chau has been a fishing town, and originally the festival commemorated the spirits of ancestors who were killed by pirates. It also honored a local deity who helped residents survive a plague two hundred years ago. Other gods are honored at the Temple of Jade Vacuity, built in 1788. The highlights of the festival include lion dancing, parades with the gods, and "flying colors," where small children stand on high-poled tiles and act out historical legends.

But the real climax is the so-called "snatching buns on the hill," in which high bamboo racks like small hills are erected with sacrificial meat buns hanging on the posts for everyone to climb and grab. According to custom, the more buns one can grab and eat, the more blessings from the gods one will receive, since the buns are meant for the gods. In 1978 participants grabbing for the

Fishing boats in the Cheung Chau harbor. Tourists along the waterfront are treated to a Lion Dance.

Children floating through the streets of Cheung Chau during the 1996 Bun Festival.

buns trampled over one another, and more than twenty people were injured, several with broken arms and legs. The government tried to put an end to this spectacle by replacing it with a more moderate ceremony of "passing out" buns—apparently to no avail. Both villagers and visitors still love the old excitement—Cheung Chau's version of Pamplona's running of the bulls.

Another religious festival is the month-long Yu Lan or Hungry Ghost festival observed at the beginning of every seventh month of the lunar calendar. During this month, ghosts roam the human world. Thus one finds at street corners and sidewalks all kinds of offerings—foodstuff, burning incense sticks, white flowers—to feed and appease these hungry spirits. Theatrical performances often take place in the same month, mostly attended by older people. Similar Yu Lan festivals are also observed in Singapore and the Chinese communities in other Asia countries. On Hong Kong island, the offerings are sometimes found indoors, in restaurants, factories, and garages. Each trade and each community have their own ghosts to appease in order to bring good fortune.

For people living in a modern capitalistic society, Hong Kongers are exceedingly superstitious and tend to honor every local deity who can shower them with good luck. In the popular imagination, the worship of gods and deities has a direct bearing on human fortune, for good or ill. Much of Hong Kong superstition is connected with *feng shui*, translated "wind and waters"—a widespread Daoist belief that the harmonious positioning of objects leads to equilibrium with the rhythms of nature and the movements of ancestral spirits. The Hong Kong government has become well versed in *feng shui* customs since the 1960s, when the construction of new buildings and highways ran into opposition from local leaders. Special funds were set aside for "religious" expenses involved in appeasing the disturbed gods. Whether the project is the Sai Kung Highway in West Kowloon or mountain roads and ditches in the New Territories, a special ceremony called Man Fu must be performed. It is a totemic appeal to the protecting deities of land, trees, wells, and graves. The ritual is often carried out in front of the shrine of the appropriate deities on a date carefully chosen by consulting the lunar calendar.

The ritual stand is a long wooden table covered with red cloth, on which are placed bamboo sticks, a ritual urn filled with sand, wine, tea, rice, cooked chicken, vegetables, as well as a candle—plus a live rooster hung under the table. At the ceremony, the officiating Daoist priests pick up the sticks, scorch them slightly in the burning candle, write "curse words" on the sand to scare away evil spirits, and then splash blood from the live rooster all over the sand urn. This is but one ritual among hundreds that have become an essential part of the lives of many Hong Kong residents. Of course similar rituals were practiced in all rural areas in China for thousand of years, until 1949, when the Communist regime banned religion. The colonial government in Hong Kong, by contrast, did not interfere with local customs, and as a result they have been kept alive, especially in the New Territories.

Religious practices in Hong Kong should not be equated with religious beliefs in the Western sense. Chinese temples are not churches, with a liturgy and organized services; they are the residences of deities, where people come to pay homage whenever they please. Chinese gods in the folk tradition were originally mortals believed to have performed miracles that deified them. The most famous of the local gods is Tin Hau, goddess of the sea and the guardian angel for fishermen In one account, Tin Hau was originally a girl from a poor Fukien family. When her father and brothers were away on a fishing trip, she dreamed that they were drowning in a terrible storm; she was trying to pull them to safety when her mother woke her. Her two brothers apparently saw a beautiful girl throwing ropes to them and towing them ashore. But she did not have time to throw a third rope to save her father before she awoke. Tin Hau did not live much longer herself, but after her death she appeared numerous times to save seafarers from disaster. In

1683 after she helped the Qing navy defeat the forces of the pirate Koxinga (Zheng Chenggong), she was elevated to the status of Queen of Heaven. At least a dozen other Chinese deities have this kind of detailed biography.

Every year more than one hundred thousand worshippers come to the Che Kung temple in Tai Wai near Sha Tin on or around the second day of the Chinese New Year. The temple has become the designated site of official fortune-telling, where each year a high-ranking representative comes to make offerings to this deity—originally a Song dynasty military commander—and seek information about Hong Kong's collective fortune. In 2003 Patrick Ho, head of the Home Affairs Bureau, drew a wooden chim stick (a bamboo stick used for divination) that predicted the worst possible fortune. Shortly thereafter, the SARS epidemic broke out, and the stock market, in response, took a nosedive. Local people in the New Territories were not surprised at these misfortunes.

Another religious building in Sha Tin that draws both worshippers and tourists is the Ten Thousand Buddhas Monastery, built in 1957. A path of over four-hundred steps, lined with life-size Buddha figures of all shapes, must be climbed to reach the monastery. The walls of its main hall are lined with over 12,800 Buddha statues, each in a different posture, made from local clay by twelve craftsmen from Shanghai. The two bottom shelves of statues are guarded by eighty-four *lohan*—representatives of Buddha's army. There is also a nine-story pagoda on the site.

The biggest Buddha statue in Hong Kong is in Po Lin Monastery on Lantau Island, founded around 1920 by three reclusive monks. Built in 1990, this immense statue of Buddha Sakyamuni sits on his lotus throne at the top of a flight of 268 stairs. The Buddha, made of bronze, is 26 meters tall, weighs 250 tons, and can be seen from a great distance. Lantau—the largest of the 262 outlying islands in the New Territories—is twice the size of Hong Kong island. Ferries from the pier in Central take visitors to Mui Wo (Silver Mine Bay) on the eastern side of the island; from there, a bus ride on a winding mountain leads to the monastery. The trip can also be made on a newly constructed sky-ride cable from Tung Chung near the airport, reachable via the MTR subway. The sky-ride offers scenic views and saves considerable time.

To facilitate tourist traffic to the newly constructed Disneyland on the eastern tip of the island, a special rail was built that links Sunny Bay on the MTR Tung Chung line to the amusement park. Thus, travel by public transportation to Lantau has become much easier in recent times. But for those who choose to drive on the North Lantau Highway, the gigantic Tsing Yi Bridge—at 1,377 meters one of the world's longest suspension bridges—or the equally magnificent Tsing Ma Bridge to Ma Wan represents a marvel of modern engineering and, on clear days or nights, a stunning view.

The bus road to Po Lin Monastery passes Shek Pik (Stone Wall) Reservoir, built in 1958–1962. During its construction, a number of archaeological discoveries were made, and in 1968–69 a pair of earthenware jars with identical blue-and-white porcelain bowls as covers, which are believed to be from the Ming dynasty, were found on a sloping hillside west of the former village of Shek Pik. Rock carvings first discovered near the reservoir in the late 1930s indicate that the island was inhabited as early as the Bronze Age, 3,000 years ago, if not earlier.

The long mountainside path leading to the Ten Thousand Buddhas Monastery.

Lantau Island is haunted by legends. The famous buccaneer Cheung Po Tsai supposedly had a base in Lantau for over fifty years in the late eighteenth and early nineteenth centuries. The Hong Kong Maritime Museum's special exhibition of 2006 on the subject of "Piracy and the World of Zhang Baozai" was directly inspired by the Hollywood box office success of *Pirates of the Caribbean*, I and II. Part III of this film trio, released in 2007, includes a Chinese pirate character, Captain Sao Feng, played by Chow Yun-Fat (who was born on Lamma Island) and based on Cheung Po Tsai (Zhang Baozai in mandarin). Cheung claimed his pirate pedigree through his foster father, Zheng I (1765–1807), who was the last of a long line of pirate-rebels from coastal Fukien whose great-grandfather had been allied with Koxinga (Zheng Chenggong), another legendary pirate.

Cheung Po Tsai, according to all accounts, was a tall, charismatic figure who was fond of fine clothes and eventually married the wife of another deceased pirate chief. In 1810 the couple commanded a fleet of 17,318 pirates, 226 junks, 1,315 cannon, and 2,798 weapons but finally were forced to surrender to the combined naval forces of the Qing government and the Portuguese from Macau—not without fighting fiercely for nine days in a November 1809 sea battle near Tung Chung, not far from today's new airport. Apparently the surrender was to the pirate's benefit. Cheung was later made a lieutenant of the Qing Imperial Navy, and his wife, Zheng Yisao, received a country estate and a pension—which did not deter her from becoming the new boss of a successful smuggling operation.

At the height of their glory in the early 1800s, pirates organized themselves into a federation of fleets, with six major groups designated by the colors Red, Black, White, Green, Blue, and Yellow. Each fleet had between 70 and 300 ships, and the total forces formed an armada of 1,800 ships and 70,000 men. The pirate federation enforced trade monopolies, purchased weapons from foreign suppliers, issued passports, and collected taxes. In the Hong Kong area, pirate lairs were located on Lantau and Cheung Chau islands, in Aberdeen and Stanley on Hong Kong, and in Lei Yue Mun in east Kowloon. Needless to say, they caused havoc among the local inhabitants. After one pirate raid, only two families were left on the island of Cheung Chau.

Piracy continued well into the nineteenth and twentieth centuries. After Cheung Po Tsai, there were Chui Apoo (Xu Yapao) and Shap-ng-tsai (Fifteenth Son). The former was a local boy, presumably from Stanley, who operated a fleet of 40 junks and 1,800 pirate followers until he was captured by the Royal Navy in 1849. Shap's fleet was chased by a joint Anglo-Chinese expeditionary force all the way to the Gulf of Tonkin near the entrance to the Red River in Vietnam. Miraculously, he escaped and disappeared. One source says that, like Cheung Po Tsai, Shap finally surrendered to the Qing and was given a commission in the navy.

Western adventurers also joined the fray, in particular the two Americans Eli Boggs and Bully Hayes. Boggs joined with local pirates in 1852 and is said to have commanded 50 junks at one time before he was captured in 1857. Hayes (the hero of the Hollywood movie *Nate and Hayes*, 1983) began his career as a pirate in Hong Kong around 1856. Among his many evil deeds was kidnapping Chinese peasants from coastal villages and carrying them off to New Zealand and the south sea islands as slaves.

While these men provided the raw materials for glamorous legends and adventure films, the problem of piracy in the real world never went away. It is still rampant in the world today. There were 329 reported incidents in 2004, 276 in 2005, and 123 in the first half of 2006, of which 52 took place in Southeast Asia.[5] Sailing in the high waters near Hong Kong is not entirely safe.

A major attraction on Lantau Island is the fishing village of Tai O on the western side. It can be reached by bus from Mui Wo or from the bus terminal in Tung Chung. This charming, remote site has been called the "Venice of the East" — an extravagant claim, but Tai O is indeed one of the oldest fishing villages in Hong Kong, with a history of human settlement going back at least to the Song dynasty. Architectural historians have taken a keen interest in a special type of housing shed built over the water, called a "pile house" or "matshed on stilts" or "stilt house." These primitive homes can still be found in fishing villages all over Southeast Asia. The prototype of their design has been traced to the Neolithic age. Originally, the roofs were curved in a triangular shape and covered with leaves, and the houses rested on stone pillars hammered into the riverbed.

Stilt houses in Tai O. Dried fish are sold nearby, in the village's daily market.

A fire in the year 2,000 destroyed some ninety of these sheds in Tai O, but they were rebuilt, and in recent times a new generation of two-story shed-houses have appeared. Each house, inhabited by one family, is separated into three zones: sleeping rooms, an area for ancestral altars, and a living room. Several houses form a group but are separated from one another by wooden platforms. The roofs are now patched together with all manner of modern building materials. Despite the primitiveness of this housing, most residents refuse to be relocated, perhaps because living close to the water has become their way of life.

Fishing is still the main profession for the indigenous residents in Tai O. Different types of fish come in different seasons and are caught by a variety of vessels and equipment. There used to be a competition among the Tai O fishermen for the greatest volume of fish caught during the year. The winning fishing vessel was crowned the "top boat of the year," and it paraded up and down the river during the Dragon Boat Festival.

Drum and gong in a Tai O temple.

SHIP BUILDING and repairing, along with salt refinement, are no longer the viable occupations they once were. Other small-scale industries — such as manufacturing watch chains, light bulbs, plastic flowers, dolls, spare parts for radios, and adapters — have come and gone since the 1970s. Slowly, as the fishing village aged, the population dropped off. But in recent years Tai O, like a few similar fishing villages in the area, has begun to attract locals intent on seeking their roots, along with tourists curious to see out-of-the way spots. Cultural heritage, especially of the authentic kind, has become a rarity, and Tai O's appeal lies paradoxically in its poverty and "underdevelopment."[6]

Some Western expats–especially young professionals — prefer the more rustic surroundings of Discovery Bay on the west side of Lantau island, which has become a popular conclave, with deluxe condos, club houses, and tennis courts. Other favorite places for resort living in village surroundings are Sai Kung on Clear Water Bay, Shek O and Aberdeen in the south of Hong Kong Island, and Lamma Island — the last unusual in that motor vehicles are banned. All of these relatively remote areas offer a retreat from the urban life on the Mid-Levels. Some of the more than two hundred other islands in the area remain unpopulated to this day.

ONE IMPORTANT SITE of historical interest in the New Territories has been all but forgotten by both locals and tourists: the old Shaw Brothers film studios, hidden on a hilly slope near Hang Hau south of Clearwater Bay Road. The old studio has fallen into disuse, though a television production studio carrying the Shaw Brothers logo has been built at Tseung Kwan O. In 1964, when Shaw Brothers (SB) founded the company on this barren piece of land, it instantly created a "dream factory" that made Hong Kong the Hollywood of the East and the world's third largest center of film production, following Hollywood and Bombay.

Sir Run Run Shaw, who lorded over his empire for half a century, is now over a century old himself and no longer makes films. But his legacy is kept alive by recent reissues of more than a hundred titles from SB's archive of over seven hundred movies. Hong Kong film scholars have held revivals and conferences in honor of SB, as they have also seen fit to honor a smaller rival company, Cathay, which also produced many high-quality films. The two companies, each with its roster of famous stars, dominated the Hong Kong film scene for at least thirty years, from the 1950s to the 1970s, until a young generation of directors — John Woo, Ann Hui, Tsui Hark, Stanley Kwan, and Wong Kar-wai among them — changed the way films were made in Hong Kong. Yet most of these New Wave directors had served as apprentices in the SB studio system.

The Shaw family started their film business in Shanghai in the 1930s. As war and revolution broke out, two of the Shaw brothers decided to seek their fortunes overseas, first in Singapore, where they ran a chain of movie theaters, and then in Hong Kong, where they formed a company modeled entirely after Hollywood's "big eight" studios. Its production style recalled MGM and 20th-century Fox in their heyday, and Sir Run Run's power and authority was comparable to that of Louis Meyer and Darryl Zanuck combined. Cathay often produced films of more artistic interest, reminiscent of those Warner Brothers made in the 1930s and 1940s.

Run Run Shaw certainly demonstrated foresight in setting his film empire in Hong Kong, not only because Hong Kong was Shanghai's sister city under British colonialism but because Hong Kong had its own history of film-making. In fact, one of the earliest film-makers in the history of Chinese cinema was from Hong Kong. In 1913 Lai Man Wai collaborated with two Americans—producer Benjamin Brodsky and cameraman Roland F. Van Velzer—to make a film in Hong Kong called *The Deformation of Chuang Chow* (or *Chuang Tue Tests His Wife*), an adaptation of an operatic play about the philosopher Chuang Tzu's testing of his wife's loyalty. Lai himself starred in the film. Historians now list that film—and Lai's contribution—among the first four films ever made (of which two were made in Shanghai in 1909). This set a precedent, and native film production in Cantonese followed. At its height in the 1940s and 1950s, hundreds of Cantonese-language films dealing with a variety of subjects (such as the folk hero Wong Fei Hong) were made.

If the Shaw Brothers were not on virgin territory when they started their own company in Hong Kong, what made them new and different was their Hollywood-style studio production system. Run Run Shaw set up his ambitious kingdom of film-making with painstaking care as well as great audacity. The Clear Water Bay compound comprised ten large studios, in which large-scale sets were built, including a traditional Chinese small town complete with streets, taverns, and shops. The majority of its actors, actresses, and crew—totaling about 1,700—were hired under exclusive contract and had to live in dormitories in the studio compound. Young starlets, in particular, were forced to attend acting classes. This living arrangement, coupled with sex scandals, caused several young actresses to commit suicide. Yet the system produced between thirty and forty films a year during its most active period. The films were shown in the company's own chain of theaters, thus guaranteeing a steady profit.

Every Shaw Brothers film carried the studio emblem (an SB on a shield) and this logo: "A Shaw Brothers product must be a good film." This was of course just a branding strategy, and the real products varied considerably. What Shaw Brothers did achieve was a vernacular film genre with several distinguishable characteristics. Unlike Cantonese films, all SB films were dubbed in Mandarin Chinese. This marketing strategy started a trend that Cathay and other small companies followed. After 1949, when films made in China were no longer available overseas, the two largest markets for Shaw Brothers films (aside from Hong Kong) were Taiwan and Singapore, where the local Chinese population spoke Mandarin.

For much of the Hong Kong audience, however, this strategy turned locally made movies into "foreign films." Chinese subtitles had to be added, sometimes coupled with English ones. Whether the experience of watching a Shaw Brothers movie enhanced film viewers' knowledge of Mandarin Chinese—and by extension mainland culture—is anybody's guess. But it is an indisputable fact that SB films changed the viewing habits of local audiences. For the first time, movies became a convenient, and often comfortable, form of mass entertainment, because the SB theaters were on a par with the deluxe movie palaces that showed first-run Hollywood films. Cantonese films, by contrast, had been relegated to small and not so comfortable neighborhood theaters. The company's publicity machine—again a copy of the Hollywood system—included two popular fan magazines that showcased SB stars, who became instant celebrities.

With its wide distribution and circulation channels, the Shaw empire extended its domain to all of Southeast Asia. In the 1970s, hoping to expand into Japan's market, SB began to hire Japanese directors and technicians and a few leading actors as co-stars. This effort at collaboration failed, but Shaw films succeeded in speaking to a huge Chinese audience that cut across national boundaries. With its influence, Hong Kong became the center of not only Chinese-language films but of a "pan-Chinese" popular culture.

Western film aficionados tend to dismiss the Shaw Brothers products as vulgar commodities of blatant violence and demure sex. But the recent popularity of Jackie Chan films has made some of them aware of SB's contribution, for Chan, like many other *kung-fu* stars, was first nurtured in the Shaw studio system. The *kung-fu* genre—for a long time a trademark of SB production—was derived from a rich tradition of martial arts films. The acknowledged masters of this genre were two veteran directors, King Hu (1931–1997) and Chang Cheh (1923–2002), both of whom are subjects of study by film scholars.

King Hu (Hu Jinchuan) began his career as an actor and directed his first *kung-fu* film for Shaw Brothers; *The Drunken Swordsman* (1966) became a surprise hit. He soon left the company and did his other celebrated films with funds from a Taiwan producer. These included *Dragon-Gate Inn* (1967) and *A Touch of Zen* (1971). In many ways Hu was not a typical SB product because his films were more historically based (mostly Ming dynasty) with a classical style. The fighting scenes are carefully choreographed—"dances" reminiscent of Peking operas rather than real fights.

The mainstay of SB directors and the doyen of *kung-fu* films was Chang Cheh, who made about a hundred films for the studio, several of which became all-time box-office hits. Like Hu, Chang was also versed in classical Chinese culture, but he decided to take a more commercial route, like many Hollywood directors. He left a distinct imprint in all his films—a style of excessive violence and explicit homoerotic display of the male torso, although the storylines stick to traditional sexual moralities. Chang Cheh personally discovered and promoted several male stars and initiated the trend from costume sword fighting to pure *kung-fu* fistfights.

When fighting scenes had to be shot outdoors, both Hu and Chang went to barren hills in the New Territories. Longtime residents could recognize, for instance, where the final immolation scene in *A Touch of Zen* was shot: right on a construction site in Sha Tin where half of the hilly slopes were already being razed. Some of the horse-riding scenes in Chang's films were shot near villages not far away. The term "going out for location shooting" thus became a euphemism for going to the rural outskirts in the New Territories.

A third famous director from the Shaw Brothers was Lee Han-Hsiang (Li Hangxiang, 1923–1997), who was the subject of a major retrospective in spring 2007 by the Hong Kong Film Archive as part of the Hong Kong Film Festival. Lee specialized in historical dramas and traditional folk-tune musicals that became enormously popular. A noted example of the latter genre, *The Butterfly Lovers* (1963), was a tear-jerker that audiences at the time (including the young Ang Lee in Taiwan) would watch again and again.

Sheer escapism and entertainment were obviously the intended effect of all these films. But taken together, they had a side-effect of which the film-makers at Shaw Brothers may not have been conscious. All these *kung-fu* films and costume dramas conjured up a historical China that seems far removed and unreal but at the same time a "generic" world of unspecific times and places, in which heroes and heroines adhere to a strict code of ethics: loyalty, filial piety, brotherhood, and a sense of justice that provides the motive for revenge. Given the real historical context in which these 1960s and 1970s films were made, they met a collective need for a Chinese culture—or more specifically a "cultural China"—that rose above political boundaries and the associated disputes.

In other words, the films inadvertently constructed an imaginary China for overseas Chinese who could identify with its vaguely Confucian ethos. At the same time, they provided emotional relief from the daily reality of hardship and the sense of social and national disenfranchisement in the Chinese diasporas. For Hong Kong audiences, this "cultural China" created in the tinsel town of the Shaw studios provided an alternative to both the People's Republic on the mainland and the Republic of China on Taiwan. At the basest level, the theme of revenge resulting in the bloody death of a villain provided a certain psychological compensation for the real difficulties, injustices, and dislocation they suffered in their everyday lives.

A special box-office teaser, the midnight preview of a new film, proved immensely popular with lower-class audiences, who would flock to the theaters and shout out their approval or disapproval. One local scholar even attributed the relatively low rate of murders and killings in Hong Kong, compared with those in New York or other major cities, to this collective ritual of emotional release. But to outsiders who knew Hong Kong only through its films, the city must have seemed like a slaughterhouse.

The fortunes of the Shaw Brothers began to change in the late 1970s. The signs were imperceptible at the beginning and came from a most unlikely source. A local comedy team, the Hui brothers (Michael, Sam, and Ricky) made a crude film called *The Private Eyes* (1976) in Cantonese was released by another company, Raymond Chow's *Golden Harvest*. Surprisingly, the film broke all box office records. This farce about three bungling private detectives who obviously imitated the Marx Brothers in demeanor and deed managed to win the hearts of the local audience and to change the Mandarin-dominated film market. After the 1980s most films made in Hong Kong shifted back to Cantonese. The Hui brothers are now legends on the city's cultural scene, especially the eldest, Michael Hui, who became a celebrated actor and director, and the more handsome Sam Hui, who became a singer.

The beginning of *The Private Eyes* was shot on a construction site in the New Territories, where the young detective Sam Hui was sent to snoop around among the construction workers. The convenient choice of location turned out to signify something more momentous: as the traditional rural landscape began to take a modern urban shape, so did the mentality of the local Hong Kong population. The refugees from China who had migrated since the early 1950s realized that they were the ones who would occupy this new high-rise public housing—and they were here to stay. For the first time in Hong Kong's history, a sense of a Hong Kong identity began to emerge, and the newly constructed buildings in these new towns became the physical world in which such an identity and a collective lifestyle began to form. It was also around this time that the colonial government began to actively promote the concept of a collective "community" in Hong Kong by demonstrating its willingness to modernize the city with new buildings, electric trains, a subway system, and cross-harbor tunnels.

In film-making and in television, not only was Cantonese adopted as the official language but the focus also shifted away from escapism to a new social consciousness. In the 1980s a generation of young film-makers, mostly educated abroad, returned to Hong Kong and found employment in the new medium of the masses, television. Administrators in the two major TV companies proved very liberal and gave them room for experimentation. Some of them—notably Fong Yuk Ping and Ann Hui—made a series of short documentaries called, revealingly, *Below the Lion Rock*, a reference to the partition line between Kowloon and the New Territories. Each of the hour-long episodes in the series contains a story and a real character drawn from the various villages and squatter areas in the outskirts of Kowloon and the New Territories (but not from Tai Ping Shan on Hong Kong island). In style and content, they were mini-films comparable to postwar Italian Neorealism, and they conveyed the same humanistic sympathies for the poor and downtrodden in a society undergoing rapid transformation.

Of course, this trend of social consciousness was soon swamped under the tide of commercialism, and some of the same directors—Tsui Hark, John Woo, and Ann Hui—eventually went into commercial film-making, where they established an international reputation. In the golden era of Hong Kong's film-making in the 1980s, the central location would change again, from the countryside in the New Territories back to the contemporary urban milieu of Hong Kong and Kowloon. The subject matter was also more contemporary: cops-and-robbers thrillers, Chinese mafia intrigues, gambling kings, and romantic comedies. Notably lacking was historical drama, a genre that has been taken over by directors from mainland China such as Zhang Yimou and Chen Kaige.

A 3,000-year-old rock carving near Shek Pik on Lantau Island.

A narrow street in Central's Lan Kwai Fong, filled with restaurants, bars, and young patrons.

7

Hong Kong Lifestyle

The Chinese talk about the "four basic requirements" of everyday life: food, clothing, dwelling, and movement, probably in that order. This truism no doubt stems from living conditions in premodern China, in which livelihood meant above all to survive before one could consider the luxury of living well. In modern Hong Kong as in urban China, starvation is no longer a pressing issue. People eat as much for pleasure and for other social reasons as for sustenance. Similarly, clothing for protection from the elements is easy to come by. The clothing shops that bedeck every shopping mall and almost every street are there primarily to satisfy an insatiable desire for fashion, especially among Hong Kong women. The requirements that preoccupy most people in Hong Kong are dwelling and movement: how to find adequate living quarters for a family, and how to move from home to workplace in an efficient way. Everyday life still revolves around these four requirements, however, and for that reason they are worth considering in some detail. In addition to these basic aspects of Hong Kong's lifestyle, I will take a look at the city's "workstyle" and also how its citizens entertain themselves afterhours.

We'll start with that most fundamental requirement, food. "Cantonese cuisine" is a generic term, and like all Chinese regional cuisines it has its own varieties. What truly defines Hong Kong's urban-vernacular taste is not the Cantonese cuisine in restaurants, which you can find in other cities, but the half-colonial and half-native hybrid found in a special eating establishment called *cha tsan ting* or teahouse. There are thousands of teahouses all over the territory, yet they are hardly noticeable. The décor inside is utterly undistinguished and the ambience

A roadside food stall in Kowloon, 1957.

pedestrian, with cheap-looking wooden or plastic chairs and tables. The menus are often written on strips of paper and pasted on the wall or printed on a sheet and placed on the table alongside the chopsticks and toothpicks. But the teahouse offers a great variety of food at cheap prices—Chinese, Western, and Asian. This includes Cantonese fish balls, wonton noodles, rice gruel with meat, but also toasts, sandwiches, fried or poached eggs for breakfast, and Hainan chicken, Indonesian fried rice, Singaporean rice noodles, and many other concoctions and combinations, as well as different kinds of snacks for afternoon tea.

But the one thing that makes the teahouses so characteristic of Hong Kong is the basic beverage they serve, called *nai cha* or milk tea, a concoction of heavy English (or Ceylon) tea mixed with condensed milk. Certainly a colonial derivation, but it does not taste like English tea with milk at all, nor does it resemble regular Chinese tea, which is taken without milk.

The *cha tsan ting* became a popular establishment only in the 1960s, replacing the more primitive street-side open-air eatery (*dai pai dong*). In colonial Hong Kong, these road stands arose to meet the needs of working-class Chinese, especially laborers who wanted cheap but substantial food for breakfast or lunch and snacks when they took a break from work. These food stands came in two varieties: those serving Chinese food such as fish balls, noodles, gruel, *cheung fen* (a kind of ravioli-shaped rice noodles), and fried flour sticks, and those offering a native derivation of Western breakfast items, such as *to si* or *sei to si* (Western toast), *yau jim to* (toast with butter and jam), *bo luo bao* (bread topped with butter in the shape of pineapples), *mak sei ko bao* (Mexican bread), and so on.

It has been said that colonialism was formally introduced to Hong Kong in the form of the English breakfast. That may be so, but the local Chinese lost no time in creating vernacular variations and new inventions. This "fusion" cuisine was eaten at the roadside while sitting on shabby stools. When in the course of urban development the government removed these stands, they migrated indoors and transformed themselves into the *cha tsan ting*. A convenient representative is Tsui Wah, located on Wellington Street in Central, which offers some prize-winning dishes.

Eating at a *cha tsan ting* is different from the custom of *yum cha*, literally "drinking tea" but accompanied by eating *dim sum*, that is, dishes of meat, vegetables, shrimp, and fish wrapped in pastry and served in bamboo steamers. *Yum cha* is offered in regular Cantonese restaurants, especially for lunch or Sunday brunch but not for dinner. This custom most likely stems from the lifestyle of the old Chinese elite, who would go to the *cha lou* (tea pavilions) for tea and breakfast. These rich dandies from merchant families cultivated their own high style by carrying bird cages to the *cha lou*, where they could have a leisurely meal while listening to the birds sing. This custom is the target of spoof in several local films, such as *Wong Fei Hung* (also known as *Once Upon a Time in China*, 1991) and *Project A* (1983).

A few *cha lou* establishments can still be found in the old town area. One of the oldest, at 162 Wellington Street on the western edge of Central (called Lin Heung Lou, or Fragrant Lotus Pavilion), originated in Canton in 1889; its first two branches were opened in Hong Kong in 1918. The restaurant, famous for its moon cakes, moved to the present site in 1996. During the 1970s the restaurant also included a small stage, with singers. At most hours of the day it is hard even to get in, and, once inside, you share a table with several strangers. I have tried twice to get in for lunch, still without success. Old-time patrons of *cha lou*

"Hegemon of fishballs, king of curries" announces the Tsui Wah teahouse sign.

establishments in Central have remarked that different crowds come at different times: the locals living nearby come for breakfast, office workers and middle-class professionals come for lunch and afternoon tea, and seedier men in dark suits, making business deals of all sorts, appear late at night.

Today, *yum cha* has become a favorite eating practice of the Chinese middle-class. Most families participate in a weekly ritual of getting together for *dim sum* around noon on Sunday. The different delicacies were once served in carts pushed around by waiters and waitresses (the latter often middle-aged women), who called out the names of the different foods. Customers could look them over and pick up what they wanted. Nowadays, to save time and space, restaurants ask customers to fill out order forms—much less fun but probably more efficient. Still, *yum cha* and eating in the *cha tsan ting* are two separate local customs. Any Chinese man or woman can participate in the former and pretend to be a local person, but only true Hong Kong natives favor the latter.

Since the *cha tsan ting* is an institution of plebian origins, it cannot be compared to the European coffee house, which was a bourgeois invention of the eighteenth century. The German philosopher Jurgen Habermas has made it part of his theory of the bourgeois "public sphere," where people from all classes congregated presumably to have a rational discourse on politics or to promote democracy. Of course, the modern coffee house culture in Hong Kong, organized mostly around Starbucks and Pacific Coffee chain stores, is the same as in other world cities, and very little philosophy or politics gets discussed there. The clientele of the *cha tsan ting*, on the other hand, gathers informally for casual food, drink, and conversation.

To get a feel for real Hong Kong food, a visitor must go to a teahouse and order a bowl of fish ball soup or wonton noodles, along with a cup of milk tea. For Westerners and nonlocals it is certainly an acquired taste, but natives who migrate to other countries often miss the flavor of fish balls from the *cha tsan ting* most of all. *Yum cha* can be had in any number of Cantonese restaurants in San Francisco, Toronto, or New York, but no authentic *cha tsan ting* can be found outside Hong Kong.

Local film-makers have added glamour and sensationalism to this Hong

Kong institution by portraying the teahouse as the regular hangout of young mafia types (called *gu wah tsai*). In Wong Kar-wai's famous film *As Tears Go By* (1988), their life in the Mong Kok and Yau Ma Tei area revolves around teahouses, and a lot of killing takes place there. More serious writers have also glorified this institution, placing it within the context of Hong Kong's unique social history. Chan Koon Chung has published a volume of three stories about Hong Kong's past, of which the last is about a *cha tsan ting* called Can Do Teahouse (which once existed). In this fifteen-page short story, two whole pages are devoted to the various new items in the bilingual menu.

IN THE HONG KONG VERNACULAR, clothing is a synonym for fashion, not for one of life's necessities. But in the nineteenth and early twentieth centuries, styles of clothing were a defining hallmark of race and class. One of the most noticeable differences between Western and Chinese elites was the clothes they wore. Colonial men wore dark suits (a custom that persists among Hong Kong bureaucrats today) or white military uniforms, and their women wore long Victorian dresses and elaborate hats. By contrast, wealthy Chinese, both men and women, wore long silk gowns, while lower-class people dressed in simple waist-length blouses and billowy trousers, in white or black.

Before the Second World War, native women still wore these traditional blouses and trousers—rather than skirts—because they had to work. Only the Hakka women in the New Territories, with their special headgear and hood, had a distinguishing look. In the 1950s and 1960s fashionable mature women began to wear the *cheung sam* or long gown—a local derivation from the *qipao* or Manchu-style gown that became popular in Shanghai in the 1930s. It was made all the more glamorous, especially in Western eyes, by the image of Suzie Wong in the 1960 film, but it has now taken on a decidedly nostalgic appeal, as in Wong Kar-wai's film *In the Mood for Love* (2001).

Among upper- and middle-class Chinese men, the postwar period witnessed a gradual transition from Chinese gowns to Western suits—a sign of modernization—and the East-West division was obliterated. Still, at formal occasions, Western and Chinese traditional styles might be worn interchangeably. The

On this typical Hong Kong street in 1955, a man wears traditional black trousers and white blouse, while women dress in the fashionable *cheung sam*. A beauty (*Meili*) parlor advertises the latest hairdo: the "permanent wave."

suits, shirts, and ties worn by Chinese men in the 1950s, mostly in black and white, look rather drab by today's standards.

Western men discovered the expertise of Hong Kong tailoring probably around the same time that Western women fell under the spell of the *cheung sam*—that is, in the 1960s. But Chinese men had been well aware of Hong Kong's fine tailors for a decade. Most of them had been transported from Shanghai, together with everything else, in the 1950s. Once in Hong Kong, however, the profession gradually modernized and professionalized, and it prospered alongside the rising textile industry. Visitors were duly impressed by the fast and efficient service: a suit could be done from measurement to delivery in forty-eight hours or less, and shirts by the dozen could be ordered from and delivered to hotel rooms.

The majority of Hong Kong's tailors are Chinese, with Indians as their close competitors. Prices vary a great deal, and the locals often go to familiar tailors in their neighborhood or to some obscure second-floor tailor shop they happen to know. Dresses can also be tailor-made, but special orders have never been as popular as shopping sprees—a universal habit among Hong Kong women who can afford it.

Matthew Turner, a longtime scholar and resident in Hong Kong, has argued that the 1960s was a watershed in the evolution of a Hong Kong identity (however amorphous and ill-defined in the beginning) and that fashion played a large role in shaping the popular self-image of Hong Kong's people. "Fashion shows, originally introduced to promote exports, were instantly adopted as social events, while ready-to-wear fashion displaced reliance on tailoring and dressmaking, and with the decline of the sewing machine, Chinese styles of *saam fu* and *cheong saam* that until the 1960s had signified Chinese identity." But modern fashion-consciousness presented a problem for Hong Kong women, since in traditional Chinese eyes a Westernized appearance was associated with bar girls. Thus, a new rhetoric of fashion had to be introduced in the late 1960s: "modernity as 'smartness' . . . to the point where the bright, efficient, diligent office girl became a personification of modern design."[1] To promote exports and attract overseas investment, government agencies played up these images of Hong Kong's modern working women, dressed in their sharp, crisp designs, and even local factory workers began to dream of office jobs in the CBD, where "Central values" were coming to life along with this new sense of fashion.

Today, for both male and female office workers in the Central Business District, black remains the favored color and fashionable suits the dominant style. The nature of jobs in banking or real estate seems to require this unisex uniform. But once they leave the office, Hong Kong women especially reveal themselves as the most trend-conscious consumers in the world. Being chic does not mean just being fashionably dressed but also conspicuously flaunting the latest styles and colors, preferably by brand-name designers, regardless of how well these designs fit any individual's body. Thus, ironically, one also sees a certain "chic uniformity" in Hong Kong—like the shoes currently worn, all sharply pointed as if to hide a secret weapon in the toes.

In recent decades, with the mushrooming of shopping malls, a glitzy new world has opened up for women and men of all ages. Buying ready-made trendy clothes has become a major goal of everyday life. It is the one act of obsessive consumerism found everywhere in Hong Kong—its importance is second only to eating. Those who cannot afford high-priced brand-names can always find cheap imitations or leftovers in the street-side bazaars in Wan Chai or Mong Kok. As fashion changes quickly, so must the clothes one buys and wears every day. Especially among women, custom-made clothing is usually worn only on the most formal occasions.

Japanese styles (and sizes) seem to suit many Hong Kong women better than Western brands, but long lines can be found in front of Western brand-name outlets for handbags and shoes. Advertisements for women's clothing are everywhere, particularly in subway stations and escalators. An aggressive advertising campaign for a new clothing store from England, H&M, drew several thousand customers on the day of its opening in March 2007. In Hong Kong, buying fashionable clothing is no longer an occasional pastime but an unquenchable fetishistic drive. As a former manager of a famous clothing store told me, a shopper is not buying new clothes so much as "buying a dream," whether or not she has the time or the body to wear it.

A high-fashion industry definitely exists in Hong Kong, but as yet not many world-renowned designers, except for a select few such as Vienne Tam, have developed distinguishing trademarks. A unique clothing shop called Shanghai Tang (a pun on the owner's surname and on a popular TV series *Shanghai Tan*) first opened in the Pedder Building in Central in 1944. The clothes in Shanghai Tang were designed in an imitative oriental style, playfully gaudy and exaggerated. For a while, shortly after the handover in 1997 this shop became very popular, when a publicity campaign called upon all Hong Kong people, Chinese and Westerners alike, to put on "Chinese"-style clothing for one day as a celebratory gesture to mark Hong Kong's return to China. But the trend failed to catch on. Hong Kong taste, by and large, still emulates the West, French and Italian fashion in particular.

Since not all human bodies are built like models, *sau sun* or body thinning has become a lucrative industry in Hong Kong, with shops and exercise rooms catering to this latest obsession. They can be found everywhere, particularly in fashion-conscious Central, Wan Chai, and Causeway Bay. Riding on the outdoor escalator or walking along an elevated passageway, one often sees young women and men in athletic wear working their exercise machines in plain view behind glass windows. Hong Kong also has massage parlors and body shops—including clinics with Chinese medicinal herbs and acupuncture—that offer a variety of so-called wonder treatments for nonconforming body parts.

Given the extremely limited space of the average apartment in Hong Kong, which has no attic or basement for storage, it is a wonder that the accumulation of old and new clothes has not overflowed into the hallways and streets. It is said that quite a few women rent storage cubicles to hoard their new purchases. Which brings us to the third requirement of daily life: dwelling.

BOTH DWELLING and transportation are shaped by one crucial condition in Hong Kong: population density. According to an SAR government publication, *Hong Kong in Figures* (2007), the population density as of 2006 was as follows: Hong Kong island, 15,920 people per square kilometer; Kowloon, 43,030 people per square kilometer; the New Territories and off-shore islands, 3,750 people per square kilometer. More staggering figures can be found in the central urban districts, where Mong Kok held the world's record, at 130,000 people per square kilometer in 2005. Density was even greater in the 1980s in some parts of Kowloon: Sham Shui Po reached 165,445 people per square kilometer, and the old Kowloon Walled City, while small, reached the equivalent of 1,934,563 people per square kilometer before it was demolished at the end of the decade.[2]

The direct consequence of putting so many people in such a small area is that living space shrinks. The story of a distinct Hong Kong "lifestyle" must therefore be told against this incredible background of population density.

An ad in Admiralty for a local fitness club.

Housing congestion within the Chinese population has always been a problem in Hong Kong. In 1874 the colonial surgeon noted the sorry state of affairs: poor ventilation and drainage, the lack of toilets, pigs running all over town and kept in houses, their "urine dropping through from floor to floor." He gave the following description and figures: "The average size of the main rooms is 26 feet by 14 feet by 10 feet high, containing eight partitions, averaging 7 feet by 6 feet by 8 feet high, over which a sort of loft is often built to increase the accommodation, and in a room of this description, from 16 to 25 people live."[3]

In 1882 the famous Chadwick Report (by Osbert Chadwick) noted that "the population of 106,000 of urban Hong Kong (including non-Chinese) in 1881 occupied 6,402 houses, averaging 16.6 persons per house," and the Tai Ping Shan area represented the extreme of congestion. As the historian David Faure narrates, Chadwick went into four Tai Ping Shan houses for close inspection and counted "between 10 to 11 people in each basement that was occupied, and between 14 and 20 people on the second floor. Where the ground was not used as a shop, it housed up to 30 people." The village houses in Kowloon were not much better: the total living space per person was 437.5 cubic feet.[4]

Despite all the ordinances issued by the Sanitation Bureau, the situation may have become worse in the twentieth century. Most Chinese people in Hong Kong—except colonial officials, privileged foreigners, and poor squatters—lived in tenements called *tong lou* that were built before 1935. A typical *tong lou* was three to five stories high and constructed on long narrow lots roughly 15 feet wide and 40 feet long. Most tenements were leased by floor but were further subdivided into smaller units or cubicles for subletting. Each cubicle unit was occupied by a family or several people. The minimum standard of 34.4 square feet per adult as recommended by the government in a 1935 ordinance was never met. Bunk beds of two or three tiers were the norm. An old three-story tenement in Wan Chai slept ninety people, many of them in bunks piled up in six tiers. In 1960 a family of seven living in one of these old tenements shared one cubicle with bunk beds in seven tiers. Individuals who rented bunks could have their bunk-cubicle fenced in with wire and locked, to prevent theft.[5]

The main reason for this state of affairs was the influx of more than two million refugees from China after 1949. Most of them thronged into these old tenements, and some of them made do with hastily built sheds on the roofs. Half a million people ended up living in squatter sheds throughout the region. But the colonial government was also to blame for Hong Kong's poor housing situation. For even in public housing, government ordinances simply required so many square feet of floor space and so many cubic feet of air space per unit, regardless of the sex and the number of persons living there. Life under these miserable living conditions can be glimpsed from the following description in

Homes from Yesterday, a bilingual book published in 1993: "A factory worker named Ah Kan, lived in Shangtung Street, Yau Ma Tei with a woman friend, the first tenant of a flat. They shared a double bed on the verandah, letting the rest of the flat to six families totaling 28 people. The rent was controlled and they collected about $20 per month for each cubicle and $16 for a bed space. One of the cubicles was home for a couple, their three children and a grandmother; another was home for a widow and her small daughter, her two children and her mother."[6]

The only ventilation and lighting came through the front or rear of the building and were often sacrificed in favor of domestic privacy. In newer tenements, one toilet served each floor. Very old tenements had bucket latrines instead of toilets, and communal cooking facilities were shared by several families. Because the communal kitchen proved insufficient, some of the cooking was done outside, on rickety balconies. The danger from fire was high, but residents were mentally prepared to flee at the first sign. When the massive fire broke out in the Shek Kip Mei area of Kowloon on Christmas Day, 1953, leaving nearly sixty thousand people homeless, only two people died in the blaze.[7]

In response to the Shek Kip Mei fire and to a continuing influx of people from the mainland, the government developed a new policy of clearing squatter areas and building high-rise public housing to replace the older tenements. Conditions improved somewhat in the 1960s and 1970s but not by much. Inside these new high-rise compounds, the flats were not a lot bigger than before, though the toilets and kitchens were no longer communal. Even when the size of a new apartment was squeezed down to just over 100 square feet, many people who needed housing still could not be accommodated. Various new plans and strategies—such as the Long Term Housing Strategy, the Metroplan, and the Land Development Corporation—were announced in the 1980s.

The trend today is toward enlarging the new satellite cities to make more and more middle-income housing available. Two rings of new towns have already emerged: an inner arc composed of Tsuen Wan, Sha Tin, and Tseung Kwan O, and an outer arc composed of Tuen Mun, Tin Shui Wai. Yuen Long, Sheung Shui, Fanling, and Tai Po. These cities were all rural villages only two decades

A tenement in Central, viewed from the Mid-Levels pedestrian escalator.

ago. Over the past half century it has taken, on average, only twenty minutes to build a domestic unit in Hong Kong, and as of May 2006 approximately half of the population lived in over one million units of public housing.[8]

The housing situation in Hong Kong is made worse by real estate prices, which are among the highest in the world. Half of the annual income of middle-class families is spent to make mortgage payments. But this fact does not stem the trend toward real estate speculation, which causes the prices of housing in choice areas to rise even higher. Since local banks offer low or no interest on savings, housing has become a form of investment for the middle class. For those who can obtain mortgages, buying real estate seems to be the best place to put their money. It is very common for a family to buy more than one flat, but this move also exposes them to great risks. In times of economic depression when the housing market has plummeted, as it did during the years right after Hong Kong's handover to China, a large number of people became "negative property owners"—a euphemism for owing more on a mortgage than the real estate is worth. After 2004 the market turned around and the housing craze set in again. Advertisements with pictures of luxurious interior décor or fantastic vistas, complete with near-naked twenty-somethings frolicking in swimming pools, were found on the front pages of daily newspapers.

This wildly fluctuating housing market dictates the mood and lifestyle of many Hong Kong residents. The uninitiated are enticed by aristocratic-sounding names for these expensive buildings—Court, Gardens, or Mansion—although the reality is nothing but another cookie-cutter high-rise. While some of these properties are in more scenic spots such as Discovery Bay on Lantau Island, most new construction is still concentrated in urban "jungles of cement" (*shek shi sum lam*). The Cantonese vernacular for cement, *shek shi*, means literally "rock shit."

Often, these new residential towers are not much different from the shopping malls built alongside them. By forming artificial communities that provide residents' daily necessities, the mall and interconnected housing compounds replicate in microcosm the model of the satellite city and in fact become its basic "town" unit. The buildings are so squeezed together that there is almost no breathing space. In relatively older housing compounds, the lack of sufficient ventilation and unsanitary conditions make them easy targets for disease. Amoy Gardens in Kowloon was one of these, and when the SARS epidemic broke out there in 2003, more than two hundred residents eventually died.

Hong Kong's vertical architecture is the byproduct of necessity. No matter how much new land is reclaimed or developed, sufficient living space seems always to be lacking. In a book titled *Hong Kong Style*, Mathias Woo launched a devastating critique of Hong Kong's "non-style" in high-rise architecture: "Hong Kong has become a prison of cement jungles for 7 million people. All of Hong Kong is filled with uniform malls and uniform big-sized and expensive residential buildings . . . Hong Kong has only the present, but no future. Rents can rise to unlimited heights. Investment is for the opportunistic." Woo blames everything on a government policy that uses money as its only yardstick and short-term profit as its only goal.[9]

Despite these negative and depressing views, communal life in high-rise housing projects does not present a picture of urban *anomie*. The reason lies in the residents' maximum use of all kinds of public space. While neighbors seldom know or talk to each other, even when they live next door (the double doors to apartments are made of wood and steel and locked from both inside and outside), they share the same neighborhood parks, which despite their generally small size are made to serve multiple functions of rest, recreation, physical exercise, and communal socialization. (In more secluded luxurious housing compounds, the club house and other common spaces offer these amenities.) Children play with one another, and people walking their dogs have a chance to chat. Socialization is also enhanced by human interaction in the neighborhood wet markets, where housewives talk amicably to their butchers and vegetable vendors and to one another.

Perhaps a bit of personal experience could serve as illustration. In 2001 my wife and I lived for one year in an apartment in a faculty housing compound on Sha Wan Drive on Hong Kong island. Each weekend we would take the minibus to nearby Kennedy Town, where we would have a traditional breakfast of Cantonese gruel in a street-corner food stand or eggs and toast at McDonald's (usually occupied on weekend mornings by elders from the neighborhood, who use it as their public forum or chat-room). We would then enter the wet market to buy groceries. We were often detained for conversation by the ever-friendly vendors, but we never haggled over prices, which were very reasonable. The whole ritual outing took no more than two or three hours, but it served to sustain our spirit for a whole week.

Indeed, one of the great ironies of living in Hong Kong—and an open secret for all residents and old-timers—is that some parts of this super-modern metropolis still preserve the "feel" of a local village. This atmosphere is produced by both the population density and the persistence of local traditions. To be sure,

Elders in Kowloon Park doing morning exercises.

Residents of Mong Kok gather at their local wet market.

the inevitable family tensions coupled with the pressure of long work days sometimes results in domestic violence and increased rates of certain mental illnesses such as depression. On the other hand, general life expectancy (according to figures from 2006) has increased in recent times: it is 79.5 years (up from 78.4 in 2001) for men, and 85.6 years (up from 84.6 in 2001) for women.[10] The fact of longer life expectancies adds to the pressure on housing, and to a small but growing demand for facilities tailored to an aging population.

THE MOST SALIENT characteristic of Hong Kong's lifestyle is the everyday mobility of its residents. Unlike Americans living in the suburbs, people who live in Hong Kong can seldom be found at home. Because of limited housing space, home nowadays is mostly a place for sleep, and young couples seldom cook meals for themselves. This is partly because of the long hours they work and partly because of a mobile lifestyle that does not revolve around the family home. People are constantly going places: to work, to eat, to shop, to meet friends or business contacts, to be entertained at movies or the racetrack or concert hall.

The number of passenger journeys via public transportation in 2006 totaled over 4 *billion*.[11] In March 2007 the MTR subway alone carried a daily load of 2.5 million passengers, for a twelve-month total of 871 million riders. There are 5,900 public buses in service, with an annual load of 406 million passengers.[12] Not to mention countless minibuses (their statistics are not available) forming a network that supplements the main bus lines and allows passengers to get on board anywhere along the route, just by flagging down the minibus. Such heavy use by 92 percent of the total population is a testament to the government's resounding success in solving the transportation problem with the most efficient and convenient system in the world. The all-purpose Octopus card, purchased from machines in subway stations, can be applied to all forms of public transportation, from trams to minibuses, and can also be used to make purchases in many small chain stores.

Movement means always negotiating for space and rushing for time. People rush into elevators and immediately push "close door" before pushing the floor button, just to gain a few seconds. The subways and trains leave every three or four minutes—and every minute or so during rush hours—and yet they are perpetually crammed. Signs urge riders to stand "behind yellow lines" on the platform, but invariably they rush into the compartments as soon as the doors open. This rush mentality establishes a tempo of *perpetuum mobile* for Hong Kong's dynamic lifestyle.

In *Culture Shock! A Survival Guide,* the veteran Hong Konger Betty Wei argues that this "need to rush" is an expression of the city's drive "to get ahead of everybody else in every endeavor . . . It is not only that people feel it essential to arrive at their destinations in a hurry, they actually need to get there ahead of everybody else. This is called one-upmanship. Western terminology perhaps, but a Hong Kong trait. At times, this quality is a positive and necessary one; it is what leads Hong Kong to try harder, in order to gain a competitive advantage over the rest of the world."[13]

But recently this Hong Kong advantage has been challenged by other Chinese cities, which seem to be developing at an even faster pace. In the face of this stiff competition, the city has been besieged with a crisis mentality. How to maintain its tempo of sustained growth through yet another transformation—from industrialization and rapid urbanization to globalization—without losing its edge has become the paramount concern of the day. Globalization is already having an impact on Hong Kong's lifestyle. Not only are the city's businessmen moving their industries to neighboring Guangdong province, requiring them to commute between two locations, but international travel for business and pleasure is also becoming a fact of daily life for many residents. The huge new Chek Lap Kok airport is always crowded with native passengers going abroad.

Yet beneath this modern veneer of mobility and independence, with its seemingly ceaseless pursuit of the four fundamentals, is a traditional society where old values and prejudices still hold sway—in particular, family values. As Betty Wei also perceptively remarks, family ties still determine the organizational structure of some of the city's largest business enterprises, and in all Chinese households youngsters are raised to obey their parents. Three generations or more regularly gather in restaurants for noisy dinners, and modern couples continue to show their filial piety by buying apartments for their parents, rather than the other way around. The younger generation of high school and university students are seldom rebellious or independent-minded and often rely on the advice and support of their pragmatic parents, who grew up in times of real hardship. Despite racy media reports and film images, Hong Kong's juvenile delinquency rate is much lower than in the United States. But its rate of suicide is high, due to the pressures of urban living at an accelerated tempo in such a compressed space.

HAVING EXAMINED HONG KONG'S variation on the four fundamentals of Chinese life, we now take a look at the city's "workstyle" and "playstyle." When announcing his ingenious formula of "One Country, Two Systems" in 1984, Deng Xiaoping indicated, almost as an afterthought, that the Hong Kong people's "mode of life" will remain unchanged for fifty years. But the colloquial phrase Deng used to convey this was *Ma zhao pao, wu zhao tiao* or "The horses will go on running; the dancing will continue." In Deng's era, this stereotype of Hong Kong's lifestyle was quite revealing, saying more perhaps about China than Hong Kong. Now that China itself has moved into the capitalist camp—though with "Chinese characteristics"—horse-racing and dancing no longer look decadent (even in Chinese eyes) so much as outmoded.

Today, horse-racing is, for the most part, just a form of legalized gambling enjoyed mostly by aficionados from the lower classes. The upper class uses it as a social occasion. Dance halls and dance hostesses were very popular in the 1960s and 1970s in Hong Kong, as they were in Shanghai in the 1930s, but they have long since been replaced by bars and cabarets in Wan Chai and Tsim Sha Tsui, which attract a clientele of tourists and local businessmen. Nowadays the young international set congregates during their afterhours in the small bars and restaurants in Lan Kwai Fong or SoHo, and they do much less dancing than drinking. This is also one of the few places where Westerners and Chinese mix and socialize. A film made in the 1980s titled *From 9 to 5* describes the bar scene at Lan Kwai Fong with considerable daring. It was a Hong Kong variation on the American television hit series *Sex and the City* (which was also shown

Patrons disembarking at a busy bar in Central.

on Hong Kong TV). The characters in the novel *Women in Kazuo Wear* (published around the same time) also frequent bars in Lan Kwai Fong. Today, the chic appeal of this area has waned somewhat. It is just a convenient place for relaxation and social gathering, situated at the heart of the CBD.

The standard time frame "9 to 5" no longer applies to most Hong Kong office workers. It is now more like "8 to 6 or 7" and can be even longer for civil service bureaucrats. The former chief executive Tung Chee-hwa used to joke that his own daily work schedule was something like "7 to 11"—sixteen hours a day and still not enough. In spring 2006 the new chief executive, Donald Tsang, announced that the six-day work schedule for all civil service personnel will be shortened to five days a week, and in the hot summer months bureaucrats should dress casually and forgo ties. To save energy, Tsang also decreed that the temperature in air-conditioned offices should be set higher, to 24.5 degrees centigrade (76 degrees Fahrenheit). But no one seems to observe the ruling. Offices and public transportation vehicles in the city, as well as hotels and malls, are still very cold inside. Visitors are advised to take a jacket, especially during the hot summer months.

The long working hours, like the need-to-rush mentality, are supposed to exemplify another Hong Kong ethos, *bok ming* (literally "Fight for your life"), which can be rendered in vernacular English as "Work your ass off." The phrase is invoked frequently as an overall description of the Hong Kong workstyle, the goal of which is *wan chin* or "Make money." The equation *Work = Money* is self-evident in Hong Kong and needs no justification. For many natives, a sufficient explanation for the "Hong Kong miracle" is, very simply, collective hard work. It was not the wisdom of British colonists but the work ethic of the colonized that made Hong Kong what it is today.

Among the short breaks for relaxation during the long work day, the afternoon tea break is *de rigeur*. It accounts for the persistence of the English colonial custom of high tea and the popularity of the teahouse. In the late afternoon, around 4, the teahouses and noodle shops fill up with customers, as do the coffee shops in hotel lobbies and elsewhere, which offer a special fixed-price "tea set" of pastries together with tea or coffee. With their energy recharged after the break, Hong Kong workers resume their posts until the late hours.

Those who are always busy also use the break for social engagements. The din of *king gai* (the colloquial term for conversation) can be deafening, especially in Cantonese, as "orality" translates from food to talk. Foreign visitors often complain about the noise level in Hong Kong's restaurants. The reason lies not only in the physical layout of most local restaurants, in which a maximum number of tables are placed in all usable spaces—thus you have to yell in order to be heard—but also in the collective propensity to talk constantly, often at a shout. The British etiquette of polite reserve and quiet conversation at meals and high tea is never observed, except perhaps in expensive hotels. On the positive side, the energy level of Hong Kong residents can be gauged by their loud banter over meals, their constantly ringing cell phones, and their endless phone conversations while riding in public transportation or walking in pedestrian corridors or shopping malls—always in a rush, of course. The rate of cell phone ownership in Hong Kong is among the highest in the world: in 2006 there were 115 registered cell phones for every 100 residents.

The official calendar in Hong Kong includes a large number of holidays, not only the usual Western ones like Christmas, New Year's, and Easter but also the Lunar New Year, Moon Festival, Mid-Autumn Festival, and Buddha's Birthday, not to mention the prescribed national holidays. This custom seems to contradict the ethos of hard work and long hours, except that the annual vacation time allotted to most office workers (including school teachers and university professors) is relatively short, normally three weeks or less. Thus the tourist arriving in Hong Kong in August, for instance, would never encounter a city half-empty, with most of the locals on vacation, as in Paris. However, during the Lunar New Year vacation period (one to two weeks in late January or early February), a large number of Hong Kong residents go abroad or to China to visit relatives. Holiday travel also takes place during the Christmas and New Year's season.

One of the most common forms of recreation and play is *hang gai* or "walking the streets." The term has become a misnomer, however: the streets are so congested with automobile traffic that people tend to walk "indoors," along the elevated footbridges and corridors that connect buildings throughout the city and in the endless multilevel shopping malls. Since dwelling space is so small for most people, they prefer to go out and wander around town after working long hours in the office. This walk habit is a far cry from what walking has meant to many Western philosophers and artists, who take the opportunity to ponder subjective space or view different urban vistas. Local walkers in Hong Kong rarely look up, since the skyline is dotted with so many high-rises of similar shape. And indoors, they are always looking around at the myriad shop windows. Since mall space is also crowded, walkers bump into one another with total nonchalance. "Excuse me" in either English or Chinese is seldom uttered, only an occasional "Sorry." The rush mentality seems to have extended to walking and wandering as well.

To speak of "commodity fetishism" in Hong Kong is to utter a tautology, because every inch of land is filled with commodity, and fetishism is ubiquitous. Desire is aroused constantly by the omnipresent advertisements that feature alluring images of mostly Western models, male and female, as well as brandnames in English and Chinese. The signs and advertisements in the more expensive malls are almost exclusively in English. But Chinese natives are inured to the semantic or semiotic references in this spectacle. The astute shopper is attuned only to the "sale" signs—also in English, and placed in the corner of shop windows. Once I passed a sign that said: "Warning—Sale Going On!" As expected, a large crowd had gathered inside. Shopping has become the *basso continuo* of life in Hong Kong—as commonplace as eating at teahouses. And like the ubiquitous teahouses, countless street bazaars and cheap shops can be found in every district. The prevalent word to describe this behavior in Hong Kong is "consumption" (*siu fai*), which encompasses all aspects of life.

The verb "play" (*wan*) can be used in so many ways in Hong Kong that it is perhaps the most common word in the local cultural vocabulary. The closely related phrase is *ho wan* or "playable" or playful. Almost anything—from stocks to postmodern theory—can be played with and is therefore playable or even playful. Play is both the companion of and antidote to work; and like work, it is also a motivating force behind Hong Kong's lifestyle. In Hong Kong's popular culture, from movies to advertisements, hardly anything "serious" has appeared since the "suffering" 1950s and 1960s. The former Executive Chief Tung Chee-hwa introduced the official slogan "Tomorrow will be better," but the average Hong Konger seems only to believe in the present, and the thing to do is to seize the moment. This may be the postmodern condition globally right now, but Hong Kong seems to go a step further than most.

One of the most popular forms of play and entertainment can be found on local radio. A variety of talk shows go on from early morning till midnight on all radio stations and are listened to by all classes of people, but especially taxi and minibus drivers. One program consists entirely of nonstop talking about stocks, while another call-in program focuses on psychological counseling. Orality as social and cultural practice is carried to the extreme in this medium. The discussions no longer venture into politics, however, after a few talk shows that were heavily critical of the government were forced off the air for one reason or another. Hong Kong critics see no need to behave as though their ideas could influence government decisions; the talk is all play.

Politicians also play with the legislative process, some more seriously than others. The government under Donald Tsang is so adroit in playing the media that the newly formed Civic Party, a serious political entity whose founding members include some of Hong Kong's most well-known lawyers, simply cannot get favorable coverage. Public marches and demonstrations are always orderly, even carnivalesque. Demonstrators are seldom passionate or angry like their counterparts in Taiwan. But perhaps the demonstrators have underestimated their power. Tung Chee-hwa's resignation in 2004 was attributed to the unexpectedly large numbers of demonstrators, more than half a million, who turned out on July 1, 2003, to force the government to withdraw its unwelcome proposal of Article 23, which stipulated certain restrictions (for reasons of national security) on people's freedom of expression. The success of the demonstration actually took everyone by surprise, most of all the marchers themselves. It seems as if "playing" is the only choice left for people whose political destiny is already decided and whose democratic form of government is now under close watch by the Beijing government. Even the clamor for direct elections seems to get nowhere. Thus, the legislators (about half of whom were not elected) can only play with politics.

The most recent media spectacle was the unprecedented television debate in March 2006 between Tsang and his opponent, Civic Party legislator Alan Leung. Following closely the model of American presidential debates, the two candidates performed twice in front of TV cameras, which were watched by the general population. The polls showed that while Leung's performance was ranked slightly higher than Tsang's, a much higher percentage of those polled (a sampling of about eight hundred people) intended to vote for Tsang, the Beijing-appointed chief designate and assured winner, who then thanked the Hong Kong people tearfully for their support. As one local columnist, Lee Yee, writing for the mass circulating newspaper *Apple Daily*, remarked: "I was never allowed to vote for you, why thank me?"

Perhaps the most representative figure of play in Hong Kong is the film star Stephen Chow, whose string of comedies have been box office hits. In two of them, which became wildly popular among college students in China, Chow plays the famous trickster Monkey in a free two-part adaptation of the classic Chinese novel *The Journey to the West* called *A Chinese Odyssey* (1994). A few lines of monologue that Chow concocted almost in passing—a kind of personal confession on love—are now regarded as "classic" and recited by Chinese students in several dialects. I was once invited to share a public forum with Chow at the University of Hong Kong, which the organizers billed as a confrontation "between modernism and postmodernism." Of course Chow, playing to a packed crowd of cheering students, pleaded ignorance of all this academic nonsense and left all the explaining to me.

Chow was the initiator of a kind of comic spoof called *mo lei tau* or "nonsensical" games. The nonsense from his comedies makes sense only in the local context, as he pokes fun at a string of screen heroes, from the king of gamblers to the god of eating, from mafia rebel to government cop. He even fashioned his own version of a super-spy, a Chinese 007 agent, in a film spoof titled *From Beijing with Love* (1994), who turns out to be a country bumpkin and a butcher. Chow scored two recent triumphs in *Shaolin Soccer* (2001) and *Kung-Fu Hustle* (2004). Somehow he has succeeded in capturing the heartbeat of his local audience. He has knowingly or unknowingly hit upon a central paradox underlying popular culture in Hong Kong: to play is the only way to be engaged.

Ironically, in person Chow is a shy actor who has worked very hard on each of his recent movies. Laughter is a serious business for him, but it must be elicited from the audience in a deadly playful mode. No other filmmaker anywhere, with the possible exception of Jerry Lewis, has approached Chow's irreverent sense of humor. But unlike Lewis or Charlie Chaplin or Buster Keaton, Stephen Chow never plays dumb in his movies; he always manages to outsmart and outwit everybody around him. He is the one and only "anti-hero" that Hong Kong has ever produced, but you have to know the local Cantonese dialect with all its colloquial idioms to appreciate his devastating jokes, which otherwise sound rather silly. For outsiders, Hong Kong comedy is definitely an acquired taste.

THE SPOKEN LANGUAGE for the largest majority of Hong Kong's Chinese population is Cantonese, a regional dialect that has several variations, including Toi San and Hakka, all within Guangdong province. These dialects are the hallmarks of a regionalism that still prevails in southern China today. Mandarin, China's national language, was not common in Hong Kong partly because its earliest residents were mostly lower-class immigrants from Guangdong and not official degree-holders (mandarins).

The Cantonese dialect has nine instead of the standard four tones of Mandarin, and therefore it is a more melodious vehicle for folk songs and opera. Cantonese opera is arguably the most significant and pervasive form of popular culture in the entire Lingnan or southern Guangdong region, and in Hong Kong it found its most splendid expression. Called *tai hei* (literally grand opera), it was itself an amalgam of several local operatic forms, including Peking opera and Kunqu, the operatic tradition from the Suzhou area. Cantonese opera also inherited a rich tradition of dramatic stories from the Yuan and Ming dynasties (thirteenth to seventeenth centuries).

In the villages, performances took place on bamboo platforms erected for festivals, especially those associated with the birthdays of folk gods. Often the whole village would flock to these performances, as it was believed that the raucous sound produced by percussion instruments could scare away ghosts. Collective exorcism was one way of forging and reforging communal cohesion. Predictably, it was this village form, called *sen gong hei* or operas honoring the merits or birthdays of gods, that was transported to Hong Kong in the early nineteenth century. It is still performed today at festive occasions in the local communities, especially in islands such as Cheung Chau and Ping Chau.

For early immigrants who maintained their village identity even while living in Victoria City, opera performances, like religious rituals, helped perpetuate a collective memory that sustained their culture. This is perhaps true of all folk operas, but in colonial Hong Kong it had a special poignancy for a people who were serving alien rulers. The main repertoire of Cantonese opera consisted of martial arts scenes and stories drawn from historical legends. The festive performances could last for several evenings. Customarily, the inaugural opera performed was *The Minister for Six States*, the story of a famous ancient Chinese diplomat, Su Qin, who managed to form an alliance of six states against the powerful Qin empire in the second century BC. No one knows for sure why this particular opera was chosen as the first one to perform. One theory is that its ceremonial setting provides a perfect opportunity for all the actors and actresses to line up on stage and display their costumes and postures. But might one detect a deeper meaning in the opera's diplomatic motif, and even a repressed nationalism? No one has ventured such an interpretation.

With the influx of richer immigrants in the mid-nineteenth century, the repertoire expanded and indoor theaters were built. The first building devoted entirely to Cantonese opera was constructed in the early 1870s, on Po Hing Fong, at the center of the Chinese quarter in Central. Other theaters were built in the next two decades. One of the most famous was Ko Shing, at the corner of Hollywood Road and Queen's Road West. The Tai Ping theater was in the Shek Tong Tsui area in the midst of brothels. Both theaters were modern constructions that could seat a thousand people.

In 1890, when Prince George V visited Hong Kong, a lavish banquet was held in his honor in Ko Shing theater, probably accompanied also by a special performance of Cantonese opera. By this time Hong Kong no longer relied on traveling troupes from Canton; local theaters had their own resident troupes. By the early twentieth century, Cantonese opera had become the most celebrated of local traditions, boasting a large roster of male and female performers. Its popularity has continued, despite vicissitudes of war and revolution, down to the present.

In the face of competition from pop songs or movie tunes, which attract large young audiences, and despite a shortage of performing venues—the old theaters have all been torn down or renovated into movie theaters or apartment buildings—Cantonese opera not only survives but constantly renews its traditions and modernizes its performance practices. In 2006 a revival of a seldom-performed opera was the major event and talk of the town. In that same year, a memorial concert for a famous opera star, Yam Kim Fai, an actress who played male roles, was staged by some of Hong Kong's most talented young artists in other fields of endeavor. They all willingly donated their time and effort to honor the memory of Yam and the actress Pak Suet Sin, her surviving partner in art and life. This celebrated female couple, both household names, seemed to embody all that was precious and glorious in the performance history of Cantonese opera in Hong Kong.

How does one account for the persistence of this traditional form of popular art in a modern metropolis? Certainly it testifies to the dynamism of a native culture that refuses to be overwhelmed by globalization. Perhaps, also, it owes its popularity to the "uneven" development of Hong Kong's modernization itself. While some sectors like the CBD or Mid-Levels are highly developed and Western-oriented, other areas and people—for instance, in the northern districts of Kowloon and in the New Territories—are still deeply traditional and protective of their entrenched customs and rituals. Still, the appeal of Cantonese opera cannot be explained entirely by geography or anthropology. It goes deeper and seems to be the *only* popular form that unites the local Hong Kong population, regardless of age, gender, or class.

Even today, Cantonese opera performances by professional and especially amateur groups are still well attended. Social gatherings of its aficionados for an evening or afternoon of singing are even more frequent. The linked names of Yan and Pak have attained legendary status, and Pak has received several honorary degrees from Hong Kong universities. Their recordings and films, now remastered as CDs and DVDs, continue to sell well. Cantonese opera holds sway wherever there are enough Cantonese people around to fill a theater—not only in Hong Kong but also in the Chinese communities of Singapore and North America.

Writers rather than composers hold the key to this art form, perhaps because its music is derived from a set of established tune patterns. The most honored of all writers is Tong Tik Sang (1916–1959), who adapted the stories and lyrics from classical masterpieces of drama and fiction, especially from Ming and Qing times. Tong's great achievement lies in his inimitable style, which combines poetic elegance in the arias—all written in the classical poetry and *ci* forms—with a lively vernacular in the spoken dialogues. It compares with the best poetry and prose of the Chinese vernacular tradition.

Tong did some of his best work for the company of Yam and Pak. Definitely the all-time favorite is *The Emperor's Daughter*. This story is taken from history: the last Ming emperor committed suicide before the dynasty fell to the rebels and the Qing conquerors. His one surviving daughter and her betrothed demanded a proper burial of her father and then committed suicide themselves. In the final act, their suicide is enacted on their wedding night, as the couple sing their last duet while drinking poison, just before consummating the marriage. This is probably the most memorable scene in the entire repertoire of Cantonese opera—aficionados can recite its passages by heart. Even the tomb scene in Verdi's *Aida* cannot compare with its emotive power.

Not only did this particular opera endear itself to the audience via the exquisite performances of Yam and Pak but it became, as one local scholar has put it, a parable for the history of Hong Kong itself. Indeed, it can be said that Hong Kong fell to two successive waves of foreign conquerors: first to British colonials in 1842, then to the Japanese invaders a century later. Some would add a third conqueror, China, when it took over Hong Kong in 1997—certainly many local opera lovers, who consider themselves the most self-defensive of Hong Kong's population, seem to share this sentiment.

Hong Kong has almost always been linked to Canton in the popular imagination. In addition to Cantonese opera, much of Hong Kong's early popular culture and many of its folk legends came from that mainland city. For example, the martial arts hero Wong Fei Hong is as celebrated in Hong Kong as he is in Canton. After appearing and reappearing in countless Cantonese movies and television dramas, he finally became an international hero in the successful series of films called *Once Upon a Time in China*. Wong, a doctor and a martial arts hero (as played by the famous *kung-fu* star Jet Li), is seen moving freely between Canton and Hong Kong and taking an active part in fighting the French navy, British colonials, Manchu noblemen, and local Chinese officials. In one version he befriends Sun Yat-sen and shows off his knowledge of traditional Chinese herbal med-

Top: Chinese opera performance for the Hungry Ghost Festival in Sheung Wan, 1997.
Left: Hong Kong Cantopop star Andy Hui, making an entrance.

icine, along with his skill in the martial arts.

Aside from opera, the musical genre that most closely links Hong Kong to its sister city on the mainland is Cantopop—popular songs sung in Cantonese. Performances by famous Cantopop singers invariably fill up the ten thousand seats of Hung Hom stadium, often for several evenings. What accounts for the widespread impact of iconic stars of Cantonese opera or Cantopop on the popular imagination in Hong Kong—an impact that goes beyond that of any politician or billionaire?

Star attraction is a universal phenomenon that needs no explanation, but Hong Kong pop stars are icons with more aura than usual and with longer shadows after they leave the stage. Famous pop singers often go on to become movie stars. In the 1980s the so-called "four super-kings" of popdom—Andy Lau, Leon Lai, Jacky Cheung, and Aaron Kwok—all starred in feature-length films. The list of female singers who launched movie careers is even longer. Anita Mui became known not only for her distinct alto voice but for her unique style of acting. The same can be said of the gay singer-actor Leslie Cheung, whose performance in Chen Kaige's film *Farewell My Concubine* (1993) left an indelible impression on audiences worldwide. Both Mui and Cheung acted in the trilogy *A Better Tomorrow*: Cheung in the first two films, Mui in the last. After they died, one following the other in 2003 and 2004, they were honored at spectacular funerals and mourned like national heroes.

Like the Beatles for the generation of the 1960s, Cheung and Mui epitomized the 1980s, when both Cantopop and film-making reached an apex of popularity. Cheung's flaunting of a bisexual persona on stage and screen—he even played a gay role in Wong Kar-wai's film *Happy Together* (1997)—must be seen as more than a titillating publicity stunt. It brings to mind the memory of Yam Kim Fai, the actress who personified the traditional elegant male scholar roles in Cantonese opera. But Cheung in modern dress stands for more: an openly gay icon who seems to attract both male and female followers and whose staged sexual confusion bespeaks the larger identity issues of his Hong Kong audience.

A different bisexual persona is projected onto the movie screen by Anita Mui, an excellent actress with a rare sense of personal integrity. Her personal life was marked by tragedy, however: she died of uterine cancer because she refused an operation that would have left her unable to bear children.

The circumstances surrounding Leslie Cheung's death were also tragic: apparently he suffered from long-standing depression and jumped to his death from the top of the Mandarin Hotel in Central on April Fool's Day, 2003, in the midst of the SARS epidemic. News of his suicide traumatized the entire population. Every year since, on the anniversary of his death, flowers have appeared on the very spot where he died in front of the hotel. For people in their thirties and forties, this is the key historical landmark on any map of the CBD.

In the 1950s and 1960s, a host of film stars, mostly women, had become top box-office draws for Shaw Brothers and Cathay after making their debut as singers of popular Mandarin songs. But beginning in the 1970s, Cantonese singers replaced Mandarin singers, and some of the latter even switched over and learned to sing in Cantonese. Every hit song or movie theme song in Cantonese that touched the collective psyche quickly reached iconic status. For example, Lo Man, who died in 2001, was always known for his singing of the theme song from the TV series "Under the Lion Rock," and as such he became the "spokesman" of the period in the 1970s when Hong Kong emerged from the shadows of poverty. James Wong, an irreverent songwriter and singer who is sometimes called a father of Cantopop, wrote the theme song for the Wong Fei Hong film series and other hit tunes that somehow captured the popular imagination. His death in 2005 was mourned like the passing of a legend.

Thus, each decade in Hong Kong's recent past has had its representative icons in Cantopop, which in turn have perpetuated the popular memory of that era. This has become a kind of oral tradition. To be sure, memory always tends to enlarge the contemporary significance of a few icons; the majority of pop singers have long disappeared from the scene, their meteoric careers—often created by the media—long since forgotten. The current crop of young Cantopop singers, from Faye Wong (now fading from the scene) to the Twins, Edison Chen, Andy Hui, and Nicholas Tse, appeals mostly to a younger audience. The subject of their lyrics is largely a paean to the pains of love. And like their predecessors, they have also embarked on movie careers. Yet how long their popularity will last in the memory of a generation whose attention span seems to be shortened by the daily onslaught of Japanese cartoons and computer games is anyone's guess. This latest crop of singers are more "packaged" products, known for their looks and bodies rather than their singing. The interplay between local and global forces of commercialism and consumption will largely determine their fate.

IS THERE ANY "HIGH CULTURE" to speak of in Hong Kong? Indeed there is, and it has been woefully neglected by outsiders. To give some noteworthy examples, more than one hundred drama troupes of all sizes make their home in the city, and the government-funded Hong Kong Repertory Theater tours around the world, most recently in Toronto, New York, and Beijing, with its own adaptation of Eileen Chang's famous short story, "Love in a Fallen City." This combination of play and musical performed in Cantonese earned acclaim even among the serious-minded critics of Beijing. The group's most recent world premiere is the play *Blindness*, based on a Chinese translation of the novel by the Portuguese Nobel Prize winner José Saramago.

In the classical music scene, Hong Kong boasts two orchestras—the Hong Kong Philharmonic with music director and conductor Edo de Waart, and the Hong Kong Sinfonietta, formed by local musicians and conducted by Yip Wing Sie, a woman who was born in Hong Kong. The Chinese Classical Orchestra of more than eighty musicians playing traditional Chinese instruments competes vigorously with the well-funded HKPO and the local-favorite Sinfonietta for box-office share. The annual Hong Kong Arts Festival from late February to early April presents scores of programs ranging from opera and symphonic music to drama, jazz, ballet, tango, and Cantonese opera. The Arts Festival is immediately followed by the annual International Film Festival in April and May, with more than a hundred films from all over the world. In 2005 a documentary featuring a lecture monologue by the Slovenian theorist and academic Slavoj Žižek drew a long line of ticket buyers. In the 2006 festival, another film starring Žižek, called *The Pervert's Guide to the Cinema*, sold out well in advance. No one can predict exactly what programs will attract which clientele, but some kind of audience always shows up for any avant-garde program, especially film. Hong Kong is without a doubt one of the most film-conscious cities in the world.

Cinema and the performing arts certainly dominate other art forms in Hong Kong. The city's fourteen museums cannot compare with those in most major European cities, and museum attendance is low, about five million people per year. Art galleries tend to be scattered about in Central, and when Hong Kong artists participate in the Venice Biennale, they receive little notice from local media. The multimedia performing troupe Zuni, under the leadership of Danny Yung and Mathias Woo, has spearheaded many innovative programs and played a central role in cultural exchanges with Berlin, Shanghai, and Taipei. Zuni leaders are also among the most outspoken critics of the government's cultural policy.

Hong Kong's "culture wars" are fought in a totally different way than those in the United States. Instead of race, gender, ethnicity, and religion, the battle lines are drawn rather between two social strata with different cultural tastes. On the one hand are the clusters of artists and critics of an avant-gardist persuasion (many of whom are openly gay) who promote "alternative" lifestyles and programs. On the other hand are the rich and conservative patrons of "high art" served by a government sub-bureaucracy called the Department of Leisure and Cultural Services. The title is revealing: culture is officially consigned under "leisure" and intended, it seems, to provide at most a diversion or pastime from people's busy lives. The bureaucrats seem to be at a loss about how to plan for the city's future, culturally. The government appoints special committees and arts councils to parcel out funds in support of the arts, but there is no Department of Culture or National Endowment of the Arts in charge. That absence is a colonial legacy.

A recent fiasco—the plan to develop a West Kowloon Cultural District— serves as an illustrious example of the government's failure to envisage a role for high culture in the life of the city. Around the year 2000 Donald Tsang (even before he became chief executive) had the ingenious idea of luring real estate tycoons into a project to turn a large piece of government land in West Kowloon into a new cultural zone, complete with museums, theaters, concert halls, and a large stadium. In exchange, a percentage of the land would be parceled out to the winning developer to build deluxe apartments. The rationale was simple: since the presence of high culture would raise housing prices, any developer allowed to build apartments at this choice location should contribute to the cost of high culture.

A competition was duly held in 2001 to select the best "conceptual plan" of the entire West Kowloon Cultural District. A committee finally selected the winning designer, Sir Norman Foster, the world-renowned architect who had recently designed the new airport and, earlier, the HSBC—a fact that led some local critics to argue that postcolonial Hong Kong was rapidly becoming "Fostertown." Foster's plan was to build a huge glass canopy that would cover the entire area. The canopy in Foster's model looked rather like a dragon, a fitting symbol for Kowloon (Nine Dragons), but otherwise this preliminary concept was rather vague on the details.

What made Foster's plan ultimately unworkable was the cost. Developers, especially in Hong Kong, care about profit, period. Culture makes no sense unless it makes business sense. The calculations of Hong Kong's real estate tycoons were focused on the percentage of land allowed for building top-price residences, and on how long they would have to wait in order to turn a profit, after building all the cultural facilities. At least twenty years or more, according to one calculation by an outside consultant. That is a long repayment time frame by Hong Kong standards, but the big developers were willing to play along, for a while. Since no single company was rich or ambitious enough to shoulder the whole responsibility, the various competitors organized themselves into three teams for the bidding game.

At this point, in 2005, the public was invited to participate. With great fanfare, the government set up a special exhibition of the competing projects from the three development groups. Each group brought forth its own glittering showcases, complete with design models, brochures, and other publicity materials. It turned out that a long list of world-renowned museums and other cultural institutions had been invited to join the various groups as partners and collaborators. The critics formed their own united front and held meetings and published reports. In a way, the whole debate served to awaken Hong Kong's weak civil society. The publicity and media blitz brought some residents to look at the exhibitions, at which they were asked to fill out an elaborate questionnaire and indicate their preferences. The final result of this unscientific survey was, according to Tsang, "indeterminate."

The clamor rose to a high pitch at the end of the consultation period (which had been extended from three months to six). Even the Legislative Council, whose members had seldom concerned themselves with matters of culture, joined the fray. The government suddenly found itself on the defensive, being attacked on all fronts. Still, the real estate tycoons patiently played along. When some of the smaller companies complained about unfair treatment, the government enlarged the housing component of the master plan so that more individual businesses could get a piece of the action. But by this point neither the developers nor their critics were happy. After a year of consultation and debate, Tsang left the thorny problems to his new second-in-command, Rafael Hui, who happened to be an experienced Western opera buff. Following more meetings and forums, Hui finally decided to jettison the entire plan and start from scratch. The process had cost developers millions of dollars, all to no avail. Various consultative committees started forming again to draw up plans for another round of public consultations, which began in September 2007. No one knows when a final master plan will ever be adopted, much less implemented.

Perhaps Rem Koolhaas's concept is right after all: the "generic city" results from a failure of city planning, through some combination of serendipity and trends in global consumption. Hong Kong has already fulfilled the three basic requirements in Koolhaas's scheme: the airport (by Sir Norman, considered by many the world's best), the hotels (some of the region's best), and the malls (certainly Hong Kong is the largest mall city in the world). One day, perhaps, an extensive "culture district" will make the Hong Kong cityscape unique among Asia's urban clones. But who can say, today, what a culture district of the future should be like? Maybe its growth should be left to chance and fashion like everything else.

WHAT DOES THE FUTURE HOLD for the Hong Kong lifestyle? Will the city look more and more like Los Angeles, which many consider the new model for a contemporary global city—a "city of spectacle" and of the "play of pure imagery" that "has developed intimate tie-ins with the logic of consumption and the selling of leisure-time lifestyles"? If this statement by the architectural historian Christine Boyer turns out to be true, the future Hong Kong will be reduced to a "non-place, existing in a state of constant flux and interfaces." Such a mega-city will cease to have any cultural identity at all.[14]

To have a future, Hong Kong culture must consist of something more concrete than merely "a state of constant flux and interfaces." In my opinion, the dynamism of Hong Kong's lifestyle springs from its mix of people. Instead of a "non-place," Hong Kong is a "hybrid place," its energy derived not only from its mixture of Chinese and Western traditions on the most basic level of people's existence, such as drinking milk tea in a *cha tsan ting*, but from the constant evolution of this mixture in people's everyday lives. In the opinion of the critic Chan Koon Chung, what distinguishes Hong Kong's cultural development is its "add-on" quality. If we look at the urban landscapes from Kennedy Town to Causeway Bay on Hong Kong island and from Tsim Sha Tsui to Kowloon Tong on Kowloon peninsula, we see a dense mixture of the most fashionable and the most old-fashioned, the most commercialized malls and the most indigenous food bazaars. Small shops, residential towers, and office buildings, as well as bars and cabarets, line the streets of both Tsim Sha Tsui and Wan Chai; bookstores are neighbors to brothels in Mong Kok. These vernacular forms of cultural hybridity provide the real motive force behind Hong Kong's accepted fragmentation.

But the government, employing a logic of excessive modernization, always wants to demolish old buildings and neighborhoods and build new projects, or do more reclamation or carve out new pieces of land to build new "centers," or embark on mega-projects such as the West Kowloon Cultural District. Such logic *appears* to be based on rational urban planning, but it is actually motivated by real estate speculation. The embedded cultural traditions of a building, a neighborhood, or a place are ignored or considered unworthy of preservation or even renovation. Finding or reinventing historical meaning in an old building or market area is almost unthinkable in Hong Kong. But even as it destroys the city's old landmarks, the government is willing to spend tens of millions to build a glass canopy in the proposed West Kowloon project, in the hope that it will become a *new* landmark—all in the name of "sustained growth."

Life in Hong Kong will continue to be congested—there is no other choice. But congestion in Hong Kong does not necessarily mean chaos. Some newcomers, especially from mainland China, marvel at its order and cleanliness. While exasperated by its human multitude, they also feel intensely its humanity or *renqi* ("human air"), and they sense that it comes from the city's creative collision of cultures.

Golden Bauhinia, a handover gift to Hong Kong from the PRC, in recognition of the city's emblem, the bauhinia flower.

8

City and Country

The Western tourist who visits Hong Kong nowadays likes to include a trip to China in the itinerary, perhaps at the end of the stay. The express train from Hung Hom in Kowloon to Canton takes about two hours. Shenzhen on the border is even closer and easier to reach by local train; at the stop in Lo Wu, tourists can get a temporary visa at the border and cross over into Shenzhen. Hong Kong residents can simply insert their identity cards into the automatic machine and pass through in a matter of seconds, just as they pass through the subway entrance with their multipurpose Octopus card. Hong Kongers who go by bus or automobile stop at any of the three checkpoints and go through the formalities with minimum fuss.

Since 2003, citizens of the People's Republic can also cross more easily into Hong Kong, by taking advantage of the week-long "free tours" for shopping and sightseeing. In the malls and subways, mainland visitors are increasingly visible and, with their Mandarin voices, audible. As money and investment from China has poured in, the Hong Kong stock market has become even more frenzied. Meanwhile, more and more Hong Kong industries have relocated across the border, as businessmen invest in construction and other projects all over China. And an increasing number of Hong Kong residents have bought new homes or second homes in Shenzhen, Dongguan, or other Chinese cities near the border, where the price of housing is considerably cheaper. As border-crossing becomes a daily routine, the border itself becomes increasingly blurred.

Yet other forms of division, even resentment, still persist. A Hong Kong permanent resident is by law also a citizen of the People's Republic but carries a

Special Administrative Region (SAR) passport that provides more entry privileges to other countries than a regular PRC passport. Is this new form of dual identity merely a matter of convenience, or does it entail dual loyalties? Hong Kong's "special" status is the result of Deng Xiaoping's ingenious "One Country, Two Systems," but this simple slogan has given rise to different interpretations. The government in Beijing focuses on "one country," while many Hong Kong residents seem to fixate on "two systems." In Deng's original formulation, "two systems" referred to the two economic modes of socialism and capitalism, and the practice of capitalism as a "way of life" (*shenghuo fangshi*) in Hong Kong was guaranteed to remain unchanged for fifty years—that is, until 2047.

However, now that post-socialist China is becoming more and more like capitalist Hong Kong rather than the other way around, does it still make sense to talk about two systems? Politically, the official designation—Special Administrative Region—seems to have legitimized Hong Kong's autonomous status, but it is still under the national sovereignty of the People's Republic. Modern nationalism, in the form of the nation-state, dictates that all regional governments are subservient to the central government, in this case the PRC in Beijing. This is clearly the stance adopted by SAR officials, who think of themselves as running a provincial government, not a national one. But some politicians, including Anson Chan, the former head of civil service and former boss of Donald Tsang, want Hong Kong to be more independent. Others argue that such an attitude is unpatriotic to the "motherland."

For Hong Kong and Macau, closeness to the motherland is unavoidable, both geographically and psychologically. Their daily water supply comes mostly from the mainland, as does much of the produce for food. Cantonese is the common language in both Hong Kong and Guangdong, albeit with slight differences in idiom and accent. Above all, Hong Kong people have become increasingly concerned about everything that affects the "motherland." Every natural disaster on the mainland elicits large relief donations from Hong Kong. The tragedy of the student deaths in Tiananmen Square on June 4, 1989, may have been largely forgotten in China and elsewhere, but it is still commemorated in Hong Kong every year, as tens of thousands flock to Victoria Park and hold candlelight vigils. This

*Going Forward!
Making Money!*
Bronze sculpture
displayed near the
main entrance of the
Langham Place
Hotel in Mong Kok
(Jiang Shuo).

demonstration of a different kind of loyalty is of course considered inappropriate by both the PRC and the SAR government but they tolerate it nevertheless.

Pro-Beijing politicians urge everyone to follow the Basic Law, which, though stipulating democratic elections in principle, does not provide a clear time frame. The pro-election democrats, who sometimes join in marches and demonstrations, demand a definite date, 2012, for direct election of both the Legislative Council and the chief executive. But others favor a gradual, step-by-step schedule leading toward direct election, with definite dates set for each step. The Beijing government keeps a close eye on all this activism without making any public statement. Tsang, a pragmatic politician, openly allies himself with the pro-Beijing parties. But after his recent "election" in March 2007, he vowed to work hard for the goal of direct election—now still seemingly unattainable.

While the debate on democracy rages, most Hong Kong residents are resigned to their fate as new subjects of the People's Republic of China who cling to the "special characteristics" of their "unchanged" way of life as guaranteed by Deng Xiaoping. Hence, "lifestyle" has become the only basis of their claim for a collective identity.

TO UNDERSTAND THE ISSUE of Hong Kong identity in relation to the motherland, we must backtrack into recent history. Before it became a British colony, Hong Kong had always been a part of China—an administrative subunit in the Xin'an county of Guangdong province under the Ming and Qing dynasties and other county or district designations in earlier dynasties. In the early period of British rule, the Chinese population moved back and forth across the border to China at will. The new and alien concept of national sovereignty was introduced by Sun Yat-sen and formalized as the Chinese Republic in 1912, but it had little effect on the population in the Lingnan region, including Hong Kong. Lives there were bound up with the sea—fishing and trading, traveling and emigrating to countries near and far.

Of course Sun himself always considered Hong Kong a base of his revolutionary operations and a center of his overseas political enterprise. He invented the concept of "overseas Chinese"—people of Chinese birth or descent who lived in other nations but whose loyalty resides with China. Nationalism was above all a collective emotion, as the French historian Ernest Renan once said, which, however, had to be actively rallied for a political purpose, as Sun fully realized. Yet before the rise of nationalism, the Chinese, like other peoples, had an awareness of only their own ethnicity (the vast majority being Han Chinese) and, together with it, a sense of regionalism. The modern concept of nationalism was not inculcated into the popular consciousness until the early twentieth century, and regionalism continued to run strong, especially in areas more removed from the political center.

Thus, in Hong Kong it is relatively easy for both elite and non-elite Chinese to subscribe to two Chinese identities (national and regional), but they cannot have dual citizenship (British and Chinese). The very concept of citizenship is new and alien, a part of the package of modern nationalism. In China under the Republican regime and the PRC, a new course in "Civics" was required in the high school curriculum, the primary purpose of which was to train students to become good "citizens"; the Chinese term for both is *gongmin.* In colonial Hong Kong, such a term was never used, and no concept of citizens' rights existed.

All of that changed on April 4, 1966, when what seemed like a slight issue— a first-class fare increase on the Star Ferry—suddenly took on ominous proportions. A single youth went on a hunger strike in front of the Star Ferry to protest the fare increase. The next day he was joined by a dozen others. A socially conscientious legislator, Elsie Tu, an English woman married to a Chinese man, initiated a movement that instantly drew 200,000 signatories. When the government retaliated by arresting the demonstrators, rioting broke out in Kowloon. After forceful suppression, Governor David Trench (1964–1971) appointed a four-man committee to study the problem of unrest. Their report mentioned, albeit subtly, the deep-seated anticolonial sentiments of the native population, while ruling out strictly economic reasons for people's objections to the fare increase. Their reasoning was that most low-income passengers presumably took second-class, and so the fare increase did not affect them. Still, given the generally low standard of living endured by most of the population, it was not hard to justify the anticolonial demonstration on economic as well as political grounds.

The worsening situation came to a head in 1967, with the Cultural Revolution on the mainland. A riot, which some called an insurrection, was led by workers' unions and master-minded by leftist leaders stirred to action by Chairman Mao's proclamations inciting the Red Guards to rebel. It all started in early May in a plastic flowers factory in Kowloon, with a dispute over new wages and terms of employment. Once again leftists were involved, and police intervention gave them a ready excuse. On May 22 a group of demonstrators led by the heads of the two major leftist newspapers demonstrated in front of Government House on Upper Albert Road. Chanting anti-British slogans and reading quotations from Mao, they demanded to see the governor. The police guarded the gates and refused entry. Brutality and bloodshed were reported. Meanwhile, the leftists gained access to the top of the old Bank of China building in Central and installed a loudspeaker to broadcast anticolonial slogans. The government retaliated with Beatles songs, jazz tunes, and Cantonese opera broadcast from six loudspeakers on a nearby building.

In late June this carnival atmosphere gave way to a situation more akin to the Cultural Revolution, as the rebels, with professed support from China, organized a general strike of factory workers and students from leftist schools. When most transportation workers joined the strike, the whole city came to a standstill. What followed was a summer of chaos and terror. When an armed skirmish broke out in the border village of Sha Tau Kok in the New Territories, leftists came to believe that Hong Kong would soon be "liberated," and they intensified their activism. In mid-July, bombs exploded in the Tai Po Market, Mong Kok, Tsim Sha Tsui, and Sheung Wan. More primitive bombs were spotted in North Point and other places—some containing explosives, others merely fakes but all marked with the warning phrase: "Fellow countrymen, do not go near!" These "pineapples," as the locals nicknamed them, were placed at street corners or sometimes thrown from buildings. They caused great havoc, many casualties, and several deaths.

The turmoil turned popular sentiment in Hong Kong against the leftist rebels, as the majority of residents, feeling that their very livelihood was threatened, began to support the local government. Governor Trench claimed to have the backing of more than six hundred organizations and 98 percent of the population. Whether these statistics were accurate or not, it was clear that the ordeal suffered by Hong Kong residents propelled them to rally around the only power they could rely on, the colonial government of Hong Kong. The Communist regime had no intention of "liberating" the colony, and even the leftists eventually realized that Beijing never harbored such a plan. A *modus vivendi* with the status quo became the only solution.

The repercussions of the 1967 riot were long-lasting. It altered not only the popular mentality but the entire attitude and practice of the colonial rulers. Governor Trench may have been the right politician to handle the crisis in a steadfast fashion, but it was left to his successor, Sir Murray Maclehose, to initiate major reforms and construction projects that turned Hong Kong from a small colony into a major metropolis and from a largely rural and underdeveloped territory and "refugee society" into a modern cosmopolitan city. For the first time, the natives could claim Hong Kong as *their* city as much as a British colony. Even the governors changed their official tune and began to credit the native Chinese population as being responsible for Hong Kong's "economic miracle."

As the urban landscape began to take shape, it was also Maclehose, the architect of modernization, who actively promoted the concept of "community" for Hong Kong and put it in practice by emphasizing the communal functions of the Urban Council and its eighteen district councils. But community was a poor substitute for citizenship, especially during a time when Britain and China were undertaking negotiations for the handover of Hong Kong. Should all Hong Kong permanent residents be given British passports or attain at least the equivalent status of British Commonwealth "citizens"? Suddenly the paradox of Hong Kong as both a city without a state and a colony without a colonial master seemed to dawn on the city's residents. Ironically, this happened just at the time when Western commentators were writing books with such tantalizing and misleading titles as *Hong Kong: Borrowed Place, Borrowed Time*. Who borrowed from whom? Who are the victims of this "borrowing"? The Western perception of Hong Kong as "unsettled" only made things worse for a people who had only recently managed to settle down at home in their city.

If in the 1970s a sense of collective belonging, however vague, was taking root, this "Hong Kong as our home" feeling was undermined by the Sino-British declaration in 1984. In the next thirteen years, before the handover took effect, a sizable segment of the city's residents, mostly middle-class professionals, relocated to other English-speaking countries—Canada, the United States, Australia, and New Zealand. But by agreement with China, Great Britain made it difficult for its former colonial subjects to seek shelter there. The people of Hong Kong were caught in limbo, the result of political maneuvering by both its old and its new masters. Still, a major survey conducted by two scholars at Chinese University found that 59 percent of respondents in the 1970s considered themselves "Hongkongers" and only 36 percent thought of themselves as "Chinese."

The feeling of uncertainty about their future became more acute with the crushing of the Tiananmen student movement on June 4, 1989. The unexpected brutality of the PRC government profoundly disillusioned even some leftists. To those who had decided to stay and not emigrate, it seemed that the nightmare of the 1967 riot had returned to haunt them. The 1990s witnessed a series of soul-searching and heated discussions about the question of Hong Kong's identity. A vociferous debate on the subject ensued, with a voluminous corpus of books and articles published. The search for a Hong Kong identity reached a fever-pitch in 1997, but since the handover it has gradually subsided.

From a national perspective, a discourse on Hong Kong's identity is meaningless because political identity after 1997 can mean only one thing—Chinese citizenship. Identity as citizens of a city is at best subsidiary to the national identity. But in Hong Kong itself, a Chinese population has become increasingly attached to their city as their homeland but not necessarily to their new country. As one scholar and long-term resident, Matthew Turner, remarked in 1995: "The population of Hong Kong came to identify themselves as 'Heung Gong Yan,' an ambiguous construction that was more that of a 'resident,' less that of a 'people.' Hong Kong identity was rather the identity of life-style, a shared recognition of similar self-images, real or desired, of existential choices, from food to education, that had to be made now that Hong Kong people could no longer be guided by Chinese tradition or (since the demise of Shanghai) Chinese modernity."[1]

What exactly were these shared self-images and existential choices that Chinese residents of Hong Kong were making in the period before the handover? Back in the 1970s, Hugh Baker, an English scholar with many years of research experience in Hong Kong, had attempted to answer this question by defining the "Hong Kong Man." He was, according to Baker,

> go-getting and highly competitive, tough for survival; quick-thinking and flexible. He wears western clothes, speaks English or expects his children to do so, drinks western alcohol, has sophisticated tastes in cars and household gadgetry, and expects life to provide a constant stream of excitement and new openings. But he is not British or western (merely westernized). At the same time he is not Chinese in the same way that the citizens of People's Republic of China are Chinese. Almost alone in the Chinese world Hong Kong has not adopted Putonghua [Mandarin] as the lingua franca: instead Cantonese holds sway. Admiration for and empathy with his compatriots Hong Kong Man certainly has, but he also now has pride in and love of the society which he has created through his own determination and hard work. He gives little credit to the Union Jack under which his success has been nurtured, and he is not necessarily happy at the prospect of the five-starred red flag presiding over his activities. Hong Kong Man is sui generis and the problems of the territory's future are more difficult to resolve because of it.[2]

Baker also provided a detailed summary of housing, education, health care, work habits (fast-paced, hard-working lives for six or seven days a week), and pastimes (eating, horse-racing, gambling, cinema-going in the 1960s, and TV watching since the 1970s). But by 1997 a new Hong Kong Man was on the scene, and, according to the local writer Chan Koon Chung, his prospects were not as sanguine. Born in the early 1950s, these postwar baby-boomers were the first generation lucky enough to grow out of dire poverty into middle-class comfort, but they received little education about contemporary China in their colonial school system. The situation on the mainland, though reported every day in the print media, was not part of the school curriculum. Courses on classical Chinese literature and culture were taught in Chinese-language schools but remained marginal in the more prestigious English-language schools. This new generation, who now comprise most of the current elite in politics and commerce, had at best a partial and jaundiced view of modern China, especially its revolutionary phase. As they entered college, particularly the University of Hong Kong, their ambition was to enter Hong Kong's civil service bureaucracy or the most elite profession, medicine.

But for some members of this generation—a minority—political awareness came in their turbulent college years, when the Cultural Revolution was raging in China and leftist riots were traumatizing the population in Hong Kong. Some became fervent Maoists; others, socialists. Their patriotic idealism found no outlet, however, for the gates to China remained closed. Yet the vast majority of HKU students (Chan included) remained passive and unaffected. When they graduated, they were all able to find new jobs created by Hong Kong's rapid modernization, which provided easy opportunities to get rich, provided they worked hard. Thus the new ethos of working hard and making money was formed that also supplied the key scenario for Hong Kong's own Horatio Alger myth—of a poor kid who made good and became a millionaire by virtue of his own efforts, but under the blessings of the new economic circumstances. Chan characterized his generation as *Homo economicus*, a population driven by the engine of capitalism.

But mainly due to its land policy, Hong Kong is not a fully free market. The government owns most of the land, and according to a special appendix in the 1984 Sino-British Joint Declaration, the annual quota that can be sold is limited to 50 acres (as compared with 216 acres in 1981). This land policy not only provided 23 percent of the government's annual income but raised housing prices sky high. Thus, for the new middle-class, house-buying became a key form of investment (aside from stocks). Consequently, the wealth of a large segment of the middle class fluctuated according to the housing market, which was controlled by the government and big developers. In Chan's view, this severely limited their upward mobility and Hong Kong's economic future.

The generation that came of age in the 1970s and prospered in the 1980s was poorly prepared for the shift in the 1990s from textiles and other low-tech manufactured products to service and high-tech industries. In Chan's view, they lacked a cosmopolitan vision; their expertise was limited to the confines and rules of the profession they chose. Now past middle age, the 1970s generation found themselves at a loss. They must either retool for a new kind of economy (hence the currently prevalent term "self-enhancement") or be overtaken by a new elite: "globalizers" from abroad—a younger and different species, mostly of Chinese origin, who can no longer read or write Chinese because they were born or educated abroad since childhood. Chan is quite critical of his own generation for not preparing their children (especially those who remain in Hong Kong) for the global challenge.

Today, both Baker and Chan would find, perhaps not to their surprise, that the children of the 1970s generation who have stayed in Hong Kong and not migrated abroad speak and write English rather poorly. Nor can they speak good Mandarin, which has made its way into subway announcements and radio and TV programs and is frequently heard in malls and other public places, because of so many visitors and recent immigrants from the mainland. Since 1997 Hong Kong Man is no longer so *sui generis*, since he is being challenged by new elements from both China and abroad.

The typical company man or woman working in Hong Kong's Central Business District now has a counterpart in all the major cities in China, where Hong Kong's urban lifestyle is emulated and even surpassed. Hong Kong men and women may still work hard and take great pride in the society they have built, but an increasing number of them are now working elsewhere: in Chinese cities like nearby Shenzhen and Dongguan, where they have moved their factories and businesses, or in Shanghai and Beijing, where they have invested. And they are losing their self-confidence, as their lives become complicated by competition, jealousy, and the peculiar feeling of inferiority that comes from having a poor command of Mandarin Chinese.

In short, the Hong Kong lifestyle is undergoing another major transformation. What does this augur for Hong Kong's future? Will Hong Kong gradually lose its identity and become just another Chinese city, like Canton? Or will it develop into a more global and less Chinese city, like Singapore (though without its political status as a city-state)? Hong Kong's current official self-image as

"Asia's international metropolis" can be both self-evident and self-deceptive. Whether Hong Kong can still preserve its unique identity as a city and a people remains to be seen, for it depends on political, economic, and cultural permutations both in China and around the world. But we can at least trace the trajectory of its more recent self-images.

THE ATTEMPT TO DEFINE a "Heung Gong Yan" (Hong Kong people) is itself a reflection of a local consciousness emerging in the 1970s which became manifest in the works of a younger generation of Hong Kong–born writers and film-makers. This was the first generation to grow up during the postwar transformation into a modern city. At a time when China was turning inward, absorbed by its own Cultural Revolution, Hong Kong was projected to the world as the "real" China, almost by default. How else does one explain the paradox that a consciousness of their native roots began to arise precisely at the time when the Hong Kong people were being uprooted by rapid modernization and urbanization? Since many settlers were beginning to consider themselves natives of the city, they felt a compelling need to tell a "Hong Kong story" that would reinforce their sense of belonging. But no true or definitive version of the story seemed possible in view of the speed of change. Nor could there be a "master narrative"—that was the prerogative of either the nation-state (China) or the colonial regime (Great Britain). Some other means had to be found.

Since Hong Kong is without doubt one of the most image-conscious cities in the world, it comes as no surprise that the first stirrings of this new "Hong Kong obsession" was a series of short documentary-style films. They were produced in the late 1970s by RTHK, a radio and TV production company owned by the government, which attracted a group of talented young film-makers who had just returned from film schools abroad. They were given a low budget but a free hand to create images from their own observations. Each segment of the series, called *Below the Lion Rock,* began with the title song, together with images of Hong Kong (including footage of the 1967 riot). As sung by the famous pop singer Lo Man, this theme song became an instant hit. The metaphor in the song's lyrics stems from a familiar proverb, "Helping one another on the same boat" (*tongzhou gongji*), and the metaphor obviously struck a responsive chord. Viewers were reminded that there were people still suffering from the hardships "we" had suffered only a few years ago, and that "we" must also help one another in times of both adversity and opportunity.

The stories of these short films (all with realistic characters played by actors) focused mainly on the world of the poor and the downtrodden: poverty-stricken fishing families, boys working in the graveyards, drug addicts and drug dealers, residents in squatter areas whose lives were affected by a pedestrian bridge, dance hall waitresses exploited by mafia types, and so on. When these segments were shown in the late 1970s and early 1980s, they may have been the first attempt to create a collective self-image of the Hong Kong people, along with a title song as the rallying cry. In 2001, when Hong Kong was caught again in an economic crisis, Anthony Leung, the financial secretary at the time, used the song to revive what he called the "Hong Kong spirit"—the spirit of hard work and survival, along with a sense of pride in the city's collective achievement. Some of these documentaries have been reissued recently in DVD form, as reminders and souvenirs.

In the 1980s, this sense of social conscience among Hong Kong's film-makers changed. As the Yale scholar Helen Siu (herself from Hong Kong's 1970s generation) notes, "Life in Hong Kong became brashly luxurious, and its impact diffused through popular media and conspicuous consumption worldwide."[3] The 1980s was the golden era of film-making, made possible by directors with similar backgrounds but diverse styles: Ann Hui, Allen Fong, Tsui Hark, John Woo, Stanley Kwan, among many others. Some of the films eventually attained worldwide popularity, even cult status. Western aficionados of Hong Kong films (including Hollywood directors like Quentin Tarantino) praised their flamboyant style but dismissed their contents as silly or superficial. However, at their best these films can be reflective as well as entertaining: the glittering veneer of their fast-moving images and staggering action sequences is punctuated by abrupt and oblique references to Hong Kong's past and future.

If a "master narrative" of Hong Kong could never be told in commercial film, these movies found a space for many "counter-narratives" of Hong Kong identity. Given the uncertainties of Hong Kong's future from the perspective of the mid-1980s, with the impending handover only a decade or so away, we will miss something important if we view the films of this era merely as entertainment or commodities for consumption. Some of them are "dead serious," albeit encased in a playful form. One good example is *Rouge* (1988), directed by Stanley Kwan—a highly evocative film whose images can be interpreted as an allegory about past and present Hong Kong.

The film's story, based on a novel by popular writer Lillian Lee (Li Bik Wah), is told in two time frames: the past of the 1930s and the present of the 1980s. The plot follows the formula of romantic ghost stories: a rich playboy and scion of one of the major merchant families (played by Leslie Cheung) goes to a dinner party in the Shek Tong Tsui brothel area, where he encounters a beautiful courtesan called Yu Fa (Fleur) and listens to her singing a tune from a Cantonese opera. Deeply touched, he sings a duet with her and falls instantly in love. He then makes her his mistress and keeps her in a rented house because he is already betrothed to another woman. The two lovers, forbidden by his family to marry, plan a double suicide, but he survives.

Fifty years later, she returns from the underworld to look for him—only to be utterly disillusioned. In the film more so than the novel, Fleur's brothel is portrayed with lavish decadence, an old world evoked with nostalgia. But the present (the 1980s) is presented with simple unadorned realism. The sharp contrast between past and present through purposeful inter-cutting is what makes the film so engrossing.

Behind its formulaic plot is a hidden allegory that many viewers and critics have tried to unpack. The story that is set in the present is told from the perspective of a young, casually dressed couple who work for a newspaper in North Point. Fleur, the ghost, wearing a traditional long red gown, appears suddenly in the office to post a missing-person ad in the newspaper. The young man is not aware of her ghostly body until he encounters her again in a tram car (not the modern subway).

The film reveals no hint of the "brash luxury" of cosmopolitan Hong Kong, but there is clearly a contrast of values between Fleur and the young couple. Fleur is capable of romantic passion, whereas the young journalists are not.

Still, they are mesmerized by her story and decide to help her find her former lover. They take her to the Shek Tong Tsui area and wait on the street corner, where modern passers-by hardly notice their presence. Meanwhile, phantom-like images of Cantonese opera performances flit across Fleur's eyes in a montage sequence that weaves the past with the present. The place is haunted, of course, only for those who cherish the memory. The quest for Fleur's old lover has become a quest for a past that no longer exists.

But because it arouses the journalists' curiosity, they go to an old shop on Upper Lascar Row and find the remnant of a newspaper that carried a brief report of the suicide. They use the phone book and dial numbers that seem to fit the secret code the lovers created at their suicide, in order to meet again, as ghosts, at a given time and place. The quest brings both an emotional truth to the modern couple and a metaphysical significance as the old city of Hong Kong itself is remapped and rediscovered in the process. History now makes sense precisely because it is filtered through the story of this prostitute.

Old Hong Kong in Kwan's film is not a colonial city; rather, it resembles the glamorous Shanghai of the 1930s, as depicted in popular novels of the "Mandarin Ducks and Butterflies" school, a school of Chinese traditional-style popular literature prevalent in the early twentieth century. Nostalgia, however, is not just a sentiment embodied in a ghost from the past but is clearly held up as a lesson for the present. It is not by coincidence that the modern couple are both journalists. The woman is busy covering the story of the first Miss Hong Kong contest—regarded by some as another emblem of Hong Kong's identity (and in the book Fleur is almost dragged into entering the contest herself). The irony in the contrast is intentional: Fleur was so passionately committed to love that she was not afraid to die for it, whereas the modern couple have no capacity for such devotion, much less the courage to act on it. But learning about her past renews their faith in love. After several trials they finally find her lover, now an old derelict working as an extra in a film studio that resembles Shaw Brothers.

At this point, we begin to realize that the film itself is self-reflexive: the story of Fleur's past has been "staged" like a Cantonese opera, and the ghost story itself is being consciously compared to the film within this film (as when costumed actresses fly around on wires over rooftops during the shooting of one scene). Kwan uses the medium of film to its greatest advantage by creating a contrast between Hong Kong's two self-images in the double time frame of the story. When *Rouge* was in production, Hong Kong's political future was being decided by the Sino-British agreement. Thus, the film's time frame takes on a new layer—"back to the future," or the past as a reminder of the future. Suddenly the lovers' fifty-year pact makes symbolic sense, as do the numbers of their secret code—even Fleur's old identity card contains the numbers 1898 and 1997.

This "numbers game," together with oblique references to Hong Kong's "terminal" future, can be detected in quite a few other films made at the time. One example is John Woo's extremely successful trilogy (1986–1997), released in the United States under the title *A Better Tomorrow* (the original Chinese title, in translation, was *The True Colors of Heroes*). In the third film in the trilogy, directed by Tsui Hark and released in 1989 in the United States as *A Better Tomorrow III: Love and Death in Saigon* (originally titled *The Song of Sunset* in Chinese), the Hong Kong hero, played by Chow Yun-Fat, finds himself in Vietnam on the very eve of the American pullout. A pointed metaphor (aside from reflecting the director's personal background) is clearly intended, and it is even clearer in *A Better Tomorrow* I (1986), when the two buddies (played by Ti Lung and Chow Yun-Fat) stand against the glittering skyline of Victoria Harbor and wonder how long this glorious spectacle will last. Woo in the 1980s certainly could not imagine that a decade or so later the harbor spectacle would be made even more glorious—if less history-bound—with animated neon lights.

As these films show, Hong Kong's self-image in the 1980s was full of ironies and contradictions. Its past was purposefully evoked not only to make sense of the present but also to project a feeling of uncertainty about the future. When compared with portraits of the "Hong Kong Man" and of Hong Kong lifestyle, these film images are more fluid and more concerned about where and how they are situated than about defining who they are and what they are like. What was most appealing about films made at this time is the high degree of interaction between film-making and the popular imagination. Hong Kong did not have an art film tradition, with movies by the likes of a Truffaut, Godard, Fellini, or Antonioni, which catered to a small minority of intellectuals. Directors like John Woo and Ann Hui were themselves nurtured by Western art films, but they all chose to make popular commercial movies that were in tune with how people felt at the time.

In the heyday of Hong Kong's film-making in the 1980s, the most popular genre was cop thrillers, followed by films about gamblers and young mafia gangs. Successors to the old Shaw Brothers *kung-fu* genre were Jackie Chan's comic and zestful cop films, *Project A* and its sequel. Chan's colonial cop speaks both Cantonese and English and has to justify his role as a defender of law and order in the status quo. *Project A* has nothing to do with the British "colonial project" nor does it contain any anticolonial or postcolonial message. Rather, it is pure entertainment strewn with a few contemporary Hong Kong references.

Tsui Hark's modern adaptation of the Cantonese legend of Wong Fei Hong in the series called *Once Upon a Time in China* evoked an old colonial Hong Kong with a modern twist. The Wong Fei Hong saga films are commercial entertainment, but director Tsui Hark puts in a pointed reminder of Hong Kong's colonial past in the very first scene of this movie. (The English title is apparently intended as homage to Sergio Leone's popular classics *Once Upon a Time in the West* and *Once Upon a Time in America*.) On a busy street (Queen's Road) thronged with Chinese and Westerners in their hurly-burly activities, suddenly the sound of a distant cannon from a gunboat is heard, and everyone stops. The scene seems to freeze a historic moment that has come to haunt the present, a moment suggesting that war and chaos would soon ensue, and the local hero Wong Fei Hong is thrust into the national stage of modern China. But this "national saga" (which in a sequel will include a meeting between Wong and Sun Yat-sen) is viewed from the perspective of Hong Kong. This peripheral and jaundiced vision also offers enough room for jokes and playful spoofs of grand history, which is something of a hallmark in Tsui Hark's films made in this period. Another example is *Peking Opera Blues* (1986), a satire aimed at Chinese warlords and, by implication, modern Chinese history itself.

Whether intentional or not, these commercial films have managed to bring Hong Kong's history to bear on its present condition. They are at once hilarious and serious and certainly a far cry from the vapid spectacles made in Hollywood about Hong Kong, such as *Tai-pan*, or the ideological spectacles made in China specifically for Hong Kong, such as *The Opium War*. (At this film's first showing at a local theater in 1997, half of the audience walked out before the movie was over.) In Hong Kong's popular imagination, history returns as neither tragedy nor farce but as "veiled" entertainment—only the messages are so cleverly implied that they easily sneak past those outside viewers who are unconcerned about Hong Kong's fate. The pains of the insider are always hidden in the films' playful allegories.

Feelings of uncertainly about the future are negotiated not only through historical references to Hong Kong's past but also through its imagined relationship with China. We can easily trace a genealogy of Hong Kong's images of China in films made in the 1980s and 1990s. In the early years before China was open, Hong Kong shared the West's view of China as a country caught in its own revolutionary turmoil. The Cultural Revolution cast a dark shadow over the city as corpses of the revolution's victims began to float into Victoria Harbor and echoes were heard in the 1967 riot. Since the 1960s, the general impression of Hong Kong residents toward China—especially on the part of recent refugees—was fear, compounded by the tragedy of the student democracy movement in 1989. The million Hong Kong residents who marched in pouring rain to protest the Tiananmen massacre were expressing both deep concern for the victims and anxiety over the impending takeover.

Films made in Hong Kong at the time reflected this fear of violence and chaos. In the popular cop thrillers made in the early 1990s, the new "bad guys" gradually made their appearance as criminals from mainland China who illegally sneaked into Hong Kong to rob and steal. The "good guys" were always Hong Kong cops or special agents (as in Jackie Chan's supercop series) who had to cope with the new situation by drawing on their innate ingenuity and courage. After the long years of no communication with the mainland finally ended, the Hong Kong cops in more recent films progressed from combating

Chinese criminals by themselves to learning to collaborate with the security forces in China, so that border-crossing becomes a two-way traffic. This "great leap forward" is clearly observable in some of the outstanding films made in the last decade before Hong Kong's handover.

Long Arm of the Law (1993) captured the mood of chaos and fear most vividly. The film follows a band of mainland outlaws who try to rob a bank on one of Kowloon's busy streets. When the plan fails, they try to hide in old Kowloon City, where the outlaws and the pursuing police have a gunfight in the city's narrow alleyways. But behind the usual cops-and-robbers formula of this movie lurks a message: just as chaos has erupted right in this "heart of darkness," it threatens to spread to the entire territory. What is to be done?

While in this film the criminal gang is violently crushed by Hong Kong's police heroes, in reality the situation would not be so simple and easy to handle. The inevitability of a Chinese takeover of Hong Kong had to be faced, and irrational fear had to be dispelled. The result was the clever creation of a rustic and crude woman character from China, a security agent no less, who crosses the border to Hong Kong to help the Hong Kong police solve murder cases. The evolution of this "cousin" character from the mainland in a series of three films (1990–1992), literally translated *Cousin, How Are You?* but released in English as *Her Fatal Ways*, reveals tellingly the gradual changes taking place in Hong Kong's images of China during the early 1990s.

In the first film, the woman detective is a glum and unsophisticated cadre figure who has to accommodate herself rather awkwardly to the lures of capitalism, very much like the heroine Ninotchka played by Greta Garbo in Ernst Lubitsch's classic film. But this Chinese agent proves competent and collaborates smoothly with the mostly male Hong Kong police detectives. In one scene, they even join forces with some aged veterans of the Nationalist Army to solve the murder case. Thus Hong Kong's role as a free "public sphere" for all contending forces of different political ideologies is revived. But in the ensuing films of the series, the mainland "cousin," rather than being corrupted by materialistic desires, becomes quite sophisticated in her appearance and demeanor and earns the respect of her colleagues in Hong Kong. What started as a negative and even farcical treatment somehow evolved into a positive portrait. "Hong Kong for Hongkongers," to be sure, but it does not hurt to have a little help from Chinese cousins in the north.

By the early 1990s, the geographical scope portrayed in Hong Kong films expanded. As Jackie Chan's supercop went out to Kuala Lumpur, Seoul, and other Asian cities (and soon to Australia and Europe) to solve cases, he and other Hong Kong film heroes also crossed the border to China to hunt down murderers and smugglers. There they had the full cooperation of the Chinese security police. While evil elements from China continued to sneak in and disturb the peace in Hong Kong, order was restored through efforts of collaboration.

In these films, the real locations in China are always somewhere in the countryside and purposefully blurred; the Chinese characters, both robbers and cops, speak Mandarin. But there is little attempt to explore their psychology and background. The images are still one-sided. Only in rare cases, such as when Stanley Kwan began to tackle mainland subjects in such films as his adaptation of Eileen Chang's *The Red Rose and the White Rose* (1994) and his film biography of the famous actress Ruan Lingyu called *Center Stage* (1992)—both with 1930s Shanghai as background—did the tone and setting change, although Cantonese was still used, mixed with some Shanghai dialect. Even in these films Kwan kept his location shots to a minimum, as he was reportedly interested not in the real Shanghai but only in its images as viewed from the perspective of Hong Kong. Kwan's most recent film, *Everlasting Regret* (2005), is an adaptation of a famous novel by the contemporary Shanghai writer Wang Anyi that chronicles the long-suffering life experience of a Shanghai woman. But it places more emphasis on a Hong Kong character played by Tony Leung, thus inserting a local—some critics say a narcissistic—point of view.

Kwan is not alone in exploring Hong Kong's subjective preoccupation with images of the self and the "other" (Shanghai). Wong Kar-wai, perhaps Hong Kong's most famous *auteur* director internationally, shares this same trait. From *Days of Being Wild* (1990) to *In the Mood for Love* (2001) and *2046* (2004), he reveals a fascination, bordering on obsession, with Shanghai. But for him it is the Shanghai of Hong Kong, the dislocated Shanghailanders in Hong Kong's

North Point, that occupies center stage. This may have been due to his own background as the son of an immigrant family from Shanghai. But Wong's central theme (some critics say his only theme, in all his films)—a spiritual quest for a lost love or a romance of the past that is irretrievable—has to be anchored in Hong Kong, itself a bewildering and lost place that the central characters still call their home. It is this romantic leitmotif, expressed in sophisticated cinematic technique, that has endeared Wong Kar-wai to local and international audiences. Film buffs from other countries have come to Hong Kong specifically to seek out the real locations behind the alluring images of Wong's films.

Thus, throughout the 1980s and 1990s, Hong Kong's film-makers continued to be preoccupied with their city and with themselves, even while they came to an accommodation with China. The stories and images of their films evinced a persistent obsession with their hometown. The impact of these cinematic images on the cultural identity of Hong Kong cannot be underestimated, since film-watching in the theaters and at home has always been a key component of the Hong Kong lifestyle. According to one set of statistics provided by Hugh Baker, there were 104 movie theaters in Hong Kong in 1969. A falling off in attendance brought the figure down to 89 at the end of 1982, but the number of visits to the cinema that year still worked out to more than twelve for every member of the population. With the opening of multiplex theaters and the availability of DVDs, movie-watching has become a pastime of everyday life in Hong Kong. Films have become a central medium in expressing and shaping the city's cultural identity. It is only within this visual universe that we can gauge the extent to which the presence of outsiders, such as China, has affected Hong Kong. Such images may not tell us exactly what makes Hong Kong's economy tick or whether Hong Kong will lose its democratic "autonomy"—questions that seem to preoccupy foreign commentators—but they have given us a vivid sense of how Hong Kong people look at themselves and the world around them.

THIS OVERRIDING SELF-OBSESSION culminated at the crucial moment of Hong Kong's handover to China in 1997. As the time of the handover drew near, both sides started their countdown. In Beijing a gigantic clock was erected for just this purpose. While patriotic pride was swelling on the mainland, it was mixed with a sense of envy. A popular song titled "My 1997" sung (and acted in a video version) by the Chinese pop singer Ai Bei became a huge hit. She sings unabashedly of the pleasures of being with her Hong Kong boyfriend: shopping, going to midnight movie previews, as well as watching the shows of famous Cantopop singers in the Hung Hom stadium. Ai Bei's song reveals a certain truth about the period. Hong Kong still enjoyed the luxury of material goods and the supremacy of popular entertainment. The younger generation of mainlanders readily acquired a taste for Hong Kong movies (via pirated VCDs) and rock stars (who began touring in China). As the handover was drawing close, some local commentators in Hong Kong began to talk about a "takeover" of China by Hong Kong culture. The motherland was being conquered by her prodigal son.

On June 30, 1997, the last day of British rule, it began to drizzle. In the early afternoon, British soldiers did their military drills on the Tamar parade grounds in front of a group of invited spectators. Not far away, a peaceful demonstration billed as an "arts fair" was taking place in tiny Statue Square. Hundreds of stalls and booths under makeshift tents were set up, selling memorabilia and other gifts. By late afternoon, the drizzle had turned into rain.

Christopher Patten, the last governor, stood on the parade stand without umbrella and made a brief speech of farewell. Departing from his prepared draft, he delivered a moving tribute to the people of Hong Kong for their contributions in making the colony what it had become. The ceremony ended with Dame Gwyneth Jones, the famous Welsh soprano, singing an old folksong, "The Last Rose of Summer," an appropriate gesture for the departing colonists who were casting their final glance at their prized possession on board Prince Charles's yacht, which was sent specially for the occasion. Both the atmosphere and symbolism were appropriate: the last colonists of the British Empire, where once upon a time "the sun never set," were leaving—not sailing off into the sunset but making their exit in the pouring rain.

Earlier in the afternoon, I had taken a "ritual" tram ride from Central to North Point with an American friend who was visiting Hong Kong for the first time. We started from Shanghai Tang, the dress shop on Pedder Street owned by the designer David Tang, a descendant of the Tang clan of Yuen Long, who originated the shop's successful brand of chic and gaudy chinoiserie. We got on board the tram near the Legco building and sat on the upper desk to have a better view. The mood of passengers was quiet and unanimated.

A man wearing the Union Jack walks past demonstrators outside the Legco building on the last day of British sovereignty.

Banners festooning Queen's Road prominently displayed the new official slogan, "Tomorrow can only be better," together with a toylike white dolphin jumping through a rubber ring. Presumably white dolphins were a precious species found only in Hong Kong's nearby oceans, and for that reason had become something of a new mascot for Hong Kong. Unfortunately, the real dolphins were now dying of water pollution caused by the construction of the new airport—not a good omen. Few local residents, except for the rich and famous, openly exuded confidence in Hong Kong's future. During the evening of July 1, under a display of fireworks, a dragon boat in the parade of ships sailing through the harbor caught fire. The local media seized on this and every other small accident as an indication of Hong Kong's new uncertainty. A joyous celebratory mood was definitely not shared by the majority.

The official handover ceremony took place on the evening of June 30 in the newly expanded convention center in Wan Chai, a massive edifice with a roof shaped like the wings of a giant bird. After speeches by Prince Charles and President Jiang Zemin were delivered, the national anthem of the People's Republic was played by a Chinese military band at precisely midnight, as the Union Jack was lowered and the Five-Star flag was raised. According to recent newspaper reports (most of which are based on a biography of Jiang Zemin), the details of the ceremony had been negotiated down to the most extreme minutia. The British were forced to lower their flag a few seconds before midnight so that the Chinese band conductor could raise his baton at precisely midnight.[4]

The royal yacht *Britannia* sailed into Victoria Harbor under leaden skies on June 23, 1997. The handover ceremonies took place in the Hong Kong Convention and Exibition Centre in Wan Chai, shown in the background.

Thus ended 158 years of British colonial rule. The new Hong Kong SAR government under Tung Chee-hwa was sworn in right after midnight.

On the evening of June 30, I was invited to attend a lavish celebration party at Kowloon's Regent Hotel. At midnight, the ballroom band played a vulgarized tune taken from the beginning of Richard Strauss's "Thus Spoke Zarathustra"—to signify a "new dawn"—and the waiters suddenly turned the Union Jack vests of their uniforms inside out to reveal a red Five-Star design. The dramatic gesture said it all: to the members of the service trades, including Hong Kong's civil service bureaucracy, a change of loyalty to a new master was a cinch. The guests carried on with their drinking and dancing as if nothing had happened. Only a few gathered around the television screens to watch truckloads of the People's Liberation Army riding into town in the dark, under pouring rain. Was this a nightmare coming true, or was this a real liberation? Ironically, it was the quiet and disciplined behavior of the PLA soldiers that gained the trust of the local population. The garrison troops were ensconced not in the Prince of Wales building but in the faraway barracks at Stanley on the southern tip of the island, where during the Japanese occupation British prisoners were held and where British soldiers and civilians were buried in a nearby graveyard.

The rain showers continued for more than a week, which some took to be a good omen while others saw it as heaven weeping for them. *Feng shui* masters were interviewed by Chinese and Western media and predictably came up with divergent interpretations. As though to cast the deciding vote, a returned scholar (myself) was called upon to talk about weather in the context of Chinese culture! At around midnight, while the handover ceremony in the convention center was going on, a small group of activists and legislators, mainly from the Democratic Party, occupied the Legco building and gave speeches on its balcony. These popularly elected legislators found their term suddenly at an end, since Governor Patten's sped-up measures for direct elections had met with objection from the Chinese government. The entire elected body was dissolved on July 1, to be replaced with a carefully controlled system of appointment and proportional representation. The demonstrators drew media attention because they were trespassers and intruders. The disenfranchised, in their frustration, were forcing their way into this august symbol of law and democracy. This was the only conspicuous sign of open dissension throughout that momentous day, and it did not amount to much.

HONG KONG'S ADAPTATION to its new situation appeared to go smoothly. But beneath the surface, popular resentment had been building up gradually since the mid-1980s, arising from a feeling that the fate of Hong Kong had been decided by British and Chinese leaders without including Hong Kong's people in any consultation. The drafting of the Basic Law did involve a few local representatives, but the democrats were barred from participation. Thus, the pent-up anger and frustration were channeled into a demand for democracy via direct popular election, as if this were the only way to assert Hong Kong's autonomy.

But democracy had never been part of the colonial legacy. As the local scholar Agnes Ku has pointed out, Hong Kong's colonial government was a paternalistic-administrative one that prided itself on its prospering economy, stable political order, and efficient administration. The new SAR government tried to draw on this success while deemphasizing the growing demand for democracy.[5] But it did not have much success at the local, national, or international level. Part of the reason was simply bad management and bad luck. After the handover, the economy took a downturn, which precipitated the near collapse of the housing market, causing those who bought houses at premium prices to lose a fortune, at least on paper. In his inaugural speech Tung Chee-hwa unveiled his new policy of building more public housing to help the poor, but that also backfired.

He proved unable to move the large civil service bureaucracy into action.

After forcing Anson Chan, its head, to resign, Tung tried to introduce a new system of administrative responsibility by installing outsiders—especially leaders from the business world—as heads of government bureaus, but this only made the situation worse. After Tung was "reelected" in 2002 for a second term (having no opponent), the SAR was hit the next year by the SARS epidemic. The similarity in the two acronyms was purely coincidental, but the nomenclature chosen by the World Health Organization certainly did not help matters in Hong Kong. During this worst year of 2003, the city's "civil society" sprang into action almost spontaneously. A march and demonstration on July 1, the sixth anniversary of the handover, drew half a million people into the streets to show their dissatisfaction with the government. As Tung watched the peaceful and orderly demonstration on television, he knew that his days of leadership were numbered. He did not finish out his second term but resigned in 2004 on the pretext of bad health. Sir Donald Tsang was appointed the new chief executive.

Domestic unrest was only a small part of Tung's problems. Far more significant was Hong Kong's postcolonial "repositioning" vis-à-vis China, which required a new vision and a new strategy. As Y. M. Yeung of Chinese University has pointed out, "The basic unit in the competitive economy of the world of the 21st century is neither companies nor nations but clusters of cities."[6] To remain competitive, Hong Kong would have to ally itself with the other cities in the Pearl River delta so as to compete with the rising economic power of the Lower Yangtze River region, of which Shanghai was the undisputed leader. However, Hong Kong's leadership status in the larger Pearl River delta region (which includes Macau) was challenged by Guangzhou (Canton), the capital of Guangdong province and a treaty port with a longer history than Hong Kong's. Even Shenzhen just across the border from the New Territories, which was designated a "Special Economic Zone," was developing fast. It took Tung a long time to make his former colonial bureaucrats understand the need for regional cooperation. Such a plan was finally announced in his annual report in 2003.

The central government in Beijing finally came to Hong Kong's rescue by lifting its tight border controls and allowing mainland tourists to visit Hong Kong individually, in the hope that their shopping sprees would boost Hong Kong's economy. This policy was followed immediately by a more comprehensive plan called Closer Economic Partnership Arrangement (CEPA) between mainland China and Hong Kong, which allowed some 273 manufacturing trades from Hong Kong to enter China without customs duty. This move seemed to imply that Beijing indeed wanted Hong Kong to be the future economic leader of the Pearl River delta region.

However, the road to full regional economic integration is still laid with obstacles. The proposed construction of a Pearl River delta bridge and highway to link Hong Kong, Guangzhou, and Macau is under negotiation. Guangzhou's construction of a new port is seen as an unfriendly move to take away some of Hong Kong's lucrative interport trade and its leading role in logistics and transportation. Added to that is lingering resentment over the fact that the first outbreak of SARS occurred in Guangzhou but was not duly reported by the city's health officials. Consequently, Hong Kong was unprepared for the epidemic. On the other hand, the arrogance and condescending attitude of Hong Kong's bureaucrats certainly did not smooth ruffled feathers in neighbor cities.

"Hong Kong governed by Hong Kongers"—this official policy statement from Beijing, originally intended to ensure the city's autonomy, also implied an unanswered question: Can Hong Kong really govern itself, as it confronts a series of unpredicted and unprecedented problems and challenges? The worst of them is air pollution. *The Economist* reported on May 29, 2007, that "Hong Kong's air pollutant concentrations are now 200% above norms set by the World Health Organization."[1] A government study a few years earlier claimed that 80 percent of Hong Kong's pollution came from mainland factories and power plants, but a report by the Institute for the Environment at the Hong Kong University of Science and Technology and Civic Exchange, a local think tank headed by Christine Loh, found that in 2006 Hong Kong's air pollution was caused more by local sources (road traffic, coal-fired power stations, and ships) than by factories in China. Local emissions were the main cause of high pollution on 192 days in 2006; emissions from the Pearl River delta caused high pollution on 132 days; and the remaining 41 days had low pollution. Another study sponsored by the Hong Kong Environmental Protection Department (HKEPD) stated that while ammonium sulfate measured in Hong Kong was of regional origin (that is, from across the border), 49 to 63 percent of organic carbon and elemental carbon came from local sources; both contributed significantly to the city's "visibility degradation."[8]

The governments of Hong Kong and Guangdong are still at loggerheads over this issue. Each side blames the other, but no joint plan to eliminate pollution has been devised, except for a vague and ineffectual agreement to "share information." The official air pollution index posted every day is a sham, according to Anthony Hedley of the University of Hong Kong, who estimates that air pollution now causes 1,600 deaths a year and 6.8 million visits to the doctor—one for every resident every year. Meanwhile, Hong Kong's skies are getting darker, even on sunny days. Blue skies have become rare, and the government's "Blue Sky" publicity campaign has had little effect: automobiles are required by law to shut down their engines if stopped or parked temporarily, but nobody observes it. The white dolphin—a proud logo at the handover—is nowhere to be seen today in Hong Kong, and never mentioned.

In spite of this ecological gloom, the mood in Hong Kong improved drastically after the market turnabout in 2004. The SAR government under Tsang claimed that in 2007 Hong Kong enjoyed the best economy in more than twenty years and that sustained economic growth could be expected. A decade after the handover, the feeling of uncertainty was gone, as Hong Kong settled into its new role as China's economic partner and special (if not so autonomous) region.

Indeed, as Hong Kong faced up to the mammoth external challenges of the twenty-first century, the issue of its self-image became much less feverish, and today the discourse of identity has all but disappeared. Surveys show that a large percentage of Hong Kong people consider themselves *both* Chinese and Hong Kongese. There is nothing surprising in this double affirmation—"China is my country, but Hong Kong is my home"—since the same formula applies to most residents of cities throughout the world. But this inclusive assertion does not really solve the identity problem, because in a sense Hong Kong's past has required a double denial: Hong Kong is my home, and neither England nor China is my country. The underlying anguish and anxiety caused by this diasporic mentality under colonialism has seldom been fully understood, much less appreciated, by outsiders.

A more ironic variation of the same statement, as Li Siu-leung has suggested, would be: "I am a Hong Kong person because I am not allowed to be completely Chinese." If so, who has not allowed it? While both England and China can be easily blamed, this attitude reflects the passivity of colonial subjects. Even today, if the average Hong Kong person were offered full Chinese citizenship in lieu of a Hong Kong identity card and SAR passport, he or she would probably say no. This reluctance to commit to the motherland is viewed as a direct consequence of Hong Kong's colonial history, which denied the growth of full-fledged nationalism. For several years now, local television stations have aired a video every evening that showcases the magnificent landscapes and technological achievements of the motherland (including an astronaut who was received like a hero in Hong Kong), while playing the national anthem of the People's Republic. Whether this will have the desired result remains to be seen.

SO TO RETURN TO a question raised in the Prologue to this book: What is so "special" about Hong Kong? To find an answer we have to go beyond politics and economics and return to the domain of culture. In the short run, it appears that the qualities that have made Hong Kong so unusual are dwindling, not due to any negligence by its own residents but because of the speed with which other Chinese cities have imitated Hong Kong and are overtaking it. In what ways is Hong Kong's lifestyle still distinguishable from that in Shenzhen, Guangzhou, or Shanghai? In this changed context, a discussion about the Hong Kong way of life is no longer a discourse in identity politics but a depiction of the city's character or "soul." Under successive waves of globalization, even localism is losing ground; the catch phrase now is "glocalism"—incorporating the local into the global, rather than the other way around. Every multinational company is adopting the slogan "Go local!" so as to make business thrive in every market and locality it chooses to enter. And most local and national governments are eager to help in this endeavor. China and Hong Kong today are no exception.

However, "glocalism" does not necessarily mean genuine empathy for or understanding of local culture and tradition, much less its collective memory. At best, this is a clever move in public relations, encouraged by the Hong Kong Tourism Board. This business plan leaves little room for any genuine appreciation of local history and cultural memory, which to the always-pragmatic businessmen and bureaucrats are elusive, intangible, and hence dispensable. In this respect, Hong Kong has indeed become Koolhaas's model of a generic city par excellence.

In his somewhat cynical formulation of this urban concept, Koolhaas hardly bothers to talk about a city's cultural character, because by his definition a generic city has none. Is this going to be the case with all global metropolises, particularly in Asia? Ironically, an increasing number of Hong Kong residents, particularly young activists, are rising to the defense of the few historical monuments that still remain. Each government project of urban renewal in Hong Kong has been challenged with a spontaneous outpouring of popular protest. The destruction of the old Star Ferry terminal in November 2006 was a recent case in point. This was soon followed in July 2007 by the movement to save the old Queen's Pier, which also failed despite the protesters' staging of symbolic action and their pragmatic offer of an alternative plan (which included building a highway underground). This new up-rising in popular consciousness betrays a certain mental desperation—to hold on to whatever remains from the past, for otherwise there will be nothing left. These material emblems and sites from the colonial era have become cultural symbols and signposts for Chinese citizens of Hong Kong, and their impending destruction has renewed a sense of anxiety.

How do we interpret this phenomenon—is it merely recalcitrant nostalgia? If so, does this yearning imply that old Hong Kong fared much better under colonial rule than it does today under the SAR government? A small minority, it seems, may indeed harbor such a sentiment. But there are other, more complex and deep-seated factors to consider. This new awakening seems to be a refrain, in a different key, of the nostalgia craze that surfaced around the time of the handover, when large quantities of old relics and mementos—photos, newspaper clippings, calendars, and cigarette advertisements—appeared on Hong Kong's street stands, especially in Central and Sheung Wan. Most of the memorabilia—calendar posters in particular—were clever reproductions from Shanghai, which, after a revolutionary rupture of some thirty years, was also trying to rediscover its own past. Thus, a common cultural memory was revived. It seemed as if Hong Kong's image-makers were actively seeking to establish a link between the two cities or to use images of old Shanghai to reinforce its own self-image, and their timing was not coincidental.

The two cities shared a common colonial background: Hong Kong was a British colony for a century and a half (1842–1997), while Shanghai as a treaty port was a "semi-colony" for a century (1842–1945), its "International Settlement" dominated by the British. Colonialism turned the two cities into cosmopolitan metropolises in the midst of a predominantly rural hinterland. Compared to other treaty ports (with the exception of Guangzhou, whose linkage to Hong Kong predated the colonial era), these two cities had a particularly close relationship forged by an intricate web of colonial ties going back to the nineteenth century. The same British imperial architectural styles, the same Victorian manners and morals, the same colonial civil service and banking system staffed by the same type of English "gentlemen," who shared the same hobbies and pastimes and moved in the same social circles, could be seen in both cities. British ships always stopped in Hong Kong before going to Shanghai; and British visitors like W. Somerset Maugham, W. H. Auden, and Christopher Isherwood made similar stops on their way to China. Horse-racing was a popular entertainment in both cities, sometimes with tycoons from Shanghai joining the races in Hong Kong. All the major banks, HSBC in particular, had headquarters or branches in both locales. At least two of the four major department stores—Sincere and Wing On, both founded by overseas Chinese—had their beginnings in Hong Kong and then developed into even bigger enterprises in Shanghai.

Despite all these linkages, however, the two cities did not influence each other in equal measure or on equal footing. Shanghai claimed a longer history before Western occupation as one of the heavily populated towns in the prosperous lower Yangtze area, whose reputation almost rivaled Yangzhou in the early nineteenth century. Hong Kong, for all its early human habitation, remained a small-town outpost in both Chinese and British eyes. Interactions increased in the early twentieth century and intensified around 1945–1949, when the civil war and the Communist victory forced large numbers of Shanghailanders to settle in Hong Kong. These new immigrants held on to their dreams of old Shanghai until they found themselves stranded forever, with no prospect of return.

Only during the four decades from 1950 to 1990 did Hong Kong really get the upper hand, as Shanghai lost its cosmopolitanism under the Communist regime. But as soon as Deng Xiaoping's new reform policy opened the doors of China, Shanghai wasted no time in laying claim to its former glory by actively courting foreign investment and encouraging joint ventures. This siren's call has attracted the world's top architects. Shanghai's new leaders clearly want to leave Hong Kong in the dust, despite the central government's stated policy of promoting both cities.

Even Hong Kong's own businessmen have joined the effort to develop Shanghai. Vincent Lo, an enterprising developer, sought out Benjamin Wood, the architect of Boston's Faneuil Hall, in planning the construction of Xin Tiandi (New World), a leisure ground of bars and restaurants comparable to Hong Kong's Lan Kwai Fong and catering to the same class of tourists and locals. But this "new world" was created out of an old alley compound (*linong*) by demolishing all its plebian houses except for a few stone arches and bricks used for decoration. Since its completion in 2001, Xin Tiandi has become the most fashionable and talked-about place in Shanghai. Lo has confided to me that he chose Shanghai not merely for economic profit but to realize his own vision of urban renewal, which was nearly impossible in Hong Kong because of bureaucratic red tape and exorbitant land prices. If money and talent from

Hong Kong continue to move to Shanghai, will Hong Kong survive the competition, or will it find itself living once again in Shanghai's shadow?

In comparison to the new Shanghai, Hong Kong has remained rather inconspicuous since the 1990s: its streets are narrow and crowded, its buildings mostly undistinguished in style and laid out in seeming disarray. Even its signature skyscrapers have a subdued look compared with those in the new Pudong district in Shanghai. Only the moving spectacle of its skyline at night still awes visitors and locals alike. But with new plans for more reclamation into the harbor, who knows how long even this view will last? As Shanghai undergoes a facelift, it is rapidly losing its old colonial charm, but only the older generation, Western tourists, and a few investors seem to care.

In spite of Shanghai's amazing advancement in the "hardware" of urban construction, Hong Kong may still be ahead of Shanghai in the "software" of culture. However, cultural life cannot be fully measured by hardware or software alone, especially when we attempt to assess a city's character and soul. A more intangible index is found in the vitality and resourcefulness of a people's lifestyle. Greater Shanghai has twice the population of Hong Kong and equally dense urban spaces, but the quality of life there has declined. Its cosmopolitan sophistication in the 1930s at the flowering of its urban culture has been inherited by Hong Kong, and perhaps also by Taipei.

One sign of this, as Western tourists have often remarked, is a certain style of sophistication in Hong Kong's "service industry." No matter how grand-looking the new deluxe hotels in Shanghai or Beijing, only in Hong Kong does one find true comfort and efficient service. Some of the best hotels—such as the Peninsula and the Mandarin Oriental—are always listed as among the top ten in Asia. And no matter how noisy Hong Kong's restaurants may be, they always guarantee polite, attentive waiters. While the new Shanghai coffee houses in Xin Tiandi or elsewhere offer glamorous décor and atmosphere, the real addicts claim that for coffee of the highest quality one must visit the small street-corner shops in Hong Kong's Causeway Bay. Local patrons of Lan Kwai Fong who have visited Shanghai have remarked to me that Xin Tiandi offers only artifice and the appearance of sophistication and culture, but not the real quality they are used to; and besides, the prices are "beyond belief" (lei po).

This comment casts light on what has been forgotten or unappreciated by the government officials and real estate developers in Hong Kong who have allowed the profit motive to cloud their vision. They have lost sight of what Hong Kong really stands for—a character that derives from its unique mixture of colonial legacy and native traditions, a character shaped through long cultural accumulation. In Shanghai one can find new variations of "pearl milk tea" (invented in Taipei) but not the real *nai cha* in Hong Kong's ubiquitous teahouses.

Yet there are some worrisome signs on the horizon that may not be so perceptible to the tourist in Lan Kwai Fong. In some ways, becoming a part of China has made Hong Kong more parochial than before. Since 1997, this new parochialism has manifested itself in a siege mentality: all outsiders, especially those from the mainland, are potential competitors and therefore threats to Hong Kong's status quo, which some locals would like to maintain at all cost. With the city's increasing density has come a decline in the general standard of English proficiency. This waning language ability, along with a lifestyle that revolves around shopping malls, has narrowed the world of the average Hong Kong person compared with what it was before. And as even more mainland immigrants pour in, the question of quotas and limits on migration is being hotly debated. Should children born in Hong Kong to mainland parents of PRC citizenship be eligible for permanent residency in the city, together with their parents? An increasing number of pregnant mothers from the mainland are coming to Hong Kong just for this purpose. A whole series of other issues remain to be solved, all in one way or another related to the SAR government's policy toward mainlanders.

Localism with a parochial face can be the most exclusive kind of provincialism. Luckily, Hong Kong's treaty port status and island geography have not allowed the reactionary inward turns that some hinterland provinces in China have taken. The more enlightened residents of Hong Kong have called for an open-door policy, to attract not only money and investment but human talent from a variety of ethnic groups. The official epithet of Hong Kong as "Asia's international metropolis" calls for a cosmopolitan vision, with a different set of standards from either a parochially local or generically global city.

The Swedish anthropologist Ulf Hannerz defines a genuine cosmopolitanism as "an orientation, a willingness to engage with the Other," which would entail "a greater involvement with a plurality of contrasting cultures to some degree on their own terms."[9] Chinese in Hong Kong have always engaged with the "Other" in the form of British colonists, and have often played the reluctant role of the "Other" in stories written by British as well as mainland writers. The most famous of the mainland writers is the legendary Eileen Chang, who achieved overnight fame with her first short stories, all set in Hong Kong. A selection of them, including her most famous Hong Kong story, "Love in a Fallen City" (which was made into a film directed by Ann Hui) has been translated into English and recently published under that title.[10] In a sense, it was in Chang's stories, first published in Shanghai's popular magazines in the early 1940s, that the legend of Hong Kong and the "tale of two cities"—mirror images of each other—was first introduced to the Chinese reading public on the mainland.

Hannerz goes on to argue that a genuine transnational metropolis must possess four social categories of people who play major parts in making it a world city: (1) those working in transnational business and international finance; (2) various Third World populations; (3) people specializing in a broad range of "expressive activities" such as "fashion, design, photography, film-making, writing, music, cuisine and more"; (4) and tourists. It seems to me that Hong Kong definitely qualifies for (1) and is actively promoting (4). But in the categories of (2) and (3) it may still be lacking, unless we count as Third World populations the tens of thousands of maids and other temporary servants imported from the Philippines, Indonesia, and Thailand. Their visibility is everywhere noticeable, especially on Sundays, but they have not become an integral part of Hong Kong's local population. The Indian minority has fared a little better but remains separated from the Chinese majority. From this perspective, perhaps the problem is that racially the local population is too overwhelmingly Chinese to make Hong Kong truly cosmopolitan by Hannerz's definition. This racial homogeneity could reinforce provincialism, made worse by its prevalent monolingualism, Cantonese.

Filipino maids gather under the HSBC on Sundays to share food and friendship.

Thus, ironically, Hong Kongers have to be thankful for the persistence of English, a colonial language that has now become the global *lingua franca*. The official government policy, which I fervently support, is *leung man san yu* or "two written scripts (Chinese and English), three spoken languages (Cantonese, Mandarin, and English)." This multilingual practice can be found in all street signs, subway announcements, and government policy papers. The influx of tourists and immigrants from non-Chinese countries will help to make Hong Kong's linguistic and cultural landscape more heterogeneous.

A truly "international" or cosmopolitan city can and should have many faces, along with a strong sense of local cultural tradition as the basis for its character. To me, the cultural hybridity in a cosmopolitan metropolis is neither "generic" nor "melting pot" but a dynamic stew of many cultural traditions, local as well as national. New York and London are prime examples of cosmopolitanism, while Paris and Vienna are not. In China, none of the major cities is yet truly cosmopolitan. Shanghai has become "supra-national" in its global profile, but the local population is hardly cosmopolitan—unlike the generation of the 1930s.

The city-state of Singapore, by contrast, can indeed pride itself as a multiracial nation, though none of its cultural traditions runs deep enough to give it a strong character. And despite the government's effort to promote Mandarin— a reversal of its previous policy—the younger generation of Singaporeans prefers English. The city's forceful imposition of a local identity has not solved all the problems resulting from its uneasy racial mix, but Singapore still has many similarities to Hong Kong, the most obvious being a common colonial heritage. Being culturally and geographically so close to China, however, Hong Kong could never become a city-state like Singapore, even if that were politically viable, which of course it is not.

What, then, are Hong Kong's options for the future? If its localism, which has given it cultural vitality, degenerates into a narrow form of provincialism, Hong Kong will become a parochial town, just another Cantonese city in the Pearl River delta, no longer an international metropolis. At the other extreme, if the government's current policies, based on "rational" planning and development with only lip service paid to the city's cultural heritage, are carried to the extreme, they will turn Hong Kong into another generic city, without character or characteristics beyond malls, hotels, and an expanded airport.

Perhaps the crucial task in protecting Hong Kong from either of these eventualities lies in what Hannerz calls "expressive activities." Hannerz's list does not go into detail about contents and forms, nor practitioners. Does this creative element belong to the international jet set who feel equally at ease in many cities, or must they be local cultural workers who make a living by trying to give expression to a unique city they call home? The Hong Kong government is also promoting "creative industries," by which it means those "expressive activities" that can make money. While investing in culture can be good for business, a culture industry invented to line the pockets of tycoons may not be expressive enough to represent a city and its people, nor truly creative. Once again the elusive element of cultural memories enters into the picture. As I hope this book has made clear, I consider these memories to be a vital contributing factor to the character of any city—past, present, and future.

A city needs to be reinvented, again and again, from the evolving shared consciousness of its people. In the process of recollection and re-creation they also give the urban environment new cultural forms. The dialectic of tradition and innovation has always been the motor of cultural creativity. The drive merely to "catch up" with global trends so that "tomorrow will be better" can lead a city to vulgar mediocrity and homogeneity. For me, the vitality of the future always depends on how we preserve and assimilate the past. Today, more and more people are becoming aware of this and are taking part in a movement to save a few remaining relics of Hong Kong's past—an old street here, a clock tower or police station there. They may fail, of course, but in making the effort they help to keep alive a collective memory which, however fragile, will shape Hong Kong's destiny. This book has been written in the same spirit.

The Rain, 1999 (Fong So).

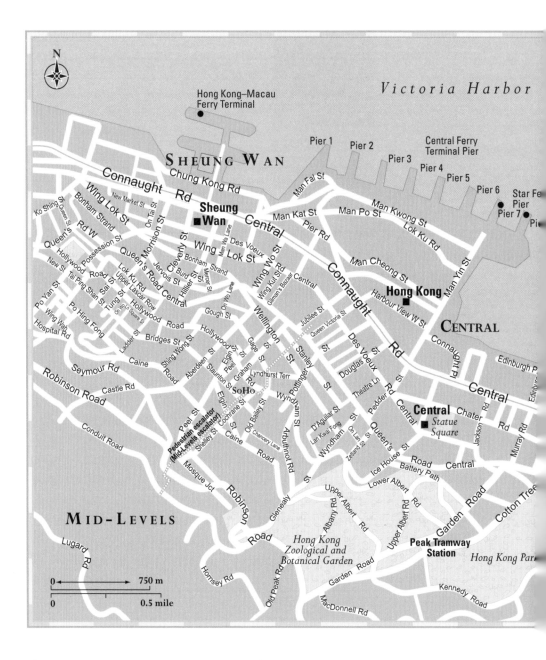

N

Victoria Harbor

Hong Kong–Macau Ferry Terminal

S H E U N G   W A N

Chung Kong Rd

Connaught Rd

Pier 1
Pier 2
Central Ferry Terminal Pier
Pier 3
Pier 4
Pier 5
Pier 6
Star Fe Pier
Pier 7

Sheung Wan

New Market St
Ko Shing St
Queen's St
Bonham Strand
Wing Lok St
On Tai St
Rd W
Queen's
New St
Morrison St
Cleverly St
Des Voeux
Central
Man Fai St
Man Kat St
Man Po St
Man Kwong St
Lok Ku Rd

Possession St
Hollywood
Road St
Lok Ku Rd
Upper Lascar Row
Jervois St
Sai St
C Burd
Hillier St
Bonham Strand
Man We Lane
Wing Lok St
Wing Wo Rd
Wing Kut St
Gilman's Bazaar
Pier Rd
Central

Po Yan St
Tai Ping Shan St
Tung St
On Lo Seare St
Gough St
Mercer St
On Wo Lane
Jubilee St
Queen Victoria St
Man Cheong St
Harbour View W St

Wing Wah
Po Hing Fong
Ladder St
Hollywood
Road
Shing Wong St
Wellington
Stanley
St
St
Des Voeux
Hong Kong

Hospital Rd
Bridges St
Aberdeen St
Elgin St
Gage St
Graham St
Peel St
Staunton St
Lyndhurst Terr
Pottinger
St
Douglas
St
CENTRAL

Seymour Rd
Caine
Rd
SoHo
Wyndham St
Theatre Ln
Pedder St
Connaught Pl
Edinburgh P

Castle Rd
Peel St
Graham St
Old Bailey St
Chancery Lane
Arbuthnot Rd
D'Aguilar St
Lan Kwai Fong
Wyndham
On Lan St
Zetland St
Central
Statue Square
Chater
Rd
Jackson Rd
Murray Rd
Central
Edinburg

Robinson Road
Conduit Road
Pedestrian escalator (Mid-Levels escalator)
Shelley St
Cochrane St
Caine
Road
Mosque Jct
Glenealy
Ice House St
Battery Path
Lower Albert
Road
Central
Cotton Tree

M I D - L E V E L S
Mosque Jct
Robinson
Road
Upper Albert Rd
Albany Rd
Upper Albert Rd
Garden Road
Peak Tramway Station

Lugard Rd
Hong Kong Zoological and Botanical Garden
Garden Road
Hong Kong Par

Hornsey Rd
Old Peak Rd
MacDonnell Rd
Kennedy Road

0 ——————▶ 750 m

0 ——————— 0.5 mile

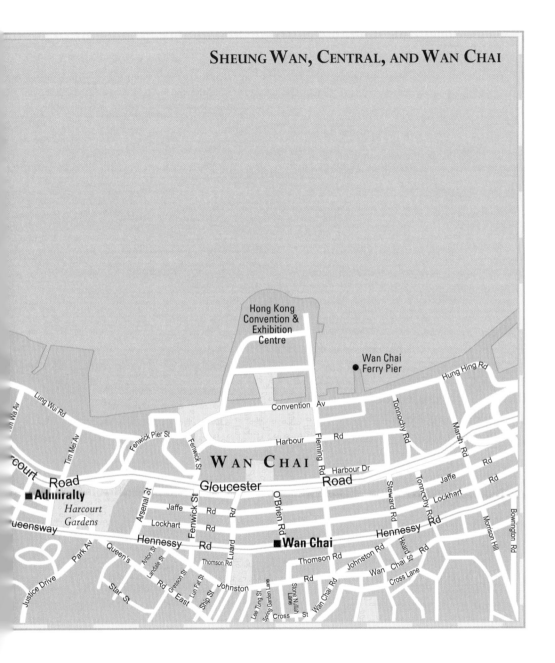

Hong Kong
Convention &
Exhibition
Centre

Wan Chai
Ferry Pier

Hung Hing Rd

Lung Wui Rd

em Wa Av

Tim Mei Av

Convention   Av

Fenwick Pier St

Harbour

Fleming Rd

Rd

Tonnochy Rd

Marsh Rd

Rd

Fenwick St

WAN CHAI

Harbour Dr

Rd

court

Road

Gloucester   Road

Rd

Jaffe

Admiralty

Arsenal St

Jaffe

Fenwick St

Rd

O'Brien Rd

Steward Rd

Tonnochy Rd

Lockhart

Rd

Harcourt
Gardens

Lockhart

Rd

Hennessy

Rd

Bowrington Rd

ueensway

Hennessy   Rd

Wan Chai

Morrison Hill

Park Av

Queen's

Anton St

Landale St

Rd

Thomson Rd

Thomson Rd

Johnston Rd

Heard St

Wan   Chai Lane

Justice Drive

Queen's

Rd

Greson St

Lun Fat St

Ship St

Johnston

Lee Tung St

Spring Garden Lane

Store Nullah
Lane

Cross

Wan Chai Rd

Johnston Rd

Cross Lane

Star St

East

Rd

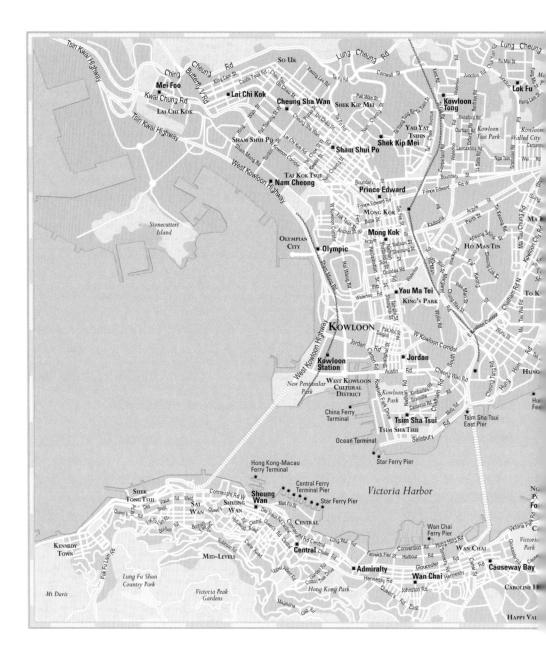

VICTORIA HARBOR AND KOWLOON

Diamond Hill

Choi Hung

Ma On Shan Country Park

Clear Water Bay Rd

Hammer Hill Rd

Tsz Wan Shan Rd

Jat's Incline

New Clear Water Bay Rd

Clear Water Bay Rd

New Clear Water Bay Rd

Fei Ngo Shan Rd

Clear Water Bay Rd

Tai Nagau Wu

Po Lam Road N

Eastern Rd

Kwun Tong Rd

Kai Cheung Rd

Anderson Road

Po Hong Rd

Fu Park Rd

Po Lam

■ Kowloon Bay

Wai Yip St

Shun Lee Tsuen Rd

Po Lam Road N

KOWLOON BAY

Kai Fuk Rd

NGAU TAU KOK

Hong Ning Rd

SAU MAU PING

Sau Mau Ping Rd

Po Lam Road

Tseung Kwan O Tunnel Rd

TSEUNG KWAN O

■ Ngau Tau Kok

Kwun Tong Rd

Yip Po Ho St

KWUN TONG

Hang Hau

Wan Po Rd

Kwun Tong Bypass

Wai Yip St

Kwun Tong Rd

■ Kwun Tong

Tseung Kwan O Rd

LAM TIN

Lin Tak Rd

Po Shun Rd

Tong Ming St

Hong Rd

Hoi Yuen Rd

Yun Ping Rd

Pik Wan Rd

Kiu Kiang Rd

Fo Yan Rd

SAI TSO WAN

■ Lam Tin

■ Tseung Kwan O

Kwun Tong Ferry Pier

Wai Yip St

Cha Kwo Ling Rd

■ Tiu Keng Leng

Kowloon Bay

TIU KENG LENG

Cha Kwo Ling Rd

■ Yau Tong

YAU TONG

Point Pier

ern Corridor

Java Road

King's Rd

Island Eastern Corridor

Lei King Wan Ferry Pier

Lei Yue Mun Ferry Pier

N

■ North Point

Temple

Pak Fu Rd

Choi Sai Woo Park

QUARRY BAY

■ Quarry Bay

Kornhill Rd

Sai Wan Ho Ferry Pier

0 — 1.5 km

■ Tai Koo

SAI WAN HO

■ Sai Wan Ho

0 — 1 mile

Shau Kei Wan Rd

Yiu Heng Road

■ Shau Kei Wan

■ MTR Train Station

• Ferry Landing

■ Heng Fa Chuen

287

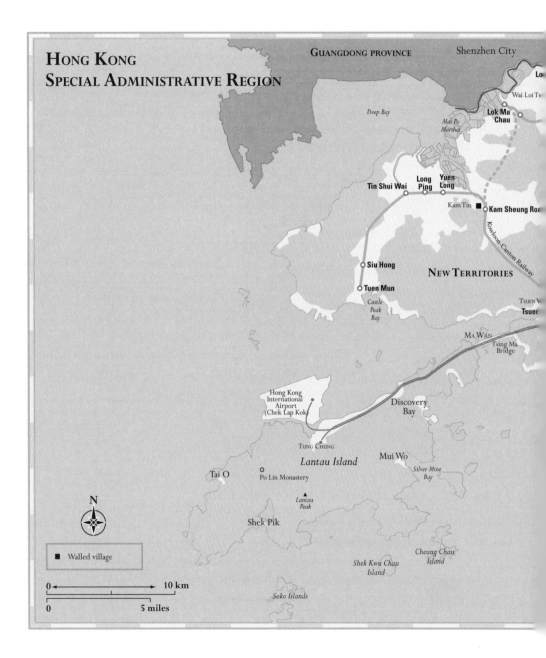

HONG KONG
SPECIAL ADMINISTRATIVE REGION

GUANGDONG PROVINCE

Shenzhen City

Lo

Wai Loi Ts

Deep Bay

Mai Po
Marshes

Lok Ma
Chau

Tin Shui Wai

Long
Ping

Yuen
Long

Kam Tin ■ Kam Sheung Roa

Siu Hong

NEW TERRITORIES

Tuen Mun

Castle
Peak
Bay

TSUEN V

Tsuen

MA WAN

Tsing Ma
Bridge

Hong Kong
International
Airport
(Chek Lap Kok)

Discovery
Bay

TUNG CHUNG

Lantau Island

Mui Wo

Silver Mine
Bay

Tai O

Po Lin Monastery

▲
Lantau
Peak

Shek Pik

Cheung Chau
Island

Shek Kwu Chau
Island

Soko Islands

N

■ Walled village

0 ◄————————► 10 km

0   5 miles

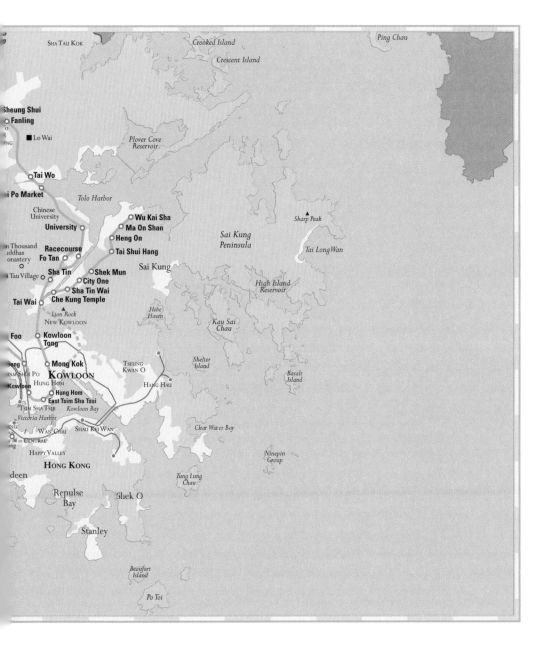

Sha Tau Kok

Crooked Island

Crescent Island

Ping Chau

Sheung Shui
○ **Fanling**
○
ING   ■ Lo Wai

*Plover Cove
Reservoir*

Tai Wo
i Po Market

Tolo Harbor

Chinese
University
University ○

n Thousand
uddhas
onastery
○
ı Tau Village ○

○ **Wu Kai Sha**
○ **Ma On Shan**
○ **Heng On**
○ **Tai Shui Hang**

Racecourse
Fo Tan ○ ○

Sha Tin ○   ○ **Shek Mun**
○ **City One**
○ **Sha Tin Wai**
Tai Wai ○ **Che Kung Temple**
▲ *Lion Rock*
New Kowloon

*Sai Kung
Peninsula*

▲ *Sharp Peak*

Tai Long Wan

Sai Kung

*High Island
Reservoir*

*Hebe
Haven*

*Kau Sai
Chau*

Foo ○ **Kowloon
Tong**

ong ○   ○ **Mong Kok**
AM SHUI PO
KOWLOON
owloon Hung Hom
○ **Hung Hom**
○ **East Tsim Sha Tsui**
Tsim Sha Tsui *Kowloon Bay*
Victoria Harbor
NG   Wan Chai
○ ■ Central
ong
Happy Valley

Tseung
Kwan O

Hang Hau

*Shelter
Island*

*Basalt
Island*

Shau Kei Wan

Clear Water Bay

*Ninepin
Group*

Hong Kong

deen

*Repulse
Bay*

Shek O

*Tung Lung
Chau*

Stanley

*Beaufort
Island*

Po Toi

NOTES

All Chinese names and terms in Hong Kong are romanized according to their Cantonese pronunciation. Names from China are done in the standard Pinyin system. To facilitate recognition, sometimes the Mandarin pronunciation of names known also in China is provided in brackets. Personal and place names with special spellings are kept as they are without alteration.

Prologue

1 Ackbar Abbas, *Hong Kong: Culture and the Politics of Disappearance* (Hong Kong: Hong Kong University Press, 1997), chap. 1, esp. pp. 4–5.

2 Rem Koolhaas, "Generic City," in Rem Koolhaas, Bruce Mau, and Jennifer Singler (ed.), *S,M,L,XL: Small, Medium, Large, Extra-Large* (New York: Monacelli Press, 1997).

3 Jason Wordie, *Streets: Exploring Hong Kong Island* (Hong Kong: Hong Kong University Press, 2002), Foreword.

1. Victoria City

1 Jan Morris, *Hong Kong: Epilogue to an Empire* (London and New York: Penguin Books, 1989; rpt. with an additional chapter, 1997), p. 303.

2 Dung Kai-cheung, *The Atlas: The Archaeology of an Imaginary City* (*Ditu ji: Yige xiangxiang de chengshi de kaoguxue*; Taipei: Lianhe wenxue, 1997). A second book, published one year later, is called *Visible Cities* in English (a purposeful counter-pun on Italo Calvino's famous novel *Invisible Cities*). Its Chinese title is more revealing: *The Glories of V City*—V for Victoria, of course, but the "glories" of its past belong to the Chinese, since the title's intended reference is to the culturally prosperous city of Kaifeng in the Sung dynasty as recounted in a classic book and a more famous pictorial roll.

3 *Apple Daily* (February 27, 2007), p. A4. This project follows the trend of many "theme parks" on the mainland that imitate old Chinese relics.

4 These population figures as well as historical information about native Hong Kong are drawn from a variety of scholarly sources in Chinese, especially Ho Poi Jan, *Moving Land and Mountains: 160 Years of Hong Kong Land Reclamation* (*Dihuan shanyi: Xianggang haigang ji tudi fazahan yibailiushinian*; Hong Kong: Commercial Press, 2004); and Wang Gungwu, ed., *Hong Kong History: New Perspectives* (*Xianggang shi xinbian*; Hong Kong: Joint Publishing, 1997), 2 vols. See esp. chapter by Elizabeth Sinn, "Social Organization and Social Transformation," 1: 157–210.

5 As described in the standard colonial histories by G. B. Endicott, they all emerge as remarkable individuals and fully capable administrators who have made Hong Kong what it is today. I do not follow this top-down approach. Only policies initiated by governors that profoundly affected the native population are discussed under their names. See also Frank Welsh, *A History of Hong Kong* (London: Harper Collins, rev. ed., 1997), p. 147; Steve Tsang, *A Modern History of Hong Kong* (Hong Kong: Hong Kong University Press, 2004), p. 24.

6 Wang Tao, "A Brief Commentary on Hong Kong" (*Xianggang luelun*), in his *Taoyuan wen xinbian* (Beijing: Sanlian, 1998), 96–100.

7 The death figure in Hong Kong was set officially at 2,552 but the real figure was much larger because most Chinese lodgers in tenements did not register with the government. Some other sources have the figures as large as 100,000.

8 Patricia Lim, *Discovering Hong Kong's Cultural Heritage: Hong Kong and Kowloon* (Hong Kong: Oxford University Press, 2002), pp. 36, 40–41.

9 Shih Shu-ching, *Her Name Is Butterfly* (*Ta mingjiao hudie*, Vol. 1 of the trilogy; Taipei: Hungfan, 1993), chap. 2. An abridged English translation of the trilogy (by Howard Goldblatt and Sylvia Lin) is called *City of the Queen: A Novel of Colonial Hong Kong* (New York: Columbia University Press, 2005).

2. Central Values

1 Lung Ying-tai, *Lung Ying-tai's Hong Kong Notebook* (*Lung Ying-tai de Xianggang biji*; Hong Kong: Cosmos Books, 2006), pp. 21–26.

2 Peter Sui Shan Chan, "A Survey Report of Historical Buildings and Structures within the Project Area of the Central Reclamation Phase III," commissioned by the Antiquities and Monuments office, Leisure and Cultural Services Department, SAR (February 2001, unpublished), p. 9.

3 David Faure, *Colonialism and the Hong Kong Mentality* (Hong Kong: Centre of Asian Studies, University of Hong Kong, 2003), p. 44.

4 Matthew Turner, "60s/90s: Dissolving the People," in Pun Ngai and Yee Laiman, eds., *Narrating Hong Kong Culture and Identity* (Hong Kong: Oxford University Press, 2003), pp. 24–26.

5 Frank Welsh, *A History of Hong Kong* (London: HarperCollins, rev. ed., 1997), p. 256. Pope Hennessy's grandson, James Pope-Hennessy, has written a book in his defense, *Half-Crown Colony: A Historical Profile of Hong Kong* (Boston: Little, Brown, 1969), which also gives a lively description of the manners and morals of colonial society in Hong Kong.

6 Welsh, *A History of Hong Kong*, p. 255.

7 Patrick Yu Shuk-siu, *Tales from No. 9 Ice House Street* (Hong Kong: Hong Kong University Press, 2002), pp. 12–13, 18.

8 Faure, *Colonialism and the Hong Kong Mentality*, chap. 1.

9 Welsh, *A History of Hong Kong*, p. 386.

10 For instance, Welsh devotes only four pages to the strikes at the tail end of his chapter 12, "Hong Kong and the Chinese Revolution," in an expanded edition of his book totaling 652 pages. Most of my account is based on Jung-fang Tsai, *The Hong Kong People's History of Hong Kong (Xianggang ren zhi Xianggang shi*; Hong Kong: Oxford University Press, 2001), esp. chap. 4.

11 Welsh, *A History of Hong Kong*, p. 373.

12 Lu Xun, "On Hong Kong," in his *Erh Yi ji*. Translations of this and other essays by Lu Xun can be found in Yang Xianyi and Gladys Yang, trans., *Lu Xun: Selected Works*, 2nd ed. (Beijing: Foreign Languages Press, 1981), 4 vols. "Silent China" is the lead essay in a short collection edited by Gladys Yang, *Silent China: Selected Writings of Lu Xun* (New York: Oxford University Press, 1973).

13 Lu Xun, "Old Tunes Are Over," quoted in Xiao Si, *Literary Promenades in Hong Kong (Xianggang wenxue sanbu*; Hong Kong: Commercial Press, 2004), pp. 28–35.

14 Ackbar Abbas, *Hong Kong: Culture and Politics of Disappearance* (Hong Kong: Hong Kong University Press, 1997), p. 113.

15 Lu Xun, "On Hong Kong," as quoted in Abbas, *Hong Kong*, p. 113.

16 John M. Carroll, *Edge of Empires: Chinese Elites and British Colonials in Hong Kong* (Cambridge: Harvard University Press, 2005), esp. chap. 5.

3. The World of Wan Chai

1 Allan Leach (Operations Manager of Hong Kong Tramways, Ltd.), *Hong Kong Tramways Handbook*.

2 Ma Kwok Ming, *The Political Economy of the Street Corner (Lubian zhengzhi jingji xue*; Hong Kong: Shuguang, 1998), chap. 1.

3 This is precisely the focal point of "street-corner politics" in Ma Kwok Ming's cultural argument. Ma himself owned a small bookstore in Wan Chai—the only bookstore that specializes in works of Western philosophy and literary theory. He is also a self-styled theorist and author of a book on Walter Benjamin!

4 Jan Morris, *Hong Kong: Epilogue to an Empire* (London and New York: Penguin, new ed., 2000), p. 85. John K. Fairbank's classic *Trade and Diplomacy on the China Coast* (Cambridge: Harvard University Press, 1964) has a similar account.

5   Frank Welsh, *A History of Hong Kong* (London: HarperCollins, rev. ed., 1997), p. 499.

6   Guy Haydon, "About the Author," in rpt. ed. of Richard Mason, *The World of Suzie Wong* (Pegasus Press, 2005).

7   Ibid.

8   Ibid.

9   Austin Coates, *China Races* (Hong Kong: Hong Kong University Press, 1983), p. 69.

10 Ibid., p. 245.

11 Jason Wordie, *Streets: Exploring Hong Kong Island* (Hong Kong: Hong Kong University Press, 2002), pp. 185–186.

12 SeSnow, "Land of Memories," *Muse* magazine (Hong Kong), No. 2 (March 2007), p. 63.

4. Views from the Peak

1   Joseph S. P. Ting and Wong Nai-kwan, *City of Victoria: A Selection of the Museum's Historical Photographs* (Hong Kong Museum of History, published by the Urban Council of Hong Kong, 1994), p. 20.

2   *Voices from the Past: Hong Kong 1842–1918*, selected and annotated by Solomon Bard (Hong Kong: Hong Kong University Press, 2002), pp. 75–76.

3   Jan Morris, *Hong Kong: Epilogue to an Empire* (London and New York: Penguin Books, 1988), p. 139.

4   Included in Leung Tin Pui (T. P.), ed., *Excerpts from the Preliminary Collection of Prewar Archives in Hong Kong Culture* (*Zhanqian Xianggang wenhua wenxian chubian tiyao*; Hong Kong: School of Design and Languages, Hong Kong Polytechnic University, 2003), pp. 56–58. This volume contains selections in both English and Chinese.

5   Article by Margot Conley, ABC News online (March 22, 2007).

6   Quoted in Leung, *Excerpts*, p. 69.

7   They provided the model for Timothy Mo's novel *Insular Possessions*, in which two rival newspapers in Canton—both fictional with one taking a jaundiced view—competed for readers' attention. Their present avatar is the *South China Morning Post*, which takes a commanding share of the English-

language market, with the *Hong Kong Standard* trailing far behind. A selection of articles from these colonial newspapers in the period 1842–1918, compiled by Solomon Bard in *Voices from the Past*, offers a few glimpses of colonial society.

8 "Betty," "Intercepted Letter," in Barbara-Sue White, ed., *Hong Kong: Somewhere between Heaven and Earth* (Hong Kong: Oxford University Press, 1996), p. 149.

9 Bard has commented: "Behind Hong Kong's apparent success and prosperity of the period, hides the ugly truth of poverty, malnutrition, and high infant mortality rate among the Chinese population." *Voices from the Past*, p. 185.

10 Morris, *Hong Kong*, p. 136.

11 E. J. Hardy, "John Chinaman at Home," in White, *Hong Kong*, p. 143.

12 Ibid. See also Leung, *Excerpts*, p. 55. Chapter 6 of Morris, *Hong Kong*, contains some vivid descriptions of life in this "Compleat Colony" in the 1880s.

13 Leung, *Excerpts*, pp. 62, 65.

14 Dorothy Dix, "Joy Ride Round the World," in Leung, *Excerpts*, pp. 75–76.

15 Leung, *Excerpts*, p. 79.

16 Morris, *Hong Kong*, p. 218.

17 Leung, *Excerpts*, p. 55; Bard, *Voices from the Past*, p. 113.

18 *Voices from the Past*, p. 38; Morris, *Hong Kong*, p. 141. Frank Welsh quotes a comment about the Chinese by "a resident" in 1845: "They were treated as a degraded race of people . . . not permitted to go out into the public streets after a certain hour in the evening, without a lantern and a written note from their European employer" (p. 165). This refers to the infamous "light and pass regulation" of 1857, which was not abolished until 1897. See David Faure, *Colonialism and the Hong Kong Mentality* (Hong Kong: Centre of Asian Studies, University of Hong Kong, 2003), p. 18.

19 Morris, *Hong Kong*, p. 52. For a more vivid description of the case, see James Pope-Hennessy, *Half-Crown Colony: A Historical Profile of Hong Kong* (Boston: Little, Brown, 1969), pp. 57–58.

20 Pope-Hennessy, *Half-Crown Colony*, p. 56.

21 Included in White, *Hong Kong*, p. 31.

22 Ibid., pp. 31–32.

23 Bella Woolf, "The Borrower," in White, *Hong Kong*, p. 177.

24 Leung, *Excerpts*, p. 73.

25 Recent archeological findings have established traces of human habitation as early as 6,500 years ago.

26 Jeffrey Meyers, *Somerset Maugham: A Life* (New York: Knopf, 2004).

27 Emily Hahn, *China to Me*, as quoted in White, *Hong Kong*, p. 199.

28 Philip Snow, *The Fall of Hong Kong: Britain, China, and the Japanese Occupation* (New Haven: Yale University Press, 2003), pp. 132–133.

29 Ibid., pp. 134–135.

30 White, *Hong Kong*, p. 177.

31 Ibid., p. 115.

5. Kowloon, Past and Present

1 Rem Koolhaas, "Junkspace," *October* 100 (Spring 2002): 175–190.

2 *Hong Kong in Figures*, Government of SAR (February 2007).

3 Frank Welsh, *A History of Hong Kong*, rev. ed. (London: HarperCollins, 1997), p. 324.

4 Hugh Baker, "Life in the Cities: The Emergence of Hong Kong Man," in Pun Ngai and Yee Lai-Man, eds., *Narrating Hong Kong Culture and Identity* (Hong Kong: Oxford University Press, 2003), p. 170.

5 Alan Smart, *The Shek Kip Mei Myth: Squatters, Fires, and Colonial Rule in Hong Kong, 1950–1963* (Hong Kong: Hong Kong University Press, 2006), p. 97.

6 Austin Coates, *China Races* (Hong Kong: Oxford University Press, 1983), pp. 133, 174.

6. New Territories, Ancient Traditions

1 Cheng Po-hung, *A Century of New Territories* (Hong Kong: Joint Publishing, 2003), p. 8.

2 I visited some, but not all, of these sites. Information about other sites is drawn mainly from Chinese sources and Patricia Lim, *Discovering Hong Kong's Cultural Heritage: The New Territories* (Hong Kong: Oxford University Press, 1997).

3 Sung Hok-p'ang, "Legends and Stories of the New Territories, Tai Po,"

Journal of the Hong Kong Branch of the Royal Asiatic Society, Vol. 28 (1988): 72. I am grateful to Hugh Baker who brought this article to my attention. Professor Baker himself has authored, among others, two most readable books, titled *Ancestral Images: An Hong Kong Album* (Hong Kong: South China Morning Post, 1979) and a *Second Album* (1980), from which I have drawn freely for most of the religious customs and rituals described in this chapter.

4 Frank Welsh, *A History of Hong Kong* (updated edition), p. 332.

5 *Piracy and the World of Zhang Baozai*, First Anniversary Exhibition at the Hong Kong Maritime Museum (Hong Kong: Maritime Museum, 2006), p. 40.

6 Several books have been written on the village, including *Tai O—Love Stories of the Fishing Village* by Wong Wai King, a bilingual book with lots of photos (distributed by Stepforward Multimedia Ltd., 2001).

7. Hong Kong Lifestyle

1 Matthew Turner, "60s/90s: Dissolving the People," in Matthew Turner and Irene Ngai, eds., *Hong Kong Sixties: Designing Identity* (Hong Kong: Hong Kong Arts Center, 1995), pp. 19, 38. Turner's essay is also included in *Narrating Hong Kong Culture and Identity*, a collection of reprinted scholarly papers in both English and Chinese edited by Pun Ngai and Yee Lai-Man (Hong Kong: Oxford University Press, 2003), pp. 24–50.

2 Most figures in this section are based on two sources: the SAR government's most recent publication *Hong Kong in Figures* (February 2007), which quotes statistics from 2006 (see esp. sections on "Population and Vital Events," "Information Technology," and "Transport, Communications and Tourism"); and a recent Chinese source on urban density by a group of eight researchers in a project on urban space and housing sponsored by the Bureau of Home Affairs called—in a purposeful bilingual pun—*The Bik* [Cantonese word for "compressed"] *City* (2006), whose statistics are based on 2005 figures. Various other sources give other numbers, which add to the confusion. Still, I hope that these figures give at least a sense of the extreme density of Hong Kong's housing space and urban environment.

3 David Faure, "The Common People in Hong Kong History," in Faure, ed., *Hong Kong: A Reader in Social History* (Hong Kong: Oxford University

Press, 2003), pp. 484–489. Faure gives special attention to various reports and debates on the housing situation.

4 Ibid.

5 These figures are drawn from Ferdinand K. H. Cheung, *Tenement Building in Light of Their Origin* (1999). According to another Chinese source, *Traveling in Space: The 100 Years of Hong Kong Architecture* (Hong Kong: Joint Publishing, 2005), pp. 54–55, supervised by the Hong Kong Architects Association, the *tong lou* tenements in 1903–1955 can be divided into six sub-types ranging from 450 to 700 square feet.

6 Fong Kwok Wing and Chan Jit, *Homes of Yesterday* (*Zuori de jiayuan*; Hong Kong: Joint Publishing, 1993), p. 29.

7 The shifts of the government's housing policies have been analyzed in great detail in a recent book (2006) by Alan Smart, *The Shek Kip Mei Myth: Squatters, Fires and Colonial Rule in Hong Kong, 1950–1963* (Hong Kong: Hong Kong University Press, 2006), p. 95.

8 Figures on time to build a domestic unit come from Hong Kong's Venice Biennale exhibit, 2006. My calculations are based on the "Property and Construction" section of *Hong Kong in Figures* (2007), pp. 33, 35, which shows a total of 1,111,000 units of public rental housing (715,000) and subsidized sale flats (396,000). See also *The Bik City*, p. 95.

9 Mathias Woo, ed., *Hong Kong Style 2: Destroy Hong Kong* (*Xianggang fengge 2: Xiaomie Xianggang*; Hong Kong: Zuni, 2006), pp. 2–51.

10 *Hong Kong in Figures* (2007), p. 41.

11 *Hong Kong in Figures* (2007), p. 35.

12 *The Bik City*, p. 96.

13 Betty Wei and Elizabeth Li, *Culture Shock! A Survival Guide to Customs and Etiquette, Hong Kong* (Singapore: Marshall Cavendish, 2005), p. 2.

14 M. Christine Boyer, *The City of Collective Memory: Its Historical Imagery and Architectural Entertainments* (Cambridge: MIT Press, 1996), pp. 46–51.

8. City and Country

1 Matthew Turner, "60s/90s: Dissolving the People," in Pun Ngai and Yee Lai-man, eds., *Narrating Hong Kong Culture and Identity* (Hong Kong: Oxford University Press, 2003), pp. 35–36.

2 Hugh Baker, "Life in the Cities: The Emergence of Hong Kong Man," in ibid., p. 178.

3 Helen Siu, "Hong Kong: Cultural Kaleidoscope on a World Landscape," in ibid., p. 126. Siu also detected from her field research in Guangdong that the popular reference to Hong Kong residents shifted since the mid-1980s from "Gang Ao tongbao" (Hong Kong and Macau compatriots) to "Xianggang ren" or "Hong Konger" (p. 127).

4 Robert Kuhn, *The Man Who Changed China: The Life and Legacy of Jiang Zemin* (New York: Crown, 2005).

5 Agnes Ku, "The 'Public' Up Against the State: Narrative Cracks and Credibility Crisis in Postcolonial Hong Kong," in Pun and Yee, eds., *Narrating Hong Kong Culture and Identity*, p. 258.

6 Yang Ruwan (Y. M. Yeung), "Two Dragons of Splendor: Shanghai and Hong Kong from City-Based to Regional Competition" ("Shuanglong tu yen: cong chengshi benwei dao quyu daidong jingzheng de Shanghai yu Xianggang") in Leung Yuen Sang and Lawrence Wong, eds., *Two Dragons of Splendor: Cultural Exchange and Interaction between Shanghai and Hong Kong* (*Shuanglong tuyen: Hugang zhi wenhua jiaoliu yu hudong*; Hong Kong: Center for Asia-Pacific Studies, Chinese University of Hong Kong, 2005), pp. 3–28.

7 "Pollution in Hong Kong: The Big Wheeze," *Economist*, March 29, 2007.

8 Hong Kong Environmental Protection Department, "Relative Significance of Local vs. Regional Sources: Hong Kong's Air Pollution," p. 3.

9 Ulf Hannerz, *Transnational Connections: Culture, People, Places* (London and New York: Routledge, 1996), pp. 103, 128–132.

10 See my *Shanghai Modern: The Flowering of a New Urban Culture in China, 1930–1945* (Cambridge: Harvard University Press, 1999), Chapter 10 "Epilogue: A Tale of Two Cities," esp. pp. 339–341.

SOURCES

This section contains only English-language sources and a few bilingual sources. The Chinese works I have quoted and consulted are not included. Chinese authors' names are rendered in Cantonese romanization except when their preference differs. Chinese book titles are rendered in Pinyin.

Abbas, Ackbar. *Hong Kong: Culture and the Politics of Disappearance.* Hong Kong: Hong Kong University Press, 1997.

Baker, Hugh. *Ancestral Images: A Hong Kong Album.* Hong Kong: South China Morning Post Ltd., 1979.

——— *Ancestral Images: A Second Album.* Hong Kong: South China Morning Post Ltd., 1980.

Bard, Solomon, ed. *Voices from the Past: Hong Kong 1842–1918.* Hong Kong: Hong Kong University Press, 2002.

Blake, Robert. *Jardine Matheson: Traders of the Far East.* London: Orion Publishers, 1999.

Booth, Martin. *Gweilo: Memories of a Hong Kong Childhood.* London: Bantam Books, 2005.

Carroll, John M. *Edge of Empires: Chinese Elites and British Colonials in Hong Kong.* Cambridge, MA: Harvard University Press, 2005.

———— *A Concise History of Hong Kong.* Hong Kong: Hong Kong University Press, 2007

Chang, Eileen. *Written on Water*, tr. Andrew Jones. New York: Columbia University Press, 2005.

———— *Love in a Fallen City*, tr. Karen S. Kingsbury. New York: NYRB Classics, 2006.

Cheng Po-hung. *A Century of Hong Kong Roads and Streets.* Hong Kong: Joint Publishing, 2000. [Bilingual guide with photos.]

———— *A Century of New Territories Roads and Streets.* Hong Kong: Joint Publishing, 2003.

———— and Toong Po-ming. *A Century of Kowloon Roads and Streets.* Hong Kong: Joint Publishing, 2003.

Cheung, Martha, ed., *Hong Kong Collage: Contemporary Stories and Writing.* Hong Kong: Oxford University Press, 1998.

Clarke, David. *Hong Kong Art: Culture and Decolonization.* Durham, NC: Duke University Press, 2002.

———— *Reclaimed Land: Hong Kong in Transition.* Hong Kong: Hong Kong University Press, 2002. [An album of photos taken by the author.]

Clavell, James. *Tai-Pan.* New York: Dell Publishing, 1986.

Coates, Austin. *China Races.* Hong Kong: Oxford University Press, 1983.

———— *Myself a Mandarin: Memoirs of a Special Magistrate.* Hong Kong: Oxford University Press, 1987.

Empson, Hal. *Mapping Hong Kong: A Historical Atlas.* Hong Kong: Government Information Services, 1992.

Endicott, G. B. *A History of Hong Kong*, 2nd ed. Hong Kong: Oxford University Press, 1964.

———— *A Biographical Sketch-Book of Early Hong Kong.* Hong Kong: Hong Kong University Press, 2005.

Faure, David. *Colonialism and the Hong Kong Mentality.* Hong Kong: Centre for Asian Studies, The University of Hong Kong, 2003.

———— *Hong Kong: A Reader in Social History.* Hong Kong: Oxford University Press, 2003.

Fong Kwok-Wing and Chan Kit. *Zuori de jiayuan (Homes of Yesterday).* Hong Kong: Joint Publishing, 1993. [Bilingual.]

Hacker, Arthur. *Arthur Hacker's Wanchai.* Hong Kong: Odyssey Publications, 1997.

————— *The Hong Kong Visitors Book: A Historical Who's Who.* Hong Kong: Odyssey Publications, 1997.

Harrison, Mathew. *Queen's Road Central and Other Stories.* Hong Kong: Phaeton, 2006.

Hayes, James. *The New Territories and Its People, 1898–2004.* Hong Kong: Hong Kong University Press, 2005.

Hennessy, James Pope-. *Half-Crown Colony: A Historical Profile of Hong Kong.* Boston: Little, Brown, 1969.

Ho, Oscar, et al. *Words about Wan Chai: Text on "Display Wan Chai."* Hong Kong: Hong Kong Arts Centre, 2002. [Bilingual.]

————— *Mapping Identities: The Art and Curating of Oscar Ho.* Hong Kong: Para/Site, 2004.

Hong Kong in Figures, 2007. Hong Kong SAR: Census and Statistics Department, February 2007.

Ingham, Michael. *Hong Kong: A Cultural and Literary History.* Hong Kong: Hong Kong University Press, 2007.

Koolhaas, Rem. "Generic City," in Rem Koolhass, Bruce Mau, and Jennifer Singler (ed.), *S,M,L,XL: Small, Medium, Large, Extra-Large* (New York: Monacelli Press, 1997).

Ku, Agnes, and Pun Ngai, eds. *Remaking Citizenship in Hong Kong: Community, Nation and Global City.* London and New York: Routledge, 2004.

Kwok Siu-tong and Kirti Narain. *Co-Prosperity in Cross-Culturalism: Indians in Hong Kong.* Hong Kong: Commercial Press, 2003.

Lee, Leo Ou-fan. *Shanghai Modern: The Flowering of a New Urban Culture in China, 1930–1945.* Cambridge, MA: Harvard University Press, 1999.

Lee, Pui-tak. *An Annotated Bibliography of Hong Kong History.* Hong Kong: Joint Publishing. 2001. [Contains both Chinese and English sources.]

Leung Ping-kwan. *Islands and Continents: Short Stories by Leung Ping-kwan,* ed. John Minford. Hong Kong: Hong Kong University Press, 2007.

Leung Ping-wa, ed. *Heritage of the Central and Western District, Hong Kong.* Hong Kong: Central & Western Provisional District Board, 1998.

Leung Tin Pui (T. P. Leung). *Zhanqian Xianggang wenhua wenxian chubian tiyao (Excerpts from the Preliminary Collection of Cultural Archives in Prewar*

Hong Kong). Hong Kong: Hong Kong Polytechnic University, 2003. [Contains materials in both Chinese and English.]

Lim, Patricia. *Discovering Hong Kong's Cultural Heritage: The New Territories.* Hong Kong: Oxford University Press, 1997.

_____ *Discovering Hong Kong's Cultural Heritage: Hong Kong and Kowloon.* Hong Kong: Oxford University Press, 2002.

Liu Yichang. *The Cockroach and Other Stories.* Hong Kong: Renditions Books, 1995.

Loh, Christine. *Being Here: Shaping a Preferred Future.* Hong Kong: SCMP Publishing, 2006.

Luk, Thomas Y. T., and James P. Rice. *Before and After Suze: Hong Kong in Western Film and Literature.* Hong Kong: New Asia Academic Bulletin No. 18.

Mason, Richard. *The World of Suzie Wong.* London: William Collins, 1957; rpt. El Segundo, CA: Pegasus Press, 2005.

Maugham, W. Somerset. *The Painted Veil.* New York: Vintage, 2004.

Mo, Timothy. *An Insular Possession.* London: Peddleless Press, 2002.

Morris, Jan. *Hong Kong: Epilogue to an Empire.* London and New York: Penguin Books, 1988; new edition, 2000.

Morris, Meaghan, Li Siu Leong, and Chan Ching-kiu, eds. *Hong Kong Connections: Transnational Imagination in Action Cinema.* Durham, NC: Duke University Press, 2005; Hong Kong: Hong Kong University Press, 2005.

Piracy and the World of Zhang Baozai. First Anniversary Exhibition brochure at the Hong Kong Maritime Museum. Hong Kong: Hong Kong Maritime Museum, 2006. [Bilingual.]

Pun Ngai and Yee Lai-man, eds. *Narrating Hong Kong Culture and Identity.* Hong Kong: Oxford University Press, 2003.

Shih, Shu-ching. *City of the Queen,* tr. Howard Goldblatt. New York: Columbia University Press, 2005.

Smart, Alan. *The Shek Kip Mei Myth: Squatters, Fires and Colonial Rule in Hong Kong, 1850–1963.* Hong Kong: Hong Kong University Press, 2006.

Snow, Philip. *The Fall of Hong Kong: Britain, China, and the Japanese Occupation.* New Haven: Yale University Press, 2003.

Sung Hok-p'ang. "Legends and Stories of the New Territories." *Journal of the Royal*

Asiatic Society 14 (1974).

Theroux, Paul. *Kowloon Tong.* London: Penguin Books, 1998.

Ting, Joseph S. P., and Wong Nai-kwan. *City of Victoria: A Selection of the Museum's Historical Photographs.* Hong Kong Museum of History. Hong Kong: The Urban Council of Hong Kong, 1994.

Tsang, Steve. *A Modern History of Hong Kong.* Hong Kong: Hong Kong University Press. 2006.

Turner, Matthew, and Irene Ngan. *Hong Kong Sixties: Designing Identity.* Hong Kong: Hong Kong Arts Center, 1995.

Wei, Betty, and Elizabeth Li. *Culture Shock! A Survival Guide to Customs and Etiquette, Hong Kong.* Singapore: Marshall Cavendish, 2005.

Welsh, Frank. *A History of Hong Kong,* rev. ed. New York: HarperCollins, 1997.

White, Barbara-Sue, ed. *Hong Kong: Somewhere between Heaven and Earth.* Hong Kong: Oxford University Press, 1996.

———— *Turbans and Traders: Hong Kong's Indian Communities.* Hong Kong: Oxford University Press, 1994.

Wiltshire, Trea. *Hong Kong: Pages from the Past.* Hong Kong: FormAsia Books, 2005.

Wong Wai King. *Tai O—Love Stories of the Fishing Village.* [Bilingual.]

Wordie, Jason. *Streets: Exploring Hong Kong Island.* Hong Kong: Hong Kong University Press, 2002.

———— *Streets: Exploring Kowloon.* Hong Kong: Hong Kong University Press, 2007.

Xu Xi (aka S. Komala). *History's Fiction: Stories from the City of Hong Kong.* Hong Kong: Chameleon Press, 2005.

Yu, Patrick Shuk-siu. *Tales from No. 9 Ice House Street.* Hong Kong: Hong Kong University Press, 2002.

MY INSIDER'S CREDENTIALS for writing this book are only half earned, for by background and experience I am not fully qualified either as a historian of Hong Kong or as a native speaker of Cantonese. I was born in China (Henan province) and educated in Taiwan, and my field of expertise is Chinese literature and culture. For these reasons and others, as a scholar and researcher I have seen fit to draw upon a range of diverse sources in Chinese as well as English. The important English-language works are listed in the Sources, which serve also as acknowledgment of my intellectual debts. The Chinese sources, though not included here, are far more numerous.

My reliance on the works of many local scholars, writers, and critics of Hong Kong will be obvious from the preceding pages. In some cases, I have intentionally simplified their views and research findings in order to introduce them to a broader readership. In particular, I am deeply indebted to a marvelous work of semifiction about Hong Kong: *The Atlas: The Archaeology of an Imaginary City* (*Ditu ji*) by the local writer Dung Kai-cheung, which is inspired by his own reading of old historical maps of Hong Kong. I have borrowed its structure to some extent, but I have separated fiction from "facts" so that readers are not confused about the many layers of history and legend in the Hong Kong story. Still, the framework and central arguments of *City Between Worlds*, however biased, are fundamentally my own.

I would like to thank my two research assistants, Cheung Lik Kwan and Kwok Sie Wing, for their special assistance in locating materials. I am grateful to numerous colleagues and friends in Hong Kong who have lent me their ears and given me advice, particularly my two colleagues in architecture, Liu Yu-yang and Wang Weijen, for their valuable information and instruction. The book would not have been written without the encouragement of Lindsay Waters, who commissioned it. The book owes its present shape to the conscientious editing of Susan Wallace Boehmer, who urged me to write several drafts, and to Tim Jones, who designed its pages. I also wish to thank the two anonymous external readers, whose valuable suggestions and many corrections I have followed closely in revising the manuscript. I am grateful to Clifford Boehmer, David Clarke, Fong So, and Oscar Ho for their generous assistance in providing illustrations for this book. Any remaining errors and imperfections are of course my sole responsibility.

To my beloved wife, Esther, who is herself from Hong Kong, my debts—emotional as well as intellectual—are beyond words. I have checked my findings against her ruthless common sense and her fund of first-hand knowledge about her home city. She has willingly borne the burden of attending to my physical and mental health during months of feverish writing and revision. Dedicating this book to her is more than a ritual gesture.

ILLUSTRATION CREDITS

AP Photos: 89, 152 (top), 155, 206, 210, 233 (bottom), 266

Clifford Boehmer / Harvard University Press: ii, iii, vi, vii, viii, 1, 10, 13, 15, 17, 20, 21, 42, 45, 47, 49, 50, 55, 56, 57, 76, 78, 79, 81, 95, 97, 106, 108, 109, 111, 137, 138, 140, 141, 143, 147, 148, 149, 152 (bottom), 156, 158, 166, 170, 173, 175, 181, 183, 187, 191, 194, 195, 203, 204, 207, 213, 216, 219, 223, 242, 245, 278, 282, 283

David Clarke: 188, 233 (top), 265

Fong So: 281

Harvard University Map Collection (Hal Empson, *Mapping Hong Kong: A Historical Atlas*, 1992): 270

Hong Kong Museum of Art: 85, 98, 99, 116, 117

Houghton Library, Harvard College Library, Department of Printing and Graphic Arts, Typ 805.43.1345 (Thomas Allom, *China in a Series of Views*, 1843): 23 (top, vol. 4), 23 (bottom, vol. 1), 145 (vol. 2).

Isabelle Lewis: 284–285, 286–287, 288–289

Library of Congress: 40, 60, 105, 113, 120, 180

INDEX